DARTMOUTH

An Enchanted Place

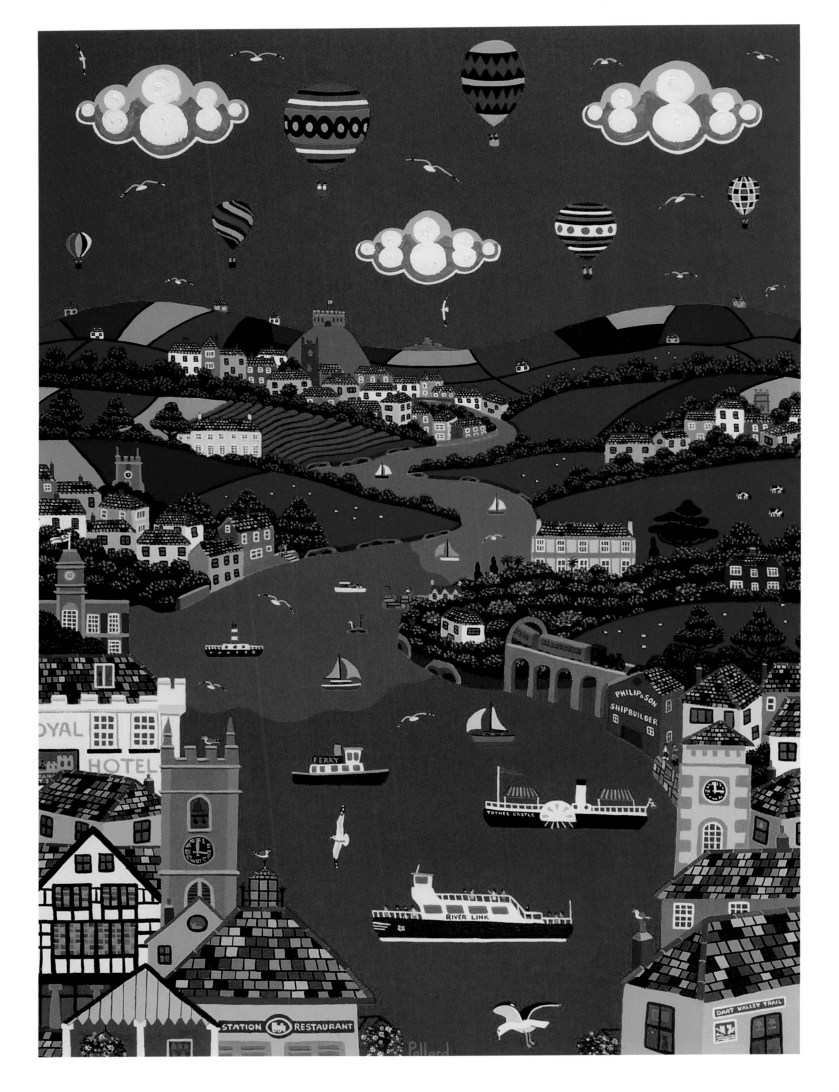

DARTMOUTH
An Enchanted Place

Joslin Fiennes

ANTIQUE COLLECTORS' CLUB
IN ASSOCIATION WITH
RICHARD WEBB

ISBN 9781851497263

British Library Cataloguing-in-Publication Data
A catalogue record for this book is available from the British Library

Every effort has been made to secure permission to reproduce the images contained within this book, and we are grateful to the individuals and institutions who have assisted in this task. Any errors or omissions are entirely unintentional, and the details should be addressed to the publisher.

Frontispiece: *River Dart: View to Totnes*, acrylic by Brian Pollard.　*Courtesy Brian Pollard*
Title Page: Dartmouth coat of arms from the stained-glass panels at Walfleet Lodge (see p.122).
　　　　　　　　　　　　　　　　　　　　　　Valerie Wills by courtesy of Mr and Mrs Otto Koeppen
Endpaper: *Dartmouth from Kingswear,* lithograph. Undated, but before October 1882, when the North Embankment closed in the boat float and the creek into Coombe mud, and after the 1830s when St Barnabas was built in Southtown, to the left on the Dartmouth side. Mount Boone, where the festival of August 1852 took place, is centred on the ridge below the skyline (see p.288).　*Valerie Wills/private collection*

Design Consultant: Laurence Daeche, Anonymous Design Company, Christchurch, Dorset
Design: Craig Holden, Antique Collectors' Club, Woodbridge, Suffolk
Colour Separation: Antique Collectors' Club, Woodbridge, Suffolk
Editor: Susannah Hecht, Antique Collectors' Club, Woodbridge, Suffolk

MIX
Paper from responsible sources
FSC® C104723

Printed in China
for the Antique Collectors' Club Ltd., Woodbridge, Suffolk and
Richard Webb, Dartmouth, Devon

www.dartmouthbooks.co.uk　　Antique Collectors' Club

Contents

Introduction: The Look in the Glass   8

Burgesses and Kings: St Saviours and Chaucer   12

Medieval Turbulence: John Hawley and a Battle at Blackpool Sands   24

The Dart Explorers: Quid Non? – Why Not?   34

The Seas That Bind   46

Slavery and Siege: The End of the Small Merchant   56

Their Day in the Sun: The Great Merchants of Dartmouth   68

My Only Secret is Damned Hard Work: Turner in Dartmouth   82

The Wild Free Life: The Dartmouth Smugglers   94

The Long Fuse: The Story of Steam   106

The 'Just-Do-It' Victorians   116

The Village and The Sea: Hallsands   132

The Frigate on The Hill   144

Touching Nature: Lucien Pissarro in Dartmouth   158

Lost Worlds: Flora Thompson and Children of Dartmouth in the 1930s   168

At War   184

Mystic River   198

Captain's Gold   210

The Mansions of the Entertainers   218

Riversong: Alice Oswold. Kevin Pyne. Brian Patten   230

The Pictures Writers Paint: Nevil Shute. Agatha Christie.   242
      Leslie Thomas. Christopher Milne

The Dartmouth Five: John Gillo. Andras Kaldor. Paul Riley.   254
      John Donaldson. Simon Drew

A Conversation with the Past   270

Last Word   276

Endnotes   278

Bibliography   282

Acknowledgements   284

Index   285

INTRODUCTION

The Look in the Glass

Everyone has their own sense of place. Dartmouth may be somewhere to live and work, to sail or to walk, to admire natural beauty or explore the past. This book looks at the town and its surrounding area through a series of features that try to capture something of their culture – the people, the artists and writers, and their ever-present history.

Dartmouth's deep, secluded harbour has always made the town's destiny. It hid 16th-century merchantmen in between piracy or privateering raids, and the navy and the Free French between secret missions in northern France in the Second World War. Explorers and pioneers, ancient and modern, set out from here. Vessels assembled here for the crusades, the Armada, emigration to the New World, and part of the largest invasion force ever combined that was to turn the tide of war in 1944. Where an early generation cast a chain between the castles at the river mouth, its descendants put an anti-submarine boom. People here lived and are living a history that is unique and yet general, local and yet cosmopolitan. This far-western place might be distant from centres of power by land, but is close to the wider world by sea.

Above: The Dart estuary, looking south, drawing by Willem Schellinks, 1665.

Österreichisches Nationalbibliothek

Opposite: Dartmouth, etching, c.1700. More like a harbour in the Netherlands, this flat coast, windmill and spires have little to do with Dartmouth's precipitous topography, but everything to do with its reputation and aspirations as the perfect harbour for vessels great and small. This is art as fantasy in the service of commerce. *West Country Studies Library*

Napoleon, after Waterloo in 1815, gave himself up to the captain of HMS *Bellerophon*, and was exiled to St Helena. The vessel stopped in Torbay in 1815 on its way to the island, and this Bellerophon Medal (inherited by a local family) was struck in commemoration.*

Private collection

The art and writing that illustrates this story often tells you what historical facts do not: about the people and their times, their attitudes, beliefs and aspirations, the influences of the foreign and the persistence of the local. And it all reflects some point of view. The medieval monks of Saint-Denis reported an imagined revenge for an actual Breton defeat at Blackpool Sands; Agatha Christie believed in the existence of evil; Nevil Shute and Leslie Thomas dramatised war; Christopher Milne told of the corrosive effects of celebrity – all themes that are still with us. The features in this book are inevitably organised around written records, but the art that goes with them tells its own parallel story. One carving on an altar table leg in St. Saviour's Church, for example, explains 200 years of merchant wealth.

There are few paintings or even etchings before the late 17th century, but when Willem Schellinks was here in 1665 he didn't record the hectic port of the explorers Gilbert and Davis,

* Single images can mark watersheds. This man closed a long chapter. When local people visited Torbay to catch a glimpse of Napoleon on his last sea voyage, receiving or perhaps buying this medal to commemorate the event, they were also saying goodbye to the merchant wealth of Dartmouth. Small places on the edge of the nation's trade never recovered from those long years of Napoleonic warfare that disrupted their commerce, took their ships and impressed their crews.

A late 19th-century Bavarian souvenir mug shows tourists were attracted by history.* *Private collection*

The Estuary of the Dart, oil, Frederick Tucker, 1880-1915. Nostalgia was strong in early 20th-century Dartmouth. As John Masefield, Arthur Norway and Flora Thompson turned away from coal ships and shipbuilding to a romanticized 19th-century of smugglers and rural hamlets, Tucker bathed rivermouth and castle in a rosy glow. *Elford Fine Art, Tavistock*

* This little mug marks another watershed. Made in Bavaria in the 1880s, it illustrates the estuary and the castle and was designed for a mass souvenir market. Dartmouth, caught late in the tail-flip of the industrial revolution, was to build ships and engage in coal bunkering until the mid-20th century, but this mug tells us that its economic future was to be tied up with people who come to Dartmouth on holiday.

but climbed up to the ridge at Mount Boone where he drew the view of the estuary out to the Castle. In the mid-16th century John Leland had written as if he, too, had climbed up to get a proper view: 'The town of Dertmouth lyith in length on a very Rokky Hille on the Haven Side, about half a mile from the very mouth of it, and extendith in lenghth [sic] about a quarter of a mile.' Some 150 years later, J.M.W. Turner was to sketch the same view, and a century after that Lucien Pissarro stood there in the nice hat that he was always losing, and made a glorious painting.

Natural beauty has always been part of the attraction of Dartmouth; in 1812 it was already on a the tourist route. Turner came to make engravings for books designed for the armchair traveller and the tourist who had been prevented by the Napoleonic wars from going to Italy. In his sketches, the painter went to enormous lengths to understand the topography, but his watercolours and engravings generally dispense with accuracy and focus on conveying the impression of the water, the land and the air, permanently changing how artists saw reality.

Contemporary local artists still see the beauty of the river. They might paint watery air and airy water in shades of grey, or capture yachts in post-impressionist blues and golds. Their subjects can also feed nostalgia – not for a past way of life, but for holidays, sunshine and sailing boats. The way they see their world is individual. Bridget McCrum goes back to pre-Christian forms, David Alexander and John Donaldson to a style that began 200 years ago with Turner and comes to them through 19th-century French painting and Pissarro. Sarah Gillespie 'photographs' the intense spirituality of nature that Frances Gynn scavenges for happy coincidences like the perfect alignment of steps found on a beach with the sea. Brian Patten applies a similar fierce scrutiny in his poetry of love, loss and the magic of childhood. And so these modern artists make an ancient connection with the uncompromising vision that looks out from the carving of the medieval mason in St Clement's Church.

Dartmouth, on the River Dart, J.M.W. Turner, engraving, *Rivers of England* series, 1822. Turner purposely distorts angles and perspective to show every aspect of the working port. *Valerie Wills/Private collection*

What the Life Coach Said, oil and beach tar, Frances Gynn, 2010. *Courtesy Frances Gynn*

Reality can still be overtly re-jigged. James Stewart looks down from above, John Gillo collapses the geometry of the huddled town around and into a swirling river. Like the 18-century etcher, these artists exaggerate to make their point, but now the intent is aesthetic.

Dartmouth and the area around it are lucky. They have good records and good historians. More importantly, their written, carved, drawn and painted heritage has been created and has survived through countless decisions of countless generations of Dartmothians. A new generation is carrying this heritage forward.

Dart and Dusk, oil, Sarah Gillespie, 2008. *Courtesy Sarah Gillespie*

BURGESSES AND KINGS

St Saviours and Chaucer

The deep, sheltered waters of Dartmouth's harbour offered destiny; with both hands, its medieval people grasped it. The sea was the thoroughfare for Englishmen setting out on the religious and secular wars of medieval times, and its harbour lent the town national importance. From here, men went off on crusades; it was the rendezvous for European vessels on the second, and an assembly point for the third, with more than a hundred ships sailing out of the port. They went on pilgrimages from here to Santiago de Compostela, thirty-seven ships 'heavily laden with pilgrims' in 1190. And after the marriage of Henry II with Eleanor of Aquitaine and the loss of Normandy some fifty years later they hammered out in early autumn across a gusty channel and the storms of the Bay of Biscay taking wool and tin to Bordeaux and bringing back wine, to underpin the town's prosperity for 300 years. Even during the great famine of 1317-21 ships brought back more wine than corn.

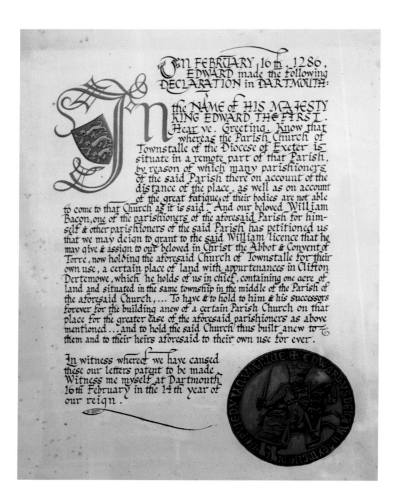

Kings came. Richard I probably visited in 1190 when he assembled the fleet for the third crusade in Exeter, Totnes and Dartmouth. Fifteen years later, King John dated a document from 'Dertemuth' when he stayed from 18-22 June, going on to Dorchester. In 1286, Edward I came, having spent Christmas with Queen Eleanor at Exeter, recognising Dartmouth's contribution of ships to his wars in Wales; and Thomas Walsingham records that he came again eight years later, sheltering from a storm with his army en route to Brittany.[1]

The ancient but undated door of St Saviour's church carries two heraldic leopards, royal emblems of the Normans, across a tree of life. Richard I, who died in 1199, used two on his first coat of arms and three on his second; and a century later Edward I used the same three leopards on the charter supporting the town's claim for a church near the port. The

A copy of the charter issued by Edward I on 16 February 1286 giving the burgesses of Dartmouth permission to erect their own church in the town. Calligraphy by Melvyn Stone, Devon Scribe, 1970.

Valerie Wills/St Saviour

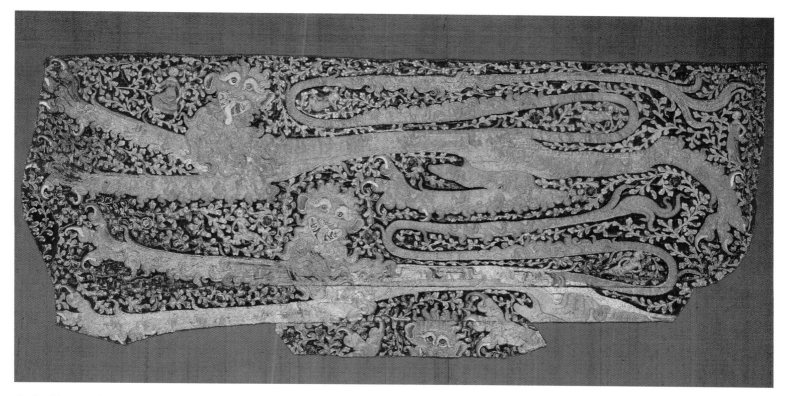

Embroidery with Leopards – Broderie aux léopards réalisée pour Edouard III d'Angleterre. Fragment of English embroidery on red velvet, c.1330-40, from the abbey of Altenberg an der Lahn. Silk, partially gilt silver thread, pearls and glass cabochons. This fragment is believed to be one of the finest surviving examples of *opus anglicanum*, highly skilful English embroidery work prized across Europe that died out after the first devastating episode of the Black Death in the mid-14th century. *© RMN-GP/Franck Raux/Paris, Musée de Cluny*

Musée de Cluny has the remnant of an embroidery that was probably the trapping of a royal horse belonging to Edward III in about 1330 showing three glorious and very similar leopards, but, unlike our more peaceful two, royally aggressive, with tongues and claws protruding. Though the similarity between the two works that are dated and the church door does not date the door, it establishes the meaning of its symbols and associates it with medieval work.

South Porch, St Saviour's church, Dartmouth, lithograph, c.1845. The ancient door carries across a tree of life the stretch leopards/ lions that were royal Norman symbols. The date, 1631, is thought to record restoration and the door and ironwork to be medieval. The similarity with a fragment of a royal horse trapping now in the Cluny Museum in Paris (shown above) is striking. *West Country Studies Library*

The Municipal Seal, thought to have been first used in the earliest mayoral document, with a copy of the grant of Mayoralty to Dartmouth, dated 14 April 1341.[4]

Valerie Wills/
Dartmouth Town Council

The interest of monarchs helped Dartmouth win independence from bishops and feudal lords.* Edward I signed a document in Dartmouth on 16 February, 1286, supporting the town's claim for a church near the port. This became Holy Trinity, eventually St. Saviour, a church built by the town for itself. At the same time, in a quid pro quo, Edward, mindful of the revenue potential of the busy port, secured for the Crown the lordship of the town, the port and the water of the Dart.[2] (The Duke of Cornwall still owns the rights to the water, the foreshore and access.) †

The sturdy independence of medieval Dartmouth must have been strengthened by the impact of the Black Death, although surviving records are silent about it. There were several episodes in the 14th century, as well as later, but the first and most virulent spread from the Caspian in 1346 along trade routes to the Mediterranean and thence westwards, arriving in Marseilles by the end of 1347, Barcelona six months later and so on to Bordeaux. We know that plague first reached England from Gascony via Melcombe Regis, Dorset, in June/August 1348 (records disagree on the exact date). From there, it spread across the country, only in early June 1349 'no longer raging in the parts that it had struck first in southern England' according to one historian.[3] Dartmouth is likely to have been hit early; the disease travelled faster by sea than overland and it is hard to believe it was not here by the autumn of 1348, when it was already in Bristol by August. Yet manorial, ecclesiastical and other records do not mention it, nor do entries show an unusual fall or other change.‡

Overall, between a third and half the population of England is thought to have died during the first plague. Local death rates varied; priests who visited the sick and those living in close-knit communities suffered higher death rates, which suggests that Dartmouth, with its tight housing huddled on the river banks, would have suffered badly. The first plague was followed by five further outbreaks before the end of the century, killing particularly the young – the second, from 1361-64, was called the Plague of Children – and there were further attacks in the 15th century.

---

* The Abbot of Torre in Paignton held St Clement, the parish church in Townstal on the hill, but as Dartmouth grew, pushing quays and shipbuilding works out into the mudflats of the river, people wanted to worship closer to home. The abbot refused to permit even a chapel.

† Dartmouth finally became a royal borough in 1327, when Nicholas de Tewkesbury conveyed the town and the port to Edward III (Watkin, 1935, p.28). In its charter of 1341, in return for giving the king two equipped 120-ton ships of war for forty days a year, the town could elect its mayor who presided over the borough court, and burgesses – later defined as only freemen – were to be exempt from a range of tolls. (These exemptions became the foundation for the wealth of the great Dartmouth merchants; Watkin, 1935, p.40). The town's first seal is on the charter: a king, torso enormous in a clinker-built boat, called a cog, a crescent over a castle to his right and a trident, symbolising dominance of the seas, to his left. Around the seal are the names of the settlements, Dertemuth-Clifton-Hardenesse.

  In 1298, when two knights from each shire, two citizens from every city and two burgesses from every borough were summoned to Parliament at York, Dartmouth sent John the Baker and William atte Vosse, blacksmith, not a Fitz Stephan, then the lords of the Townstal manor. (Until 2010 there was still a blacksmith's shop, Middletons, near the bottom of Brown's Hill, where William's father had had his smithy.)

  The burgesses continued to maintain their independence. Under Charles I, in 1627, they were asked to choose as MP an outsider, Robert Dixon. They refused, replying firmly that 'by their ancient custom, they have usually made choice of men, free of the Corporation, and well known to them.' (Freeman, 2007, p.90, citing Devon Record Office, DD62257.)

‡ There is some circumstantial evidence: the vicar of St Clement's was replaced in January 1349, when he could have died of plague, and over 1349-51 there were extraordinary disruptions at the Abbey of Torre. Rival factions competed for abbot, the abbey was attacked and robbed by riotous mobs – 'chalices, vestments, books and other ornaments of the church and other goods of the abbot' were carried away – and one contender for abbot was imprisoned and murdered by a kinsman of the other. The events were put down to the Black Death relaxing discipline (Seymour, 1977, pp.53-5).

Above: A symbolic cog, as in the town seal, bronze. The workhorses of medieval trade, cogs were square-rigged, generally single-masted and round-hulled, with a raised castle for fighting on the stern. *Richard Porter/BRNC*

Left: An early town roundel, carved wood, in a 17th-century relief design, showing a burgess dominating the cog, a symbol of the town's independence.

Valerie Wills/Dartmouth Town Council

The social impact of the plagues was enormous. With half the tenants dying on country estates, the survivors found they could dictate their terms, and manors were deprived of labour as people moved to the towns. The Peasants' Revolt of 1381 was the first major sign of tectonic shifts in society, and although it was unsuccessful, the feudal system of power devolved from the king became less reliable. It is likely that those who died in Dartmouth were replaced by migrants from the countryside looking for a better life and attracted by the self-reliance of the burgesses, ready to resist their bishop and their king in a new way.

Assuming that Dartmouth did not, uniquely, escape the plague, the continuation of the records shows that, despite the enormity of the disaster, its civic institutions did not break down. The manorial courts continued to work, burgesses exchanged, sold and gifted tenements, and complaints about illegal exports of corn and piracy were dealt with. Civic sense here was developed early, and was strong.

Medieval Dartmouth prospered. Based on tax records, the population in 1377, after five outbreaks of plague, was some 650-760, and 970-1120 if you add in the suburbs of Southtown and Norton.[5] This made it the third largest town in Devon, after Exeter with some 1666 people and Plymouth with 1549.

The town was on the sea and the seas were active. There had always been coastal trade, and wool and tin were ferried downriver from Totnes and out across the channel. Calais was a destination for wool after the mid-14th century, closer to Dartmouth than the dominant Flemish

St Saviour from the fosse in the 19th century, drawing by Helen Hunt.

Private collection

* As a contemporary poet put it:
...in sundry wises
Into this land with divers marchandises
In great Caracks...
With cloth of gold, silke and pepper blacke...
Oyle, woad ashen...good gold of Genne...

From 'Libellus de Politia Conservativa Maris' in *Hakluyt's Voyages*, by Richard Hakluyt (J.M. Dent & Sons, 1926). First published by Thomas Wright in *Political Poems and Songs*, 1861.

markets. But Devon's wool and cloth were never the best, and the port was better placed for the lucrative wine trade with Gascony. Dartmouth's position at the western reaches of the Channel, on the trading routes to the Flemish markets, also made it ideally placed for piracy and privateering. Contemporary chroniclers record rich Genoese and Spanish carracks bringing exotic goods up the western channel to exchange for wool and 'wollen cloth of ours of colours all' in Flanders.* Many of these goods arrived in Dartmouth harbour.

In August 1373, Geoffrey Chaucer, who spoke Italian and had recently been on a diplomatic mission to Genoa and Florence, was sent to Dartmouth by Edward III. His mission was to

The Shipman, with his verse below, from a 1561 edition of *The Canterbury Tales*, by William Chaucer.

Reproduced by kind permission of the Syndics of Cambridge University Library (Keynes S.7.9)

A Sailor was there, hailing from the west:
For aught I know, he was from Dartmouth.
He rode upon a nag, as well as he could,
In a gown of coarse cloth to the knee.
A dagger hanging on a cord had he
About his neck, extending under his arm.
The hot summer had made his hue all brown;
And, certainly, he was a good fellow.
Full many a draught of wine had he drawn
On trips from Bordeaux, while the importer slept.
Of delicate conscience took he no heed.
If he fought, and had the upper hand,
By water he sent them home to every land.
But concerning his skill to reckon his tides,
His currents and the dangers that beset him,
His harbour and his moon, his pilotage,
There was none such from Hull to Carthage.
Hardy he was, and shrewd in his ventures;
With many a tempest had his beard been shaken.
He knew well all the havens, exactly as they were,
From Gottland to the Cape of Finisterre,
And every creek in Brittany and in Spain;
His barge was named The Madeleine.*

enquire into the arrest by the mayor and bailiff of the Genoese cargo boat *St Mary and St George* belonging to Johan de Nigris, merchant of Genoa.[6] Thirteen years later, when he sat down to write *The Canterbury Tales*, the poet was to remember Dartmouth and left us a vivid picture in the prologue of its typical burgess – the Shipman. Ridiculous onshore riding on a 'rouncy', a nag, he's an honest fellow, dressed in coarse cloth, a dagger hanging from a cord at his side, brown from the summer sun, and a good drinker of wine. On the Bordeaux run he is happy enough to tip enemies overboard and steal cargo, but is an experienced and talented sailor 'noon swich from Hulle to Cartage. Hardy he was, and wys...' and knows the heavens from Gottland to the Cape of Finisterre 'And every cryke in Britayne and in Spayne.'[7]

Chaucer remembered Dartmouth as a town of travellers. Churchwardens' accounts for 1430-31 record 7 shillings received for ringing St Saviour's bells at the burials of a Breton, a Dutchman,

* Vincent F. Hopper, *Chaucer's Canterbury Tales, An Interlinear Translation*, Barron's, 1970, pp.25-7.

Engraving of the interior of St Saviour, Rock & Co., 1855, showing the new galleries and seats.

West Country Studies Library

a man from London and three men from Gaul.[8] Medieval Dartmouth was cosmopolitan. From northern France, records list people called Breton and Normand, and from further east many Holands, Flemmings and Flanders, and Gascoynes and even Italians from the wine run. The Walshes and Scots and their many variants were all here in numbers with the Irysh and Irlands and there was a plethora of names of places along the southern and eastern coasts, from Bristol and Fowey to Lyme, for Lyme Regis, Hastings and up to Lynn for King's Lynn and Donewiche, a great herring port near Norwich, soon to be submerged under the sea. Surnames were still being established in the 14th century, so most of the holders of these names would have been the first generation to have them. The town had strong Norman and Breton influence; historians believe the first houses and port facilities were built by Frenchmen. People would have spoken a mixture of English and French, and surviving records were written in Latin and French.

On a knuckle of hard ground to the west of the fosse stands St Saviour's church, one of the finest churches in Devon. It is truly a town church, built despite the opposition of the Abbot of Torre and Bishop of Exeter, enlarged and maintained by the corporation and embellished with the finest crafts the people could afford or make themselves. As well as devotion, the church stands for determination and civic pride. It contains virtually no grand personal monuments, but its glorious carving, masonry and mosaics display a long tradition of artistic achievement, and a couple of brasses and a gallery of 17th-century shields identify some of the burgesses who made it what it is.

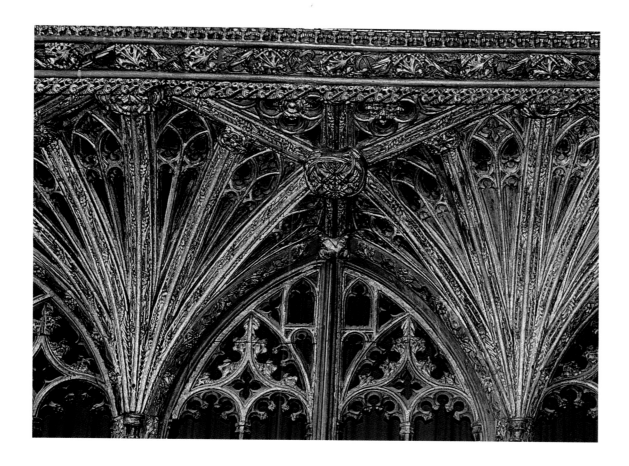

St Saviour, rood screen, 1496. *Valerie Wills/St Saviour*

Almost a century of resistance from abbot and bishop followed Edward's approval of the town's request to have its own church. Before the official consecration by a new Bishop of Exeter, Thomas de Brantyngham, in 1372, the burgesses had already built a chapel illegally, and a fraudulent Bishop of Damascus had consecrated it in 1344. The church was only built after the Bishop of Exeter, Bishop Grandisson, who was building his own magnificent cathedral, had died. After Henry VIII confiscated the wealth of the church during the reformation in the mid-16th century, the burgesses determinedly, and bit by bit, bought back the abbot's lands in the parish of Townstal and controlled the church from 1586 until 1835. During that time, they paid over £1,000 for a major rebuild in the mid-17th century with finishing touches added for the visit of Charles II in 1671. The church lived by the town's wealth from the sea: the wool, the wine and the fishing trade.

St Saviour, 1619, detail from map of Dartmouth by Nicholas Townesend, 1619. *Devon Record Office/Dartmouth Town Council*

The interior of this stalwart medieval building with its 17th-century reconstruction tells you what the town created, cared about and kept. The great oak door with its royal leopards still stands in the oldest part of the church, thought to pre-date its consecration, and near an ancient, plain and probably Norman font. In sharp contrast, the rood screen spanning the width of the medieval nave is richly intricate. It is almost unique in Devon with its fine traceries and magnificent friezes topped by carvings of ropes entwining grapes, symbols of Dartmouth's early trading wealth. The scratched-out faces of its saints are a distant echo of some terrifying unrecorded assault.

Next to this delicate sophistication, the exuberant seven-sided stone pulpit is a shock. Thought to be 15th-century, so fairly contemporary with the screen, the narrow panels were probably made for carvings of saints, but the motifs there now – the letters CR for Charles Rex in a wreath, a portcullis, harp, fleur-de-lys, thistle, rose and a crowned lion, all surmounted with crowns – were added for the visit of Charles II two centuries later. Was the screen bought in, made perhaps by foreign craftsmen, and the pulpit local? Or is the pulpit much earlier, as its enormous leaves suggest?

The chancel, thought to have been financed by the prosperous ship-owner John Hawley in the late 14th century, has on the floor his brass, one of the most important in Devon. The brass shows him flanked by his two wives, their heads to the west where the good winds come from (see the next chapter for more on Hawley and an illustration of his brass).

In the chancel stands a communion table that marks another stage in the history of the town. It is plain, with crudely magnificent figures of the four evangelists, now across the front but originally forming the legs. It is Elizabethan, made during a puritan period by a local craftsman used to ships' carving (see the chapter 'Slavery and Siege' for an image of St Matthew now on one corner of the table).*

The stone pulpit is encrusted with massive decoration, thick uprights bearing a frieze of enormous leaves over narrow panels with wooden masons' and royal badges made for Charles II.

Valerie Wills/St Saviour

* The town showed prudence during the difficult times of Henry VIII's reformation, followed by Catholic Mary, and then Protestant Elizabeth. After the dissolution of the monasteries in 1539, the corporation (sailors all, and sensitive to winds a-changing) gradually merged the church accounts with their own, so that by 1547 there was only one set: the town accounts. (Watkin believes these accounts to be the oldest in the country; see Watkin 1935, p.295.) The Church Goods Commissioners could thus only identify a small amount to confiscate under their State of Superstitions when they visited sometime after that. Sir John Skinner, chantry priest of St Saviour in 1538 and chaplain until 1574 outlived the death of Henry VIII in 1546, Edward VI a year later, Catholic Mary Tudor who lasted until 1558, and the arrival of Elizabeth I. He took away the Catholic furnishings – including altar, reredos and cross – for Henry, and put the Ten Commandments up on the wall. For Mary, he painted out the Commandments, mended the Catholic furnishings and put them back. When Mary died, he took them away again. The altar and the cross never re-emerged, and shortly afterwards the corporation bought the advowson for the church, and this puritan table appeared. You can imagine all those involved with the church then would have agreed with Emelina Petyfen, characteristically a Dartmouth woman, who is recorded as exclaiming, when it all began with Henry and Anne Boleyn: 'The devil take the king and his lady also'.

Mason's head on pillar at rear of nave, St Clement's church, Townstal. Crudely carved but full of life, this medieval man looks out, tough and independent.

Valerie Wills/St Clement's

There is history in furnishings that have gone. In the early 19th century, the corporation installed new wooden galleries and seats for themselves. The seats were designed by Arthur Howe Holdsworth in the contemporary gothic style and were magnificently carved. But they darkened the church, and as fashions changed, they were removed. Inside the seats, the carpenter, Reuben Lidstone, slipped a note that was discovered when they were repaired in 1887. 'When this you see', he writes, 'Remember me that I am not quite forgotten...that the times are very bad...for working men get 14 shillings a week, and flour 5 pence a pound, potatoes 1 shilling a stone...and one half the men can get no work. You may depend their pride is come to grief, for instead of ducks and geese they are forced to eat sheep's head.' [9]

The saints honoured in the church reflect the pride of the medieval town – first, Holy Trinity, then, by 1431, St Saviour.[10] Both dedications mirror those of the Abbey of Torre. Their church finally built, a confident town could propitiate its abbot, and move on.

MEDIEVAL TURBULENCE

John Hawley and a Battle at Blackpool Sands

Blow the wind high, blow the wind low, It bloweth fair to Hawley's Hoe.

John Hawley was one of Dartmouth's most famous medieval sons. He had such a following that the day of his death was celebrated for 150 years, and more than 600 years later ferries called *Hauley* criss-cross the Dart between Dartmouth and Kingswear opposite. His reputation lives on in popular song (above).

There were three generations of John Hawleys in medieval Dartmouth, but the hero is the second. He lived from about 1340 to 1408 through the end of the long reign of Edward III and the chaos of Richard II, whose murder ended the Plantaganet supremacy, and the early days of Henry IV and the house of Lancaster. Three facts defined his time and fortune: England's hundred years' war with France; Dartmouth's strategic position at the outer reaches of the western Channel, only ninety miles from Normandy; and the relative weakness of the king.

Richard II bestowed these arms on Hawley in 1395. They show Hawley's aspirations – heraldic horns stand for high pursuits and arrows for martial readiness. The arrow could also be a visual pun on the Dart (medieval people were fond of puns). Black stands for constancy and red for military fortitude and magnanimity.

Dartmouth Museum

Previous Spread:
Blackpool beach where medieval Breton knights fought and lost.

© 2013 Nigel Evans

Hawley was only one of the seafaring merchants of Dartmouth who prospered then, but he captured popular imagination and became a symbol for the rest. Perhaps he was just that bit more courageous and entrepreneurial, so there are more records of him receiving important commissions and being called to account for overstepping the limits.*

Agent of the king, pirate or merchant? Hawley was all three. In 1379 he was licensed with others to go to sea for twelve months at his own expense under the protection of Richard II 'to attack and destroy his enemies' with three of his ships, *la Mighel*, *la cog Johan* and *la Jouette*.[1] This official invitation to plunder, repeated many times, made him a privateer, permitted to take any enemy vessel and keep a percentage of the proceeds, sending the rest to the king.

But it was a time of shifting alliances and truces, and sometimes Hawley was caught out. Capturing ships of neutral countries or of enemies suddenly made friends turned him from privateer to pirate. An order to arrest Hawley, among others, and bring him before king and Council for capturing a Genoese vessel went out four times in 1386-87, with different people appointed to carry it out. Medieval records frustratingly don't tell what happened, but within months, Hawley was back in

John Hawley, detail of brass, St Saviour, Dartmouth. Almost certainly not a likeness, he lies between his two wives, holding hands with his first – surely on personal instruction – in the chancel he funded. Concerned for his image, although never knighted, he is in knight's armour.

favour, pardoned for seizing a Flemish vessel.[2] Did the agents refuse to arrest him? Had Richard II given up? Or did Hawley go to Westminster and restore the Genoese goods? All we know is that by 1395, the year he bestowed a coat of arms on Hawley, Richard had made Hawley's son John 'King's esquire...retained for life to stay with the King', almost certainly to help control his wayward father.[3] Not that it worked. Hawley still had a good decade of trawling the seas before him and in 1406, only two years before he died, a frustrated Henry IV was to imprison him in the Tower of London.

Some seizures may have been returned, but the rest made Dartmouth a thriving, important town. Hawley became wealthy. In the 1377 poll tax, he was assessed at two shillings; only Thomas Asshenden, another ship-owner, was assessed more highly, at three shillings.[4] From 1389 he began buying up from the king the sequestered Cornish estates of a Robert Tresilian, Chief Justice and friend of Richard II, executed the previous year, paying enormous sums for those days.[5]

* The king depended on wealthy merchants who could put ships to sea for him. At the siege of Calais in 1347, England fielded 738 ships and almost 15,000 seamen. Of these, Edward III sent only 25 ships. In contrast, Dartmouth sent 31 ships, only exceeded by Fowey, with 47 and Yarmouth, 43 (Karkeek, 1880, p.4). Merchants like Hawley were needed and this gave them leverage.

Hawley's Fortalice, drawn from historical evidence by James Stewart.[6] Part of the curtain wall at the top still stands.

James Stewart for Dartmouth History Research Group

Despite his conflicted relationship, the king could not avoid Hawley when things needed to be done. When an invasion from France seemed likely in 1374, Hawley got the commission 'in consideration of the damage and reproach which might befal the town of Dertemuth – to survey and correct all defects in the said town and port, fortify the same, array the men of the town'.[7] The fortalice, the first version of Dartmouth Castle, was thought to have been begun belatedly by Hawley sometime after 1389, and the agreement he negotiated with the king whereby Dartmouth became the sole exporter of tin for three years from 1390 was probably to pay for it. (The tin monopoly would also certainly have increased the prices he earned from his new Cornish tin mines.) He was enrolled in many commissions, a significant one in March 1382 in the wake of the Peasants' Revolt. Called a 'commission of peace to

The Cherub on Higher Street, being restored (probably circa 1940s), revealing timberwork believed to date from the late 14th century.

Dartmouth Museum

Today, the Cherub is a pub. Once a merchant's house, it is one of the town's few obviously medieval houses to survive, although more are believed to exist behind later façades.

Brian Head

Hawley's house is thought to have been next to the old Guildhall on Lower Street, demolished in the 19th century to make way for road widening. The 'Hoe', referred to in the jingle, is thought to have been his warehouse on Fosse Street, then backing onto the river where his ships could moor.

establish quiet in the country', that for Devon included such notables as the Earl of Devon, several knights, the prior of Plympton, and the Abbot of Torre Abbey in Paignton, who owned the local parishes. Hawley was the only representative from Dartmouth.[8]

There are clues to his personality. He was frustrated by committees. A record dated 1388 appeals to Richard II for an 'exemption for life' for Hawley 'from being put on assizes, juries, inquisitions etc and from being made mayor, sheriff, escheator, coroner, collector of tenths etc...or other officer or minister of the King, against his will.'[9] It was a vain hope – among other duties, Hawley was mayor of Dartmouth nineteen times, nine of them *after* this appeal. As his arms, he chose bugles or horns with an arrow, symbolising high pursuits and martial readiness; despite his wealth from booty, he saw himself as a protector of the realm. And either he or his son chose to have him remembered dressed as a knight, which he never was, in the brass over his grave in St Saviour's chancel. The image he wanted to leave was of a noble life.*

The Bretons were the likeliest threats to Dartmouth's wine fleets sailing down to Bordeaux, and its natural competitors for the merchant ships sailing up the west coast of France and turning into the Channel towards the markets of Calais and Flanders. It was a time of constant attack and reprisal. Incidents of piracy, privateering and truce-breaking involving the Bretons and the Devonians pepper French and English records, with monarchs alternately trying to impose peace and arresting those who broke it and then licensing the same seamen to make war. The game intensified in the early 15th century. In 1403 the Bretons 'attacked Plummouth by night and burnt the town' under their leader Guillaume du Châtel. Three Dartmouth shipowners including Hawley were commissioned 'to make war on men of Britanny' in reprisal and Sir William de Wilford and a fleet from Bristol and Dartmouth ravaged the Biscay coast.[10]

To give the English 'une rude leçon', a Breton force set out in April 1404 to attack Dartmouth. By then, defences had been built on either side of the Dart estuary, and the Bretons veered away to land at Slapton, meeting an English force at Blackpool Sands. The *Chronique de Saint-Denis*, a broadly accepted contemporary French record, describes a disaster of French leadership, 'Everything was lost through a rashness bordering on madness'.[11] A force of 300 ships with 2,000 knights and men-at-arms left Brittany under the command of three leaders. But on the way, part of the Breton fleet was distracted by some Spanish wine ships, and part disliked the proposed landing place, so only a small force of lightly armed men, but including all the knights and squires, landed under two of the leaders, de la Jaille and du Châtel.

All records agree broadly on what happened. The forces met on either side of a tidal ditch full of water at Blackpool Sands. De la Jaille, ignoring du Châtel's sage advice to go behind the English, led the charge, fighting over a narrow crossing. Many knights drowned, many were killed, including du Châtel, *la fleur des vaillants*, and three lords and twenty knights were taken prisoner. The rest, sensibly, fled.

French and English records do, however, differ in their detail. The *Chronique* records an English army of 6,000 well-trained troops forming an impenetrable defense at the ditch, and that the Bretons, before succumbing, managed to massacre 1,500. Thomas Walsingham, on the other hand, records women and peasantry repulsing the invaders with fury, killing them without mercy. Ray Freeman describes Hawley, forewarned, despatching an army of ill-equipped local countrymen, none of them knights.[12] (There's no record of Hawley taking any other part in the affair.) Perhaps it was this victory of peasant over knight, many captured and good ransom potential, that created such a fuss in London, astonishing the court and inspiring Henry IV to order a *Te Deum* in thanks.

As to what happened then, the *Chronique* records that du Châtel's brother, Tangui, immediately put together another force. A month later he attacked Dartmouth, entering without resistance, and burnt it to the ground, leaving only ruins. For the next two months he reportedly ravaged

* In 1403-04, records show that Hawley, with others, brought into Dartmouth a 'barge laden with iron and other merchandise of Spain'; the *Seint Nicholl* of Orio (Castile) 'laden with 108 tuns of wheat, 2 tuns of peas, 4 half cloths 'Darafroll' and 50 yards of cloth and other harness, goods and armour amounting to 1300 crowns of gold'; 'the *Seint John* of Vermew (Castile) with freight of 787 crowns of gold, 125 quintals of iron of Spain, 250 dozen goatskins and 70 ox-hides, etc.' (Watkin, 1935, p.377.) Dartmouth had to have had a sophisticated network to unload, store, market and distribute all this along the coast or up the mule tracks out of town. At the same time, Hawley pursued legitimate trade, sailing in convoy down to Bordeaux to exchange his wool for wine every year, employing some 600-700 seamen, although his own ships were attacked just as he attacked others. *John Hawley: Merchant, Mayor and Privateer*, by Michael Connors (Richard Webb, 2008) gives a comprehensive account of the man and his time.

The stream over which the Bretons and Devonians are believed to have fought still comes down to the sea across Blackpool Sands.

the coast, pursued by the English king in person, returning safely, exhausted, burdened with immense booty. But local English records dated from the summer and autumn of 1404, after the presumed pillage, show Dartmothians being pardoned for debt, raising bonds, and transferring lands while the usual commissions are established for the restitution of booty.* There is no English record of any attack. In fact, there is a record of Tangui requesting the mayor to return his brother's remains, and another suggesting that Tangui himself was imprisoned (see below) suggesting that this part of the *Chronique* cannot be correct.

While there are no records of Henry IV pursuing Tangui across the Devon countryside, there are records of him pursuing Hawley for a share in the ransoms of the twenty captured knights. Within five days of the battle, Nicholas Aldewyche was commissioned to bring the king 'five, six or seven of the more valid and sufficient of the King's enemies captured near Dertemuth', and on 25 May, the sheriff of Devon and the mayor of Dartmouth were told to bring five named knights and 'a certain Welsh esquire...that the King may have colloquy with them and learn the secrets of his enemies'.

* Most of our local knowledge of medieval times comes from records of local court decisions, land transactions, charters and correspondence with the king and ecclesiastical and naval events and decisions. These are inevitably patchy, although those for Dartmouth are far more comprehensive than they might have been had they not been rescued by two heroic historians. Stuart A. Moore documented them in 1879-80, and found an iron cupboard to put them in, and more than half a century later, Hugh Watkin recovered them from the town gaol, transcribed a précis of each record, indexed them and in 1935 published the first volume of his enormously valuable work.

Letter from John Hawley to King Henry IV, 1404, probably written by a scribe. Occupied with quelling rebellions in Northumberland, Henry still had time to pursue his share of the ransoms of the knights captured at Blackpool Sands.

© The British Library Board
(MS: Cotton MS Cleopatra F.III)

A letter in Norman French from John Hawley to the king on 14 July 1404 shows how the negotiation over the French knights proceeded.[13] 'Touching the prisoner Oliver Avelle, a Breton' writes Hawley 'Richard Keyne came to me and offered to sell the moiety in the said prisoner in "*le scomfiture a Blakpolle*", the which prisoner, Your Majesty, I have sent to your Majesty's presence. And, if it please your Majesty, know that I have, and have purchased of Anthony John the moiety in Tange Castelle, brother to the Lord of Castelle, prisoner, the which Tange is at your Majesty's disposal, that it may please your Majesty to ordain for me and for no other.' So, far from ravaging the southern coast of England pursued by Henry IV, Tangui was, according to Hawley, a prisoner being fought over by the same king. A January 1405 document shows the end result, recording Henry granting his wife Joan his own share of the ransoms paid for the knights, probably 50 percent of two.[14]

The letter shows why Hawley became a legend – a man able to bargain with his king, offering him one ransomable prisoner in exchange for another for himself. The first part of the letter is similarly firm. 'May it please your Majesty to know', he says, 'that I have received your gracious letter making mention that I ought to appear personally before your Majesty...may it please your Majesty to hold me excused...know that I have been suffering from so severe a disorder in one of my legs for more than a month that I cannot ride, and am not well able to walk.' Perhaps he was ill, he was certainly old, and due to die within four years, but he was not awed by any command from a monarch with divine rights.

By the end of the 15th century the male line of the Dartmouth Hawleys had died out. Watkin finds a small brass in the south transept of Wells cathedral to a Henry Hawley, who died in 1573.[15] And in 1630, another Henry Hawley appeared as Governor of Barbados, installed by the Earl of Carlisle. He ruled with an iron hand, imposing arbitrary taxes, granting land to supporters and punishing opponents with a particularly nasty ruthlessness. He made James Futter, a large landowner who accused the Earl of Carlisle of drinking and his Bench of whoring, stand outside at midday 'it beinge then soe parchinge hot that the Sunne peirced his skull'.[16] Hawley was replaced by an equally fearsome governor and disappeared from the records. But it is intriguing to think of Hawleys reappearing in the Caribbean, on the route taken by Dartmouth cod-traders sailing the trade winds up to Newfoundland, two centuries after the family had died out in the port that had made them great.

Knights Assaulting a Castle, miniature, from *Romance of Knight Zifar*, 1464. The miniature is almost contemporary to the battle at Blackpool Sands and the rendering of the knights is thought to be accurate. A royal Spanish copy, taken by Napoleon, is held by the Bibliothèque nationale de France. Detail from text above shown left.

M. Moleiro (moleiro.com)

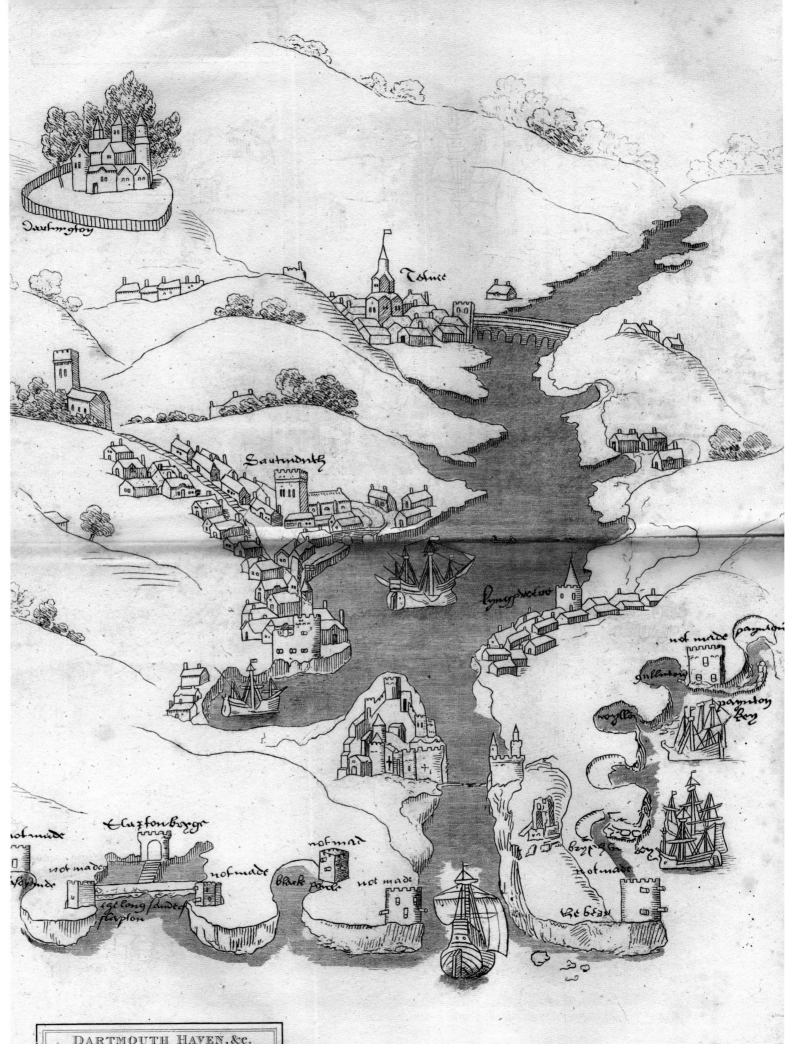

Dartmoton

Totnes

Sautmonth

Kyngysweron

not made paynton

gallaton

woyston

paynton
bay

not made

Cluzton brygge

not made

not made

brygge

not made

not made

not made

blak parke

not made

the bran

egg long sande
fleyton

DARTMOUTH HAVEN, &c.

From a Chart drawn in the Reign of K. Hen. VIII.
preserved in the British Museum.

THE DART EXPLORERS

Quid Non? – Why Not?

Dartmouth harbour took the town out of the medieval era and into the heart of Elizabethan enterprise. It came of age when English sea power and empire were founded. After glory, its explorers sailed up to the inhospitable Arctic Circle, to the Azores and Panama, and across the Pacific to Sumatra. '*Quid Non?*', the motto of Sir Humphrey Gilbert of Greenway House up the Dart from Dartmouth, symbolises their ethos. After profit, its pirates and privateers harried Spanish fleets laden with treasure and spices and its traders lined up behind to establish a trans-Atlantic cod-fishing business that was to prosper for another two centuries and more.

Politics and opportunity drove Elizabethan explorers and privateers as much as courage, inspiration – and money. Men from Dartmouth had always plied the seas for profit, travelling regularly to the southern Mediterranean and across the Atlantic. But now sea travel had become a tool of high politics. By the mid-1500s, the Spanish crown had organised a great empire in the Americas, based on Mexico, Peru and Chile, bringing back across the Atlantic fabled treasures of gold and jewels. Meanwhile, following Bartolomeu Diaz who rounded the Cape of Good Hope in 1487, Portuguese merchants had found the southern route to Asia, establishing trade in silks, spices, pearls and other luxuries. The English were not to follow for another century.*

The Dart produced two major Elizabethan explorers: Sir Humphrey Gilbert and John Davis, who was probably from a farm in Sandridge near Greenway. Sir Walter Raleigh, half-brother to the Gilberts, who spent time with them at Greenway when he was young, supported both men. With the land route to the east closed after the Ottomans had captured Constantinople in 1453, both Gilbert and Davis worked at 'the chimera' of a north-west passage via Labrador. Davis, that most determined seeker of the passage to the Indies, eventually sailed there on the southern route when the Portuguese monopoly was finally broken.

The Davis Quadrant to estimate latitude.

Previous Spread:
Three-masters still sail away past the Castle towards the open sea. © 2013 Nigel Evans

* These Iberian empires affected the power balance in Europe, while exotic riches from the east excited envy and competition. But the sources of the wealth and the routes to them were jealously guarded monopolies. While privateers and pirates made fortunes harrying the great carracks and galleons transporting treasures back to Portuguese and Spanish ports, explorers worked at discovering alternative routes to their sources.

Dartmouth Haven, map by Daniel Lysons during the reign of Henry VIII, showing the estuary up to the bridge at Totnes and beyond. 'The town of Dertmouth lyith in length on a very Rokky Hille on the Haven Side, about half a mile from the very mouth of it, and extendith in lenghth [sic] about a quarter of a mile. There be good Marchaunt Men in the Towne; and to this haven long good shippes...There is a fair Church in the Towne.' (Quoted in Windeatt, p.2.) So wrote John Leland in 1534-43, with the cadence of the King James version of the Bible, to be published some sixty years later. *West Country Studies Library*

Grey Fox, Mark Catesby. This painting of the seed of the pepper vine, shown here with a grey fox, was published in *The Natural History of Carolina* (London, 1754). Pepper was a prized object of the East Indian trade, and is still the world's most popular spice. The Portuguese brought it mainly from India's Malabar coast to Europe, where it was used as a seasoning and for medicinal purposes.

© *National Trust Images/John Hammond*

Davis made three Arctic trips to Baffin Island and Labrador between 1585 and 1587, leaving from and returning to Dartmouth. He sailed as far north as 73 degrees, convinced a way could be found through the ice and then west to Asia, leaving behind local names still seen on maps today – the Davis Strait, Totnes Road, Exeter Sound. Off Greenland 'we found many fayre sounds and good roads for shipping, and many great inlets into the land.' They met Inuits, friendly at first, but on the second voyage Davis describes them as 'marvellous theevish, especially for iron, which they have in great account. They began through our lenitie to shew theyr vile nature: they began to cut our cables...'[1] From his voyages, Davis established that Greenland was separate from North America and that there was clear, ice-free water quite far north into Baffin Bay.

Davis is a very attractive explorer, although sadly there are no fine portraits of him. Always a mariner who spent his life at sea rather than at court, he became the foremost navigator of his time – he discovered the Falkland Islands in 1592 – and was a professional who kept meticulous charts and records of his voyages. His *Traverse Book* written during his third voyage to Labrador became the model for ships' logbooks, and his *World's Hydrographical Description*, published in 1595 summarises contemporary knowledge of geography. A practical man, he invented several navigational aids; his Davis Quadrant was still being used in the 18th century to estimate latitude from the angle of the horizon to the sun. And his *Seaman's Secrets*, published in 1594, is a compendium of useful information, such as tables to estimate tides and ways to track the movement of the sun.

* Funds for the north-west passage dried up after the Spanish annexation of Portugal in 1580 and England's destruction of the Armada eight years later allowed inroads on the Portuguese monopoly of the southern routes to Asia.

Davis made three voyages to the East Indies via the Cape of Good Hope.* When the great treasure ship *Madre de Deus* came to Dartmouth, it carried 'In a case of sweet Cedar wood and lapped up almost an hundredfold in fine Calicut-cloth, as though it had been some incomparable jewel'

Map of Dartmouth, Nicholas Townesend, 1619. Drawn from a boat in the harbour, the map shows the houses concentrated in Clifton around St Saviour's church, with quays at the bottom of Smith Street, and Foss Street a path leading to Hardnesse along the dam where two mill wheels turned on the tide. Shipyards were on the river side of Clarence Street and beyond to the north. It makes a pair with the map in the chapter 'Slavery and Siege'.

Devon Record Office/Dartmouth Town Council

information on trade with China and Japan. Within ten years, Davis would be there. He went first in 1598, with a Dutch expedition led by Cornelius Houtman – Davis called in on Dartmouth to see his sons at Sandridge on the way – that rounded the Cape of Good Hope and reached Sumatra.

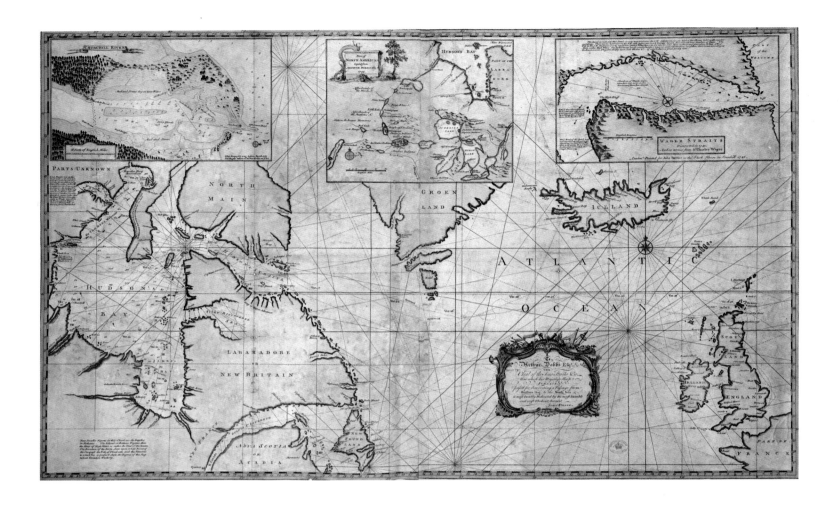

Davis next went on the first expedition of the new English East India Company in 1601. He was then forty-seven, and chief pilot to John Lancaster as commander. The Company had been founded in 1600 by a charter from Queen Elizabeth that granted it a monopoly of English trade in Asia and the Pacific. Having left from Woolwich in February, the weather was so bad and the expedition so delayed that it was taking on more water and provisions in Dartmouth by Easter; the five ships with 500 or more crew finally sailed on 18 April. All the ships returned in September 1603 with a valuable cargo and an established future for the Company. But a full third of the men had died. On Davis's previous voyage with the Dutch, many had been killed in an ambush laid by the Sultan of Aceh in Sumatra. This time, primed by Davis, Lancaster so impressed the sultan – with a letter from the queen and extravagant presents – that he was able to negotiate a trade treaty and load up with pepper, cloves and spices, leaving behind a small group to establish positions. The East India Company was on its way. By the 18th century it was to become Britain's most successful enterprise. Davis's third voyage to China and Japan was to be his last. He was killed, aged sixty-two, by Japanese pirates off Sumatra.

The Gilberts – John, Humphrey, and Adrian – close contemporaries of Davis's, lived at Greenway. Their half brother Walter Raleigh, born in 1552 when their widowed mother remarried, spent holidays there with them. They were neighbours of Davis, and their support was often critical in his career. But they were different animals – well-connected soldiers, courtiers and administrators.

It was their mother's aunt from Modbury, Kat Astley, or Ashley, who gave these West Country men their chance. 'The Gentlewomen Katheryne Chambernowne and three others' were on a list of 'Personages appointed to attend on the Lady Elizabeth, the King's daughter' in October 1536[2] and she seems to have been the future queen's governess from 1545, the year she married John Astley. A small portrait of her shows a plump, serious face, not a beauty or lady of fashion, but a strong person choosing to appear insignificant. She was well educated, and Elizabeth was to write to the Protector 'She brynketh me up from the cradell to the throne'.[3] When Mary became queen and Elizabeth was imprisoned, Kat seems to have been imprisoned too. In May 1555 a letter from the Privy Council enjoins Sir Roger Chomeley 'to set at liberty Katheryne Assheley who hath of long time remained in his custodie'.[4] Kat probably introduced Humphrey Gilbert to Elizabeth after she was released. 'Such was his countenance, forwardness and good behaviour, that Hir Majestie had a special good liking to him, and verie oftentimes would familiarlie discourse and confer with him in matters of learning.' [5]

Kat Ashley, unknown artist, governess to Princess Elizabeth and aunt to the mother of Sir Walter Raleigh and the Gilberts.

Courtesy Lord Hastings

As England's relations with Spain deteriorated, Elizabeth turned two blind eyes towards privateering raids on Spanish fleets and American possessions, and the Gilberts and Raleigh, with Sir Francis Drake and Sir John Hawkins from nearby Plymouth, were all periodically involved in them.

The East India Company's First Venture, 1601, oil, by David Cobb (born 1921).

Dartmouth Museum

SYR
HVMFRYE · GILBER
KNIGHT · DROWNE
IN · THE · DISCOVE
OF · VIRGINIA
ANNO 1584 ·

QVID NON

Sir Humphrey Gilbert, oil,
c.1584, at Compton Castle.
© *National Trust Images/*
courtesy of Geoffrey Gilbert

Opposite: Queen Elizabeth I,
studio of Nicholas Hilliard, at
Hardwick Hall. The queen's
clothes were essential to
the image she projected of
herself and England –
confident, opulent and
awe-inspiring. The jewels she
wore encrusted on her
dresses were often presents
from her courtiers, who
had acquired them from
the Spanish and Portuguese
treasure ships. She would
have them removed and re-
sewn onto different garments
as she changed them.
© *National Trust Images/*
John Hammond

Humphrey Gilbert – who Thomas Westcote, writing in 1630, called 'that high attempting spirit' –
was as obsessed as Davis with finding a northern route to China and India, writing *A Discourse
of a Discoverie for a new Passage to Cathay* for Queen Elizabeth in 1566. After a first, disastrous
attempt to reach Newfoundland from Dartmouth in 1578, he landed successfully in 1583, claiming
the island for England, mapping the coasts and recording details of the climate, products and
population. The Europeans who had been fishing there during the summers for at least fifty years
must have wondered how his claim would affect them, but the island was not to be settled
permanently by the English for another century. As for Gilbert, much of his fleet was lost, with
all his records. In the end, two ships set off for home across the Atlantic, Captain Hayes in the
Golden Hind and Sir Humphrey in the tiny 10-ton *Squirrel*, named after the squirrel on his coat
of arms. Gilbert never made it, going down in a storm off the Azores.

Sir Walter Raleigh, the untiring supporter of the Dart explorers, was born in 1552 at Hayes
Barton near East Budleigh. A soldier and explorer, he was an accomplished writer and poet, a
courtier and an intellectual and by 1583 Raleigh had made his fortune soldiering in Europe and

Sir Walter Raleigh,
miniature by Henry Bone
(1755-1834) at Wallington,
Northumberland.

© *National Trust Images/*
Derrick E. Witty

Ireland. But being a favourite at court grounded him in London. Precluded from leading explorations himself, he put his experience, money and ideas into others' voyages, including those of Davis and Gilbert, and early and unsuccessful colonisations of Virginia (see the chapter 'The Seas that Bind' for more on these settlements.) He always kept strong contacts with the West Country, being Warden of the Stannaries of Cornwall and Devon from 1584, Lord Lieutenant of Cornwall from 1587, and Vice Admiral of Devon from 1585, when he managed England's coastal defences and military levies during the Armada. Contemporaries say he never lost his Devon accent.

In 1591 the queen imprisoned him in the Tower for marrying Elizabeth Throckmorton, one of her ladies in waiting, without permission. She released him to go to Dartmouth in 1592 to secure the royal share of the cargo of the treasure ship, the *Madre de Deus*, and Robert Cecil describes in a letter Raleigh's state of mind when he saw his half brother, John Gilbert, there. 'His heart is broken for he is extremely pensive longer than he is busied...The meeting between him and Sir John Gilbert was with tears on Sir John's part, and...whensoever he is saluted with congratulation for liberty, he doth answer "No, I am still the Queen of England's poor captive".' [6]

Raleigh made two trips to South America in search of Eldorado, the presumed source of Spanish gold that attracted so much attention from English privateers, exploring modern Guyana and eastern Venezuela. After Queen Elizabeth died in 1603, James I had Raleigh arrested at the Exeter Inn, Ashburton and imprisoned for allegedly participating in a plot against him. After being released to make his second attempt to find Eldorado in 1616, he was re-arrested and executed to appease Spanish anger at a raid by some of his men on a Spanish garrison on the Orinoco. His tragic death confirmed him as an Elizabethan hero.*

Davis never made any money from his voyages and most explorers at one time or another went on more lucrative expeditions to rob the Spanish. This was made easier after Spain annexed Portugal and England then routed the Armada. Dartmouth history contains a fine example of why the early Portuguese monopoly of trade to the east was so enticing.

In September 1592, into Dartmouth harbour came the *Madre de Deus*, 'the largest of the great and fabulously wealthy carracks from the East Indies'. It was the biggest vessel England had ever hosted, and 'a sight altogether extraordinary' says a history of the event.[7] It was an enormous 1600-ton Portuguese carrack, reportedly with seven decks stuffed with spices, perfumes, drugs, like frankincense and camphire, fabrics – silks, calicos, canopies, tapestries and quilts – carpets, dyes, pearls, musk, civet as well as Chinese porcelain, ivory and ebony. Even at the time, the description was probably exaggerated. She also carried those valuable documents on Asian trade described so unforgettably by Hakluyt. She had been intercepted by privateeers including Sir John Burroughes on Raleigh's *Rowe Bucke* near Flores Island off the Azores on her way back to Lisbon from her second voyage to India.

Pandemonium broke loose when the *Madre* arrived. 'All Devonshire was in an uproar... Thousands flocked to the shore; letters to friends in London brought down other thousands...to

Portuguese Carracks off a Rocky Coast, oil, circle of Joachim Patinir, early to mid-16th century. This is thought to be the *Santa Catarina de Monte Sinai*, not the *Madre de Deus*, and is one of the very few contemporary paintings of early carracks. © *National Maritime Museum, Greenwich, London*

fill their purses.' Court commissioners were sent from London to Dartmouth with instructions to bring 'the cargo...by the Queen's order...to the Thames afore our house of Greenwich'.[8]

One of the commissioners was Lord Burghley's son Robert Cecil, who reported smelling the amber and musk on peoples' clothes within seven miles of Exeter – forty miles from Dartmouth. He complained he had never met with 'fouler weather, desperater ways, nor more obstinate people', but judiciously found 'an armlet of gold, a fork and spoon of crystal, with rubies, which I reserve for the Queen'. Elizabeth sent Raleigh, recently imprisoned in the Tower, hard on his heels and Cecil writes that his 'poor servants to the number of one hundred and forty goodly men and all the mariners came to him with... shouts of joy.'[9] Raleigh recovered enough treasure to load ten ships to take to London, where it was valued at £140,000.*

Accounts of the actual amounts of goods carried by the carrack vary; one says she had 425 tons of pepper alone. Elizabeth received enough pepper to risk flooding the London pepper market and cause a price collapse, so the city authorities were told not to sell any pepper until the queen's share had been placed.

* Robert Cecil instructed the local gentry to pursue the pilferers of the loot into their own homes. In a letter to him, dated 1592, Richard Champernowne of nearby Dartington Hall at Totnes describes finding 'of an emerod made in the form of a cross 3 inches in length at least of great breadth who of the Company sold hytt hys name set down... that won Mr Chychester who went in thys fleete sold 41 diamonds. We finde of an other that sold 21 dyamonds some very fayrr...We finde of 1400 very great Pearles who sold them. We found a chest of won Capteyn Norton worth 300£1...'.
(C.E. Champernowne, unpublished manuscript, 1954, p.134.)

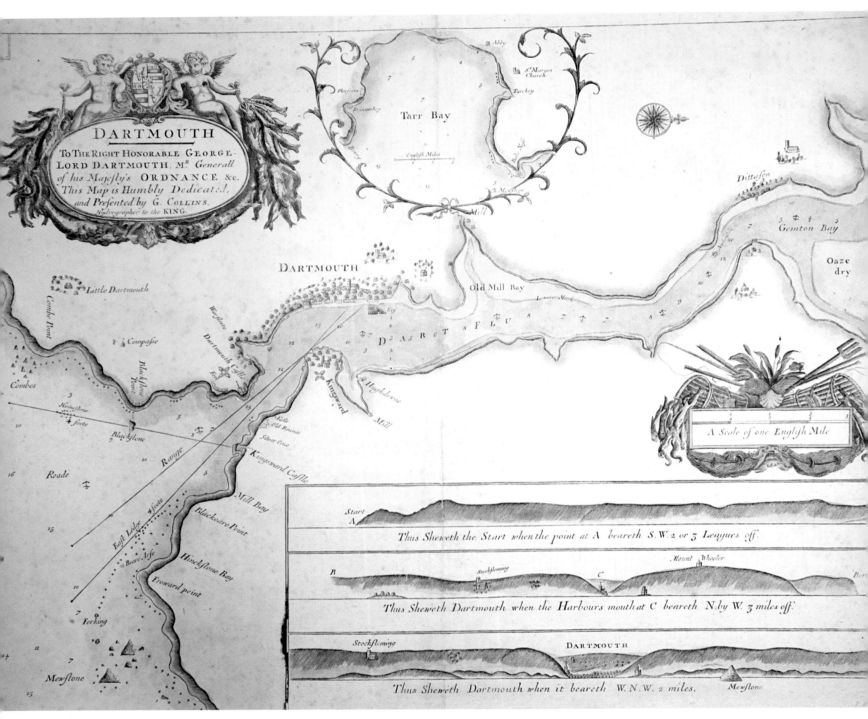

Map of Dartmouth, c.1693. Inscribed 'Dartmouth, to the Right Honorable George, Lord Dartmouth, M
Generall of his Majesty's Ordnance &c. This Map is Humbly Dedicated, and Presented by G. Collins,
Cartographer to the King'.

Valerie Wills/Richard Webb

Previous Spread:
The Mayflower and Speedwell in Dartmouth Harbour, Leslie Wilcox, oil, 1971. The 120-ton *Mayflower*
towers over the 60-ton *Speedwell*.

Pilgrim Hall Museum, Plymouth, Massachusetts

THE SEAS THAT BIND

North America was a natural destination for Devonians. Following the trade winds down to Iberia, out of the gales of the Channel and the Bay of Biscay and into the long swing of the easterlies across to the Azores and then up the east coast of America and home on the westerlies, the trip took about three months. Where explorers went, settlers followed. Exploration brought glory – and land. When, in June 1578, Sir Humphrey Gilbert received his royal licence it was 'to discover, search, find out and view such remote heathen and barbarous lands...not actually possessed of any Christian prince or people'.[1] The queen wanted colonies, but not, then, to annoy the Spanish. Since the latter were already in Florida, Sir Humphrey reconnoitred the east coast of America to the north. High politics determined where Devonians went in America.

Dartmouth played a minor role in early settlements. In 1602 Bartholomew Gosnold, captain of the Dartmouth *Concord*, with Bartholomew Gilbert, son of Sir Humphrey, took thirty-two men on an unusually direct course from Falmouth, sighting Cape Elizabeth on the Maine coast seven weeks later. The town encompassing the Elizabeth Islands is still called Gosnold; with a population of seventy-five, it is the smallest town in Massachusetts. Dartmouth Massachusetts, within sight of the Elizabeth Islands, may well be named after Gosnold's voyage. Three years after Gosnold, Captain George Waymouth called in at Dartmouth en route to New England in the *Archangel*. He stayed two weeks and took on more crew. They travelled the Maine coast, trading with Native Americans and bringing back five,* with two canoes, which they gave to their financiers, Sir Ferdinando Gorges and Sir George Popham.[2]

Peace with Spain after 1606 made colonisation safer. King James chartered two companies: one in London and one in Plymouth, under Sir Robert Cecil and Sir John Popham respectively. Raleigh Gilbert of Greenway, Sir Humphrey's youngest son, was a promoter of the London company expedition that established the first permanent English colony in Jamestown in May 1607; Gosnold died there. Gilbert chose, however, to sail with the Plymouth company and 120 settlers to the mouth of the Kennebec River in Maine. This was much less successful. The settlers built Fort St George, but more than half went home in December, leaving only forty-five to endure the winter. Their stores burnt, Popham died and Gilbert came home with the remaining settlers in the spring. Gilbert then inherited Compton Castle as well as Greenway and set out no more.

The Champernownes and Shapleighs from Dartmouth were typical of the next emigrants. Not explorers but merchants, they went where they traded. Both families were solidly grounded in Dartmouth and Kingswear. They were related, had adjoining houses and wharves at Kittery, owned privateers in common and were both prominent local merchant adventurers.[3] The Champernowne estate, Dartington Hall, was near the head of the tidal Dart. Built by the Earl

* Bringing Native Americans back was not unusual; they were used as publicity to interest new investors. There are baptismal records of three Native Americans in Devon: Raleigh at Bideford in 1588; Adrian the Indian (after Adrian Gilbert of Greenway) at Stoke Gabriel in 1597; and Gifferdandgorge (after Gorges) at Plymouth in 1602. John, an 'Indian of the Fort', buried in Plymouth in February 1613, may have been brought back by Captain Waymouth. (Gray, p.30.)

Hotel Champernowne, Kittery Point, postcard. Built in 1890 and torn down in 1927, in between it hosted many Shapleigh reunions.

of Huntingdon, John Holand, half-brother to Richard II, at the end of the 14th century, it was the grandest residential palace in the West Country. Champernowne connections were to trigger the emigration. Sir Ferdinando Gorges, prominent in the Plymouth company, was Arthur Champernowne's brother-in-law, and granted him in 1636 'two tracts of land...within...New England, bordering on the eastern shore of the Piscataqua River and at its mouth'.[4] Francis Champernowne, Arthur's son, set out that year at the age of twenty-two, and it is highly likely that Alexander Shapleigh and his son, Nicholas, sailed with Francis on their 160-ton *Benediction*.

The two families established themselves at the mouth of the Piscataqua River and gave their new homes names that recorded their old: Gommerack, Kittery, Dartington and Greenland. Remarkably, after 450 years, Devon and the Portsmouth area of New England still have these names. There are still Shapleys (no longer Shapleighs) around the Dart and a vigorous community in Maine. Until quite recently, Maine Shapleighs turned to Kittery Court in Kingswear for a sprig of myrtle for their wedding bouquets. Both countries have a Kittery and a Modbury or Madbury. Kittery is the earliest town in Maine with a population of some 9,500 in 2000. The Devon Kittery usually refers to Kittery Court, a house south of the quays, its gardens spreading along the waterfront called Kittery Point. Kittery, Devon, is in a charter of c. 1180 recording a gift of land there as Kittetorra, or Kite-Tor, the hill of the kites, birds that still swoop and hover above the Dart.[5] The charter records that the recipient of the land gave the donor, William de Vascy, 'a gold piece, Juliana his wife, a silken wimple and his son, Walter, a silver ring.'

Greenland, where Francis made his first home in the Strawberry Banks area on the south shore of the Piscataqua Bay, is now a town of some 3,000 in the Portsmouth district of New Hampshire. As late as 1899, Charles Tuttle was talking about 'the "old farm" of Captain Champernowne [as he called Francis] with grand old English oaks, planted as tradition has it, by the Captain's own hand.'[6] In 1902, Francis Gawayne Champernowne from Dartington visited his namesake's grave in Maine, and in a letter home he notes that '...the country round is very pretty and reminded me of the lower reaches of the Dart.'[7]

The Champernownes and Shapleighs may be the best documented, but over 1620-42 some 58,000 British emigrated to America and the West Indies.[*] Over the thirty years from 1654, 10,000 sailed from Bristol alone – farmers, tradesmen, mechanics, husbandmen. Servants and apprentices were actively recruited in Devon to work in the new colonies. Many travelling across the Atlantic to fish, simply stayed.

Others were driven by conditions at home. In 1625 and following years, Devon had a bad outbreak of plague, Ashburton losing 450 people, Dartmouth at least 90. After 1629, Charles I ruled without a Parliament, and split loyalties destabilised families and towns. Puritans left to avoid discrimination after Queen Elizabeth's parliament had passed her Statutes of Supremacy and Uniformity, the latter confirmed by Charles II in 1662, forbidding clergy from using any liturgy or service not from the established church. Many left for better lives abroad as the civil war and wars with Spain and Holland took their toll on trade.

* When Gilbert found '36 sailes' at St Johns, Newfoundland, in 1583, fishing was mainly seasonal but it is thought that thousands of English and Irish sailing to Newfoundland in those years went on to New England, where from 1615 new fishing grounds had been developed by West Country fishermen off the 'maine' coast. This winter cod business was eventually to drive out the English trading from England. (Dickinson, 1987, p.71.) Like many others, Arthur Champernowne was commissioned in 1622 to trade and fish in New England; it was a short step to stay and trade from there.

A glint of glory came to Dartmouth when a fortuitous leak in the ineptly-named *Speedwell* brought the Leyden Pilgrims into port. By the time they reached Dartmouth on 11 August, 1620, the Pilgrims on the *Speedwell* must have been frustrated. They had bid farewell to their fellow congregationalists at Delfshaven in Holland on 22 July and sailed in the *Speedwell* to join the *Mayflower* in Southampton. After the *Speedwell* had undergone her first repairs, they had set out for America on 5 August. Still in the Channel, in a calm sea with light winds, the *Speedwell* sprang leaks again and the captain dared not face the open sea. Dartmouth was the nearest port; there they went and there they stayed until 23 August, when they weighed anchor for another attempt. During that time, the *Speedwell*, 'as open and leaky as a sieve', was thoroughly overhauled.

But the passengers were apparently unable to enjoy their enforced respite. The log-book for 13 August remarks drily: 'Lying at anchor with Speedwell leaking badly in Dartmouth harbour. No passengers, except leaders, allowed ashore.' According to a letter written four days later by Robert Cushman, a leader of the English community in Leyden, Master Christopher Martin had insisted that passengers be kept on board 'lest they should run away'. Cushman was embittered by being demoted to Martin's assistant when the latter, from the London group, had been elected the ship's 'governour', and the log entry for 16 August records 'much dissatisfaction between passengers,

Dartington Great Hall, mixed media, John Piper, c.1946. Dartington was massively restored by Leonard and Dorothy Elmhirst in the 20th century but Francis Champernowne would have recognised this view, although the roof of the great hall was decaying in his time.
The Dartington Hall Trust Collection

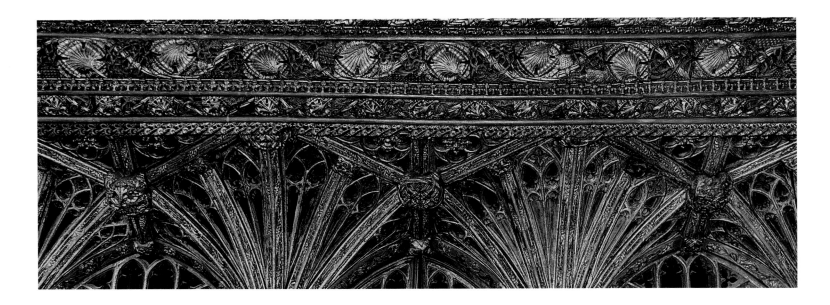

SLAVERY AND SIEGE

The End of the Small Merchant

For sixty years from about 1580 until the civil war arrived in Dartmouth in 1643, the town enjoyed a surge in prosperity. Not so much from the glory days of the explorers as from the efforts of its many small merchants, who were developing the Newfoundland cod fisheries in earnest. Their ships, at first only forty to fifty tons, battled down across the Bay of Biscay in the March storms to join the trade winds across the Atlantic. They spent the summer in and off Newfoundland, catching and salting the cod, pressing trayne oil from the livers, to exchange for wine and fruit in Iberian and Mediterranean markets on their way home in the autumn.

These Dartmouth merchants were different from others. English trade was largely monopolised by mostly London-based chartered companies, such as the East India Company, with which John Davis sailed, or the Levant Company, which controlled trade into the Mediterranean. But in Dartmouth, any small entrepreneur who could raise enough to fit out a 100-ton vessel for forty men was free to do it, sharing the profits equally between shipowner, victualler and master and crew. And they were successful. By the end of the 16th century, the Dartmouth fleet was thought to make up a fifth of the 250-400 English ships on the east coast of Newfoundland.[1]

The top rail of the screen in St. Saviour shows the ropes and grapes symbolising the sea trade in wine that made Dartmouth rich.

Valerie Wills/St Saviour

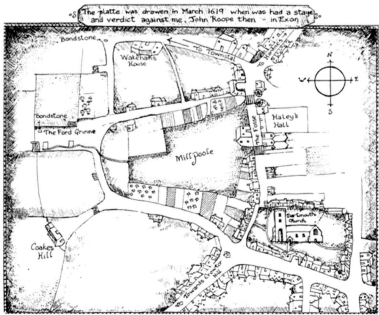

The platte was drawen in March 1619 when was had a stage and verdict against me, John Roope then - in Exon

The Butterwalk, watercolour by Matthew Rooke, late 19th century. These four extravagant houses were built between 1635 and 1640 on newly reclaimed land at the bottom of Duke Street. They cost about £2,500 (building a farmhouse then cost £40)[2] and signal the wealth of early 17th-century Dartmouth. Charles II was entertained here on 27 July 1671. Rooke was associated with the work of John Ruskin and William Morris to preserve England's early buildings.

Valerie Wills/Dartmouth Museum

Map of Dartmouth in 1619, by John Roope. It was drawn to support his case that there was no right of way between Clifton, centred on the church, and Hardnesse across the Foss, where he owned the bridges for the mill. He lost, and we now have Fosse Street. The map shows the new quay on the river side of the church wall with its first three houses.[3]

Sally Hill

The town prospered and expanded. Contributions from citizens, court fines and graveyard fees financed a building boom. The population is thought to have more than doubled from about 900 people in 1523-24 to some 2,200 in 1660-61.[4] More than half the names of families in Dartmouth in 1643 had not been there a century earlier.[5] Unable to expand up the hills, the town corporation reclaimed land, tipping waste and rubble into the river below the walls of St Saviour's and north of it, building a large new quay and about a hundred fine houses, including on the Butterwalk, many of which still stand. St Saviour's and St Petrox churches were beautified and extended.

Yet even as the opulent expansion of the town advertised its success, its foundations were weakening. The small entrepreneurs were being badly damaged by increasing lawlessness on the seas and were ultimately to be destroyed by the royalist siege and occupation during the English civil war. Vessels on the high seas carried one man's treasure and another's quarry. 'The Enemy seem'd to me as monstrous ravenous Creatures' wrote the adolescent Joseph Pitts of his capture off the Spanish coast in 1678 'which made me cry out "O Master! I am afraid they will kill us and eat us". To which his captain had replied "No, no Child,...they will carry us to Algier, and sell us".'[6]

Joseph Pitts' vessel had been surprised not by European or American privateers but a growing and terrifying menace – the Barbary pirates from Salé. These 'Sallee Rovers', as they came to be known, joined other pirates from north Africa to make the 17th and 18th centuries one of the worst periods of piracy the Atlantic and Mediterranean had ever seen.

Piracy in the Mediterranean had been on the rise since the first expulsion of the Moors from Spain in 1212. Then, in 1610, Phillip II of Spain expelled the last of the Moors: the *Hornacheros*, the tough group who went to Salé. The Sallee Rovers made the seas far more dangerous. As well as xebecs, small lateen-rigged boats, they used square riggers, which took them out into the north Atlantic and up to Scandinavia. Harsher, more capricious and wider ranging than other pirates, they followed trade routes, attacking Dartmouth vessels both off Newfoundland (where the cured cod was loaded) and off Oporto (where it was taken).* Within fifty years, every coastal port in the West Country had been affected.

The north Africans were after slaves. Algiers had most, with an estimated 25,000 at any one time between 1550 and 1730, and sometimes almost double that.† The steady population of English slaves was predominantly from the West Country. In 1635, of an estimated 20,000 British at sea, about half were from Devon. In a list of some 300 slaves rescued from 'Sally' in 1637 by a government fleet, 89 were from Devon and 22 from Dartmouth, the same number as from London. Only Plymouth and Dungarvan accounted for more. (There are Dungarvans in Ireland and Cornwall; perhaps the list conflates them.)[7]

In 1615, pirates inflicted an enormous £8,000-worth of unspecified losses on Dartmouth. In 1620 the town contributed £89 towards an unsuccessful expedition to Algiers, and later records many payments to 'poor mariners taken by the Turks' who trickled home. Two years later, the mayor excuses a 'small contribution of £30' towards another expedition 'by reason of the loss of six ships of this port this year taken and carried away by the Turks,...each of them of a burden

* By 1617, they were reconnoitring the Thames and the English, French, and Irish coasts, and in 1625 there was a major attack on Cornish ports and Lundy Island in the Bristol Channel was overrun. At Mount's Bay off Land's End, an eye witness recorded that Moors in *djellabas* wielding scimitars crept up on villagers in church, dragging off sixty men, women and children. The mayor of Plymouth told the Privy Council that raids on Mount's Bay and Looe had lost the West Country '27 ships and 200 persons taken', and by the end of the summer he estimated 1,000 skiffs had been destroyed and as many villagers captured and taken off to Salé into slavery. In some small places, almost the entire population was captured. By 1635 there was annual alarm along the coast that the returning Newfoundland fleets would be attacked by Barbary pirates lurking around the Scillies. (Bhanji, 1996, p.40.)

† Allowing for those who died, were ransomed, escaped, or converted to Islam – called *renegados* – this meant some 8,500 captured annually. A record of 1682 gives 160 British ships taken by the *al-ghuzat*, or soldiers of Mohammed, of Algeria between 1677 and 1680, which would translate into 7,000 to 9,000 seamen taken as slaves by Algeria alone. Most were southern European, especially Spanish, but the records show there were also Icelanders, other Scandinavians and Americans. (Most of this information comes from Milton [2004], which is based on published and unpublished records of the Salé slave trade. The estimates are from Milton p.271; it is corroborated by other sources, but comes from the French padre, Father Pierre Dan, who was in Algeria during the 17th century.)

A Fight in Boats with Barbary Pirates, by Willem van de Velde the Younger, c.1685.

© *National Maritime Museum, Greenwich, London*

150 tons and upwards, all laden with fish and merchandise, and in them 130 men now remaining captive in Algiers, many of them being of this place whereof wives and children are now left for most part to be relieved by the town.'[8] (Pirates were called Turks irrespective of origin.)

Thomas Newman of Dartmouth lost his 120-ton vessel to Barbary pirates in 1615, and was enslaved for a year in Algiers before being ransomed for £200 (the annual income of a London shopkeeper was £10). According to his own affidavit and mayoral records,[9] he lost £1,500 to pirates between 1612 and 1620. We don't know whether this included his ransom. To be able to afford his ransom at all, the Newmans must have been wealthy, but it did take them a year to collect it. Over 1609-16, the *al-ghuzat* of Algiers captured 466 English trading ships passing through the Straits of Gibraltar.

Newman left no description of his capture, but many escaped or ransomed slaves did. Pirates greased the hulls of their xebecs so they glided through the water, low enough to be missed by larger vessels, fast enough to emerge suddenly right up against their prey. Surprise was key; out of the blue, sailors found a noisy menacing crowd right on top of them on deck, disabling the craft by hacking down the masts and rigging. 'It is a terrifying thing to see the frenzy they work themselves into when they attack the ships. They appear on the upper deck, sleeves rolled up, their scimitar in hand, bawling all together in a most terrifying fashion' wrote a contemporary chronicler.[10]

Negotiating the Release of Slaves in Algeria, *Histoire de Barbarie*, Pierre Dan, Paris, 1637.

Taken back to Algiers, Newman would have had a 1½ lb shackle riveted around his ankle and attached to a chain. Until the slave auction he would have been kept in an underground cell, fetid, crowded and dark. Likely looking men would have been fed well, on 'fresh vittels once a daye and sometimes twice in abondance, and good white breade from the market place.'[11] At the auction, dealers checked age, health and strength – slaves were paraded like horses, limbs poked and teeth tapped. 'Their first policy is to look in their mouths' wrote William Okeley in his memoir 'and a good strong set of grinders will advance the price considerably.'[12] Signs of wealth meant the possibility of ransom. Abraham Browne records that common seamen usually fetched £30-£35; Newman's £200 ransom was high.*

Newman was lucky to have been captured by Algerians. Robert Adams, taken by the Sallee Rovers in the 1620s, wrote to his West Country parents that he was made to 'worke at a mill like a horse, from morninge untill night, with chaines upon my legges, of 36 pounds waights a peece.' Held in an underground cell, he ate 'a littell coarse bread and water'. His hair and ragged clothes swarmed with lice and fleas until 'I am almost eaten up with them'.[13] Violent beatings, maiming and even decapitation were possibilities if you happened to be unlucky enough to work for the sultan.

Stories about slavery were common London gossip. Samuel Pepys, in his diary entry for 8 February 1661, records going to the Fleece tavern with 'many' sea commanders, including returned slaves from Algiers. They 'made me full acquainted with their condition there. As, how they eat nothing but bread and water. At their redempcion, they pay so much for the water that they drink at the public fountaynes during their being slaves. How they are beat upon the soles of the feet and bellies at the Liberty of their *Padron*...How the poorest men do use their slaves best.'[14]

Galleas, drawing, Arthur Howe Holdsworth, 1798. A galleas was similar to a xebec and used widely in the Mediterranean during the 17th century.

Private collection

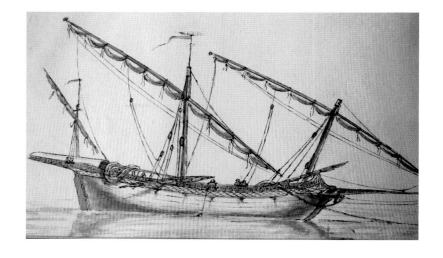

'The strength and boldness of the Barbary pirates is now grown to that height...as I have never known anything to have wrought a greater sadness and distraction in this court than the daily advice thereof.'[15] Thus Sir Francis Cottingham, one of King James' counsellors, in the early 1600s, wringing metaphorical hands over the government's impotence.

'Go tell the King of England, go tell him from me,
If he reign king of the land, I will reign king of the sea.'

This couplet from a contemporary ballad about John Ward, a notoriously vicious and active *renegado*, or convert, says it all about the corsairs' dominance of the seas.[16] Official reluctance to field an effective naval fleet is symbolised by Sir Ferdinando Gorges' resignation in 1629 as Governor of the Forts and Islands at Plymouth

The Bombardment of Algiers, 27 August 1816, oil, by George Chambers, c.1836. This attack led to the slave markets of north Africa finally being closed.

© *National Maritime Museum, Greenwich, London*

because 'the pay of his men was three and a half years in arrear and his forts in ruin'.[17] Successive British governments were harassed by mayors, merchants, wives and widows, and monarchs from Charles I to George III sent mostly small and futile missions to the Barbary Coast. Until 1816, none were successful in putting an end to the problem. In 1602, after a petition from West Country ports, including Dartmouth, the Privy Council sent two men o' war, and in 1613 the City of Exeter was authorised to fit out ships and pressgang crews to defend merchant ships, commissioning the *Hopewell* of Dartmouth. By 1656 there were regular convoys for ships from Dartmouth, Topsham, Lyme and Weymouth crossing the Channel to St Malo and Morlaix, but not any further. Complaints of losses and petitions for protection continued.

Many slaves died, a few escaped or were ransomed, but most never saw their families again. Some converted to Islam. Thomas Norton of Dartmouth, captured by Algerians in 1620, escaped to Salé where he first became a carpenter and mariner, and then a ship's captain for the corsairs after he had bought his freedom. Once at sea, he seized a Dartmouth ship with its crew, but was driven onto the rocks at La Rochelle and taken by the French. The Christians were released and the Turks sent back to Morocco. Norton came back to Dartmouth, and

*The government tried to organise ransoms, but ineptly. In 1643, Parliament ordered church collections for a ransom fund. Mostly, the people affected raised the money – families, friends and neighbours, rich and poor, clubbed together or borrowed. A petition to the Privy Council in 1624 by Nicholas Spicer, an Exeter merchant, to get £137 10s back from Thomas Spurway and William Neyle of Dartmouth to pay a London merchant for redeeming 20 captives in Algiers indicates the networks of the wealthy like Newman. The record that 156 inhabitants of Stoke Gabriel (up the Dart) gave £5 5s 1d to redeem captives in 1670 shows the determination of the poor to get their people back; two groats, tiny-value coins worth about 4d, were given back as obsolete. (Bhanji, 1996, p.26.)

The *Cleveland*, in which Charles II came to Dartmouth in 1671, from a work by Willem van de Velde the Younger. Historians differ on why the king came, what he did and how long he stayed. All agree he was making a progress down the Channel to inspect the new citadel in Plymouth. Beating against an easterly wind, the fleet bore away from Lyme Regis back into Dartmouth. *Valerie Wills/Dartmouth Museum*

In the midst of all these travails, Dartmouth was to receive a royal visit – its first since Edward I was driven in by storms in 1294.[22] Charles II arrived in the *Cleveland* with a fleet of retainers on 23 July 1671. The mayor, Emanuel Woolley, another conforming puritan (note his Christian name), paid £36 6s 8d for His Majesty's ushers, waiters, sergeants at arms, marshalls, porters, harbingers, trumpeters, footmen, boatmen, barbers and for the sewers of the Chamber, among other expenses.

Did Charles II intend to visit Dartmouth? Historians refer to elaborate preparations – the castle had a new flag, using '74 yards of bunter'; Christopher Lock, painter and gilder, smartened up St Saviour's, the town jewel, painting the coats of arms of prominent families and benefactors, judiciously excluding non-conforming puritans. How long did the king stay? He was almost certainly entertained by Woolley in his fine panelled house in the Butterwalk. Many years later some square wax candles with the royal arms painted on them were discovered there.[23] Did he see St Saviour's? All we know is that the next day Charles II was at Exeter en route to London. The payments to the boatmen suggest he was ferried to Kingswear, and the Hody family then at Nethway House (the manor behind the settlement) have a record that he spent the night there. And 'there is in St Saviour's church' says Freeman 'a stained glass coat of arms to Charles FitzCharles, the bastard son of the king, whom he created Earl of Dartmouth [according to local legend] because he was conceived on his travels to Devon.'[24] (The boy died young.)

Modern Pirates

Dartmouth is a town of long-distance sailors, and piracy is again stalking the seas they cross. On 22 October 2009, Rachel and Paul Chandler set off across the Indian Ocean for Tanzania from Mahé in the Seychelles in their 38-foot yacht, Lynn Rival. The Chandlers are a Dartmouth family, and Rachel and Paul came here after their ordeal. "We chose to opt out of the rat race and go cruising for as long as our health and savings would allow," said Rachel. "For ten years we worked towards this dream."

In the early hours of the following morning, less than sixty miles west of Mahé and still within Seychelles waters, they were assaulted and captured by pirates from Somalia. Rachel, who was on watch, just had time to light the torch as she heard engines. Almost instantaneously, the pirates were slamming their skiff against the hull, and heaving themselves on board, crashing their AK-47s on the coaming, yelling and screaming.

The parallels with 17th-century Barbary piracy are remarkable. These pirates were wide-ranging; the Chandlers were captured some 800 miles off the Somali coast, where the pirates were based. They operated out of small vessels – 16-foot flat-bottomed skiffs instead of xebecs. Their motherboat, in which they had travelled 800 miles, was small, open, and full of storage drums, half with diesel and half with water.

The pirates, hardly more than youths, wielded impressive weapons, not scimitars but AK-47s, rocket launchers and rocket-propelled grenades. Surprise and noise were key to capture, terrifying their victims. And they functioned with impunity; once captured, it took them a full week to land the Chandlers in Somalia. During this time, an emergency signal activated briefly by Paul had been picked up and the Seychelles coastguard had sent out a search vessel, a helicopter had spotted them, and they had conversed with a warship, being forced to say 'Turn away or we'll be killed'.

It had taken a year to ransom Thomas Newman in 1615, and it took slightly longer than that to ransom the Chandlers almost four centuries later. In both cases the ransom was arranged privately; the British Government took no part in it. We know more about why it took so long in the Chandler's case: it was mainly because of the gangsters' stubbornly high expectations, which the family could not match. But the personal cost – the fear, the bullying, the highs and lows of hope and disappointment combined with physical discomfort, constant moving and separation – must have been similar for Newman.

The Chandlers, like Newman, fell victim to the inability of nations to police the seas. But their story had an unexpected conclusion. While the family were negotiating and trying to raise money, the publicity had made a young Somali boy in East London ashamed to play football with his friends. His father, Dahir Abdullah Khadiye, flew to Nairobi and Mogadishu to begin the process that finally led to their dramatic release, months after the family had done everything they could.[25]

Living their dream; *Lynn Rival* and the Chandlers at sea.   *Paul and Rachel Chandler*

THEIR DAY IN THE SUN

The Great Merchants of Dartmouth

Here, mid-century, is Arthur Holdsworth, Governor of Dartmouth Castle. For well over a century after 1715 his family would dominate Dartmouth; they were Whigs, supporters of Walpole, free-traders. Five generations back, a Holdsworth had moved to nearby Modbury from Astey in Yorkshire, as vicar. The family had thrown itself into what Dartmouth did best – commerce – rising to become shipowners and merchants with properties in Newfoundland and Portugal. Arthur's grandfather bequeathed him his grand house of Widdicombe and an estate at Stokenham, with its wide views across to Start Bay and up the coast towards Dartmouth.

Though the painting shows him as an 18th-century aristocrat – gracious, landed and leisured – Arthur was in fact a merchant, his friends were business associates, and the river was their wealth. The painting depicts Stancombe bringing news of a lost ship – a fact of mercantile life. From 1713 and the Treaty of Utrecht that ended the War of Spanish Succession, wars with the Spanish, the Dutch and the French, particularly over the Americas, directly affected Dartmouth's trade. Uncertain times encouraged pirates and privateers with royal letters of marque, giving them the right to attack enemy vessels. The family was into privateering too: between 1739 and 1748 the Holdsworths and the Newmans had shares in fifteen privateers. Privateers operated on all sides of the conflict. The Holdsworth's *Tygress*, fitted out in 1745, captured three prizes, but was then taken by the French and ended up in Martinique.

This family business involved the whole town. Ships were built locally at Hardness or Coombe Mud and crewed by local sailors. The Holdsworths recruited hundreds if not thousands for the cod trade. 'Green' men signed up for two summers and a winter, or three summers and two winters in Newfoundland in exchange for free passage, keep and £15–£40 at the end. Few came back, settling there or moving on to New England. Historians believe this is why the population of Dartmouth was static between 1674 and 1801. Ships were usually financed by

Arthur Holdsworth Conversing with Thomas Taylor and Captain Stancombe by the River Dart, oil, by Arthur Devis, a painter of 'conversation' pictures, 1757. A merchant, Holdsworth chooses to be painted by Dartmouth Castle, of which he is Governor, and above the river where the ships that made his fortune were built. Taylor was Arthur's brother-in-law and Stancombe a Holdsworth captain. Arthur's relations with Stancombe were close; Arthur was an executor of his will, to receive 'one guinea to buy a ring', perhaps a bereavement ring. They would both have had money in Arthur's lost ship, said to be the subject of the 'conversation'.
Paul Mellon Collection, courtesy of the National Gallery of Art, Washington

The Newman barquentine *Retriever* at Harbour Breton, Newfoundland in 1887. The Newmans traded with Newfoundland throughout the 19th century, but by then had diversified to Africa and Asia and no longer depended on the cod-port business.

Private collection

Defoe tells of a perfect harbour and a vibrant town, where people are entrepreneurial and fish plentiful and cheap. His robust blend of description, anecdote and numbers all persuade us that he was here, and did and saw these things... but 500 ships? 40,000 pilchards? And surely the fort was a castle? Fact and fiction are interleaved. But does it matter? His message is the same as the etcher's: Dartmouth, small as it was, had an image as a significant port. And it was: foreign-going ships registered there more than quintupled between 1709 and 1770.

The 17th century was the peak of a mini-ice age. In 1672 three Dartmouth vessels with 180 men on board struck ice and went down off St John's, the main port that was the centre for Dartmouth's fishing off the Newfoundland banks.[4] 'Striving to be first in harbour' wrote a contemporary chronicler, 'and have the deepest places to make their fish upon, they bear such an overpress of sail as no seaman are the like in any part of the world. When fogs are thick and nights dark and they cannot discern the length of three ships on the way before them, and the ice flows threatening much peril, yet on runs the ship amain...when commonly most of the company are fast asleep with extreme hazard of their lives.'[5]

The ice caught *Charming Molly*. The text to the upper left of the drawing (opposite) tells you what is going on. Carpenters are 'cuting and whewing of ice to ease ship', the ice being 'in ilands and large panes'. Sails and sheet cables are converted to fenders to prevent *Molly* from being crushed. Someone is waving his hat to men setting off on the ice towards the shore and to more men coming back 'after 26 hours away'. Another man is ringing bells – to guide the sailors back? And the Captain is 'caling to his men not to go to far'. Meanwhile,

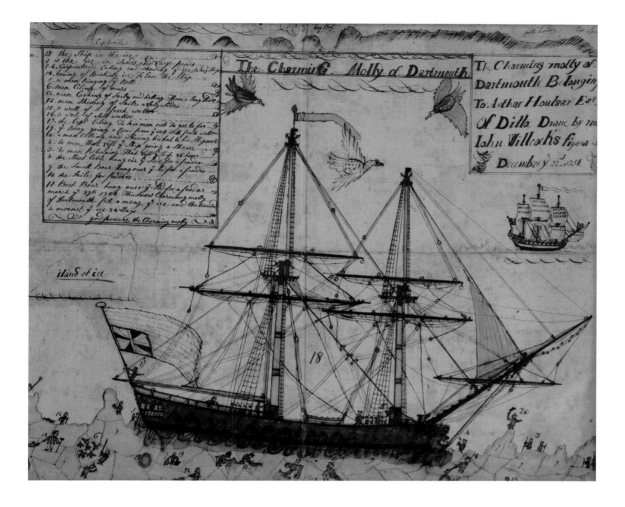

Charming Molly *in the ice off Newfoundland*, 1704, by John Willcocks. She belonged to the second Arthur Holdsworth, 1668-1726, and the story of her sojourn on the ice and her eventual release is told in this heavily annotated drawing.

Private collection

others are making the most of the mishap, 'caching of seales and halling them' and 'skinning of seales alongside'.

But a positive-looking dove is flying above *Molly*, and a miniature on the right shows her under sail on clear seas. The story ends happily. The drawing is dated 29 March 1754, and notes 'Charming Molly of Dartmouth fell among the ice and continued amongst the ice 24 days. God preserve the Charming Molly'. She got off.

The *Charming Molly* was owned by one Arthur Holdsworth, who, at least for a time, was a working sailor and a fishing admiral on and off from 1701-11. He later bought and rebuilt Widdicombe and it is his grandson we see at the beginning of this chapter relaxing under a tree overlooking the Dart some thirty years later in the painting by Arthur Devis.

Fishing admirals captained the first vessels arriving at St John's, Newfoundland in the spring, and had first choice of 'fishing rooms' to offload and cure fish and authority over competitors. With their vice- and rear-admirals (who arrived second and third) they held courts to consider petty crimes, like theft, and civil disputes – usually over property. Criminal matters were referred back to England – in 1671 the Dartmouth mayoralty received a warrant to try offences committed in Newfoundland – but very few made it to trial because of the cost of sending the suspect and witnesses home. Justice seems to have been straightforward. A letter from about

1827 in the archive of merchants Hunt, Roope & Teage, records 'an editor whose ears were cut off for having written in a disrespectful way of a Newfoundland merchant.'[6]

This cheap (for the government) and cheerful (for the admirals) governance was not to last. Admirals had to meet contracts, cure fish and ship it out – leaving little time to hold courts, and there is no record of Arthur holding a single one. When they did, they were policing competitors; this conflict of interest was a serious flaw. By the 1720s settlers were taking over the seasonal installations, and needed a less footloose legal institution, so in 1729 the naval commodore was appointed governor from spring to autumn and naval officers held courts all year round. Magistrates began to take over.

Arthur had come out to Newfoundland at a hard time. Until 1677, when William of Orange married Mary, the eldest daughter of King James, English seamen were harried by the Dutch and the Spanish. At the start of the second Dutch War in 1665, Admiral de Ruyter attacked St John's, destroying ships and property, and two years later the Dutch besieged Dartmouth. (The same year, 1667, de Ruyter was to sail up the Thames, burning the docks and shipping at Chatham, and blockading London for some weeks.) A petition to the Privy Council in 1666 records that Thomas Newman and Ambrose Mudd, merchants of Dartmouth, lost 'The Pilgrim of Dartmouth...laden with 1,250 quintals of dry Newfoundland fish for Aveiro in Portugal...surprised by a Spanish man-of-war'. They claimed 'near £4,000' damages and the English ambassador in Spain was charged 'to use his utmost endeavours to procure satisfaction for the petitioner'. Local merchants had national leverage.[7] Dutch privateers were to capture twenty-seven Dartmouth ships in 1672 alone during the Third Dutch War, over half en route home from Malaga.[8]

The fishing admiral Arthur Holdsworth was thirty-two when he went to St John's in 1701. Accounts suggest he focussed mightily on trade imperatives – harrying competitors, currying favour to

A Merchantman Entering Dartmouth Harbour, oil, Thomas Luny (1759-1837). A stormy sea, a brig under full sail coming into the secure harbour past the castle, in the distance a fishing vessel and in the foreground townsmen and women with dinghies ready to unload. Luny, a prolific painter, was Cornish, and moved to Teignmouth after a career in London, painting Dartmouth a great deal. *Private collection*

pursue contracts, and adapting the rules to suit himself. He was proud, duelling with an army officer over some slight. Two years after he left Newfoundland in 1711, French possessions there were ceded to England in the Treaty of Utrecht; peace reduced privateering and reopened markets. Although wars returned in earnest in 1739, Dartmouth recovered. Foreign-going ships registered there: some over 825 tons in 1709 increased dramatically to 4,492 tons by 1770. Arthur prospered; not only had he bought Widdicombe but he also owned a fine town house, Mount Galpin, on Clarence Street in Dartmouth, where he was twice mayor. (The house, large and solid, is still there.)

Dartmouth merchants in the century after the restoration of the monarchy were to create the extraordinary story of the cod-port trade and the ties between England and Portugal that have lasted until today.[9] The same Dartmouth names from Newfoundland begin to appear in the mid-17th century as shippers and agents in the trade of Red Portugal, a light astringent red wine from Viana do Castelo some forty-five miles north of Oporto. The predecessor to the Dartmouth firm Hunt, Roope & Co. already had warehouses there in 1654. Within twenty years they were also operating from Oporto on the Douro, better wine country, and by 1678 some 1,400 pipes of Douro wine (1 pipe is 115 gallons) were exported to England from there. Under the 1703 Methuen Treaty, Portuguese wine imports attracted less than half the duty of the French and by the end of the century wine exports from Oporto to England were 55,000 pipes.[10]

Port was to become as English as rosbif. 'Claret is the liquor for boys; port for men' intoned Dr Johnson, a three-bottles-a-sitting man himself, in 1779. Port, in the early 18th century, was still a table wine, drunk with food, often with water added, but just as quality was being improved, so new forms were being developed. Over the 18th century, Red Portugal wine, at first even despised by the Navy, was improved and then fortified by brandy, initially in small amounts to stabilise it during shipment. By the end of the century, the trade was already big business; heavy investment in infrastructure and controls had improved quality and the Alto Douro, where the finest wines are grown, was opened up. By 1840, the process of adding more brandy to arrest fermentation had been perfected and we had what we know as port. In the

Oporto, View of the Banks of the River Douro, by Dervy, c.1860. English merchants had 'port lodges' at Vila Nova de Gaia on the left of the river where the port was stored before being shipped; many of these lodges are still there.   *Valerie Wills/Private collection*

early days, Dartmouth merchants had bartered Newfoundland cod and English woollen goods in Portugal for salt and wine, and it was discovered that the wine, taken to Newfoundland en route to England, improved by being matured over the fishing season. This became company policy. Ambrose Mudd, merchant of Dartmouth, had wine with his oil and fish at St John's as early as 1667. A market developed in matured port wine, slender bottles were produced that could be laid on their side and binned to replace the squat wide bottles suitable for 'plonking' on tables. In 1775 Oporto produced the first vintage port – twelve years before Chateau-Lafite marketed their first vintage claret.[11]

Taylor & Newman; Holdsworth, Olive & Newman; Newman, Land & Hunt; Hunt & Newman; Hunt, Newman & Roope; Hunt, Roope, Teage & Co... the same names in different associations indicate which Dartmouth families were in the port trade. Most are still here today.

Many families were linked with the Oporto office of Robert Newman & Co that operated out of Dartmouth from 1679 until the end of the Napoleonic wars in 1815, when its head office moved to London. Although it continued to build ships in Dartmouth, and there were Roopes, Teages, Newmans and Hunts still living in Oporto after 1815, it was the 18th-century generations of these families who were the real Dartmothians. The men went first as passengers, to buy wine, organise collection and shipping, and then to return. Bradford describes 'How these early pioneers came to make their way up the Douro, jouncing on the backs of hired mules and ill-fed horses along perilous stony tracks over the great purple ridges of the Serra do Marao. Sweating in their heavy wigs and greatcoats, they spent comfortless nights in vile inns, where the food was villainous and the beds a battleground for vermin; hot tiring days haggling with the incomprehensible Portuguese over the price of their wine.' [12] As she says, the rewards must have been substantial for them to endure such discomforts. Their families followed. Many generations were to live and die there, as English Portuguese.*

Sailing to Oporto had its hazards. A letter from Thomas Woodmass in 1703 to his father describes the standard run to Viana do Castelo, recording bad weather, pirates, damage to the ship and losing crew to the navy.

*At first, conditions were tricky. Portugal was very Catholic and the Inquisition uneasy with Protestant ways. 'In spite of the friendship that should exist between the nations, they stick not to call us Hereticks and doggs', merchants were to complain. A state paper of 1654 records that Oliver Cromwell sent a fleet under Colonel Popham to assure the King of Portugal, then João IV, of his anxiety to preserve the ancient alliance, but instructed that if certain English merchants were not immediately set at liberty, and reasonably recompensed for their 'violent detention', the English fleet would attack Lisbon until 'the King, our dear ally, acknowledge our claim.' (Sellars, 1899, p.24.) The fleet never attacked; a peace treaty was to lay the basis for England's commercial dominance, and by 1700 most of the great names in English port were settled there.

Just out of Liverpool 'we fell in with very bad weather...and I was fain to lie down. The master had not thought to see land again, the gale being so severe.' ... 'When we were in Biscay we did see a brigg with short sails...Our skiper, not liking ye look of ye stranger, took a more westerly course'. But the brigg caught up and boarded them, telling them they were prisoners and would be taken to Cherbourg. At which point 'Our skiper had opened the case of wine you gave him and he was not steddie for some time, but when he did get better he was much taken aback at his losse.'

They were freed in the Channel by an English vessel, the skipper churlishly complaining 'that ye prize money would be great'. They put into Falmouth for repairs, still on English soil after all these travails, but not necessarily safe – although Thomas noted with relief that 'Ye bay was free from privateers inasmuch that none did molest us'.

En route again, and off Finistère, they came up against the English fleet under Sir Cloudsley Shovell. It could have signalled security, but did not; he promptly impressed two crew. The rest of the trip to Viana seems to have been uneventful.[13]

'Campo Pequeño', house of Nicholas Dixon Land Teage of Dartmouth outside Oporto, drawing, about 1845. Dixon Teage eventually came back to a very fine house, Sanders, in Stoke Fleming near Dartmouth, used by his fifteen children when they were at school in England, so perhaps his standard of living in Oporto was not so very much higher. But for many English, life in Portugal was better than struggling at home.

Private collection

Teage family and their retinue on a day trip to the countryside outside Oporto, drawing. The bullock carts carry some of the children, the donkey others, but the ladies walk. The torches carried by the servants are thought to be eucalyptus to ward off the insects.

Private collection

By the end of the 18th century, wine exports were booming, the Inquisition had receded, and life in Oporto was good. Captain Costigan, visiting in 1778, was impressed: 'Here the Christmas pies, the fat turkies, the fine sirloins, the jellies and creams of all kinds and every other delicacy are to be met with in abundance. The Foreign Merchants, especially the English, who are by far the most numerous, ...live in affluence themselves, and much better than the same persons would do in London...' He goes on, 'I find the English merchants here...a worthy, friendly and hospitable set of Gentlemen, as attentive to their counting-rooms and business, every day before dinner, as they are to their dressing, cards and other amusements in the evening'.

'They take a trip' he says '...in parties of pleasure with the ladies, to some spot they have fixed upon, whither they send a good dinner beforehand; there they dance, eat and drink heartily, play at cards, and return in the evening...'[14] The illustration above shows one of these trips in hand, a lively group weaving its way with its ox-carts across a dry valley, graceful hats, long dresses, a happy, and very English group.

These families kept their ties with the home country. In September 1817, Mary Piggott was writing from Dartmouth to Dixon Teage in Oporto: 'All the good things from Porto arrived safe, your Uncle has Grapes, Melons and Onions and Limons, all of which I had part of'.[15] The Roope family, who owned Greenway on the Dart for most of the 18th century, brought back seeds and plants, including camellias that still do so well there. The Portuguese sun shone on Dartmouth for many years.

Envelope addressed to John Teage in Oporto. Many families like the Teages had sons in Dartmouth and Oporto who travelled between the two and called either place home.

Private collection

MY ONLY SECRET IS DAMNED HARD WORK

Turner in Dartmouth

J.M.W. Turner was thirty-six when he came to the Dart in the summer of 1811. He was already a successful painter, a member of the Royal Academy, with his own gallery and established patrons. In 1808 alone he sold £2,000-worth of paintings from his gallery. His visit in 1811 was followed by another in 1813, part of an established routine of sketching tours around England while the Napoleonic wars put the European continent off-limits. The painter had Devon connections, telling Cyrus Redding, a journalist who accompanied him on excursions from Plymouth in 1813, 'that he was a Barnstaple man'[1] although it was in fact his father, William, who came from Barnstaple.

The painter's tours to the West Country were partly because the engravers, W.B. Cooke, wanted drawings for series of prints of England for the armchair travellers who could not afford

Previous Spread:
Dartmouth Cove and Sailor's Wedding, coloured engraving, J.M.W. Turner. Turner's original Dartmouth engravings were in black and white (see p.87); he is known to have worked on proofs himself. This fantastic motley of colours is a far cry from his water-colour of the wedding, with its ladies in cream and muted brown and the sailors in faded blues. It shows the 19th century had a market for livelier versions of coastal scenes.
Private collection

J.M.W. Turner, oil, by John Linnell, 1838.
© National Portrait Gallery, London

84

paintings. Turner's prints of the Dart were eventually included in three series: *Picturesque Views of the Southern Coast*, and the incomplete *Rivers of England*, both engraved by Cooke, and *Picturesque Views in England and Wales*, engraved by Charles Heath. Turner made sketches as he travelled, then worked up watercolours in his London studio, and the engravings followed. Four engravings exist from Turner's Dartmouth visits. These began as sketches *in situ*. Throughout his life, Turner would sketch while he toured and paint watercolours or oils later. We are lucky to have a good number of sketches from Turner's Dartmouth visits to relate to the engravings.[2] Many are faint, but they are fascinating, both in their own right as a record of what caught his eye and because they, with the finished prints, allow an insight into how his memory and imagination worked.

The striking feature of these previously unpublished sketches is their topographical accuracy. They are still – given changes in some buildings – instantly recognisable. They show that Turner wants to get it right. They also show restless activity, as the artist clambers up the ridges and criss-crosses the river to see Kingswear from Dartmouth and vice versa, sometimes sketching several versions of similar angles.

Dartmouth, on the River Dart, J.M.W. Turner, engraving, *Rivers of England* series, 1822.

Valerie Wills/Private collection

On the Dart, J.M.W. Turner, 1811. The full structure of the Warfleet landscape is there, trees and buildings positioned and light and shade marked, down to the few vertical strokes establishing reflections in the water. 'Corfe to Dartmouth' sketchbook.
© Tate, London 2013

On the Dart, J.M.W. Turner, 1811. The donkeys are going up a steep hill at Warfleet towards the castle along a rope walk (a track still exists along the route), and Turner records the lime kilns centre foreground. 'Corfe to Dartmouth' sketchbook.
© Tate, London 2013

Going along the Dart on the Dartmouth side, he studies the cove at Warfleet, making magical drawings that as far as we know were never taken further. Boats are drawn up at the mouth of the creek and moored alongside the shore where Nicholas Roope had built his house in about 1600. In Turner's day, Paradise Fort was on the top of the hill, and the lime kilns were on the left. The Quay House is now Driftwoood Quay, but still there; Paradise Fort became George Bidder's Ravensbury in 1860 and then today's Paradise Point.

The sketches record what people were doing and where. Look at the old farmhouse in Warfleet, with its stepped chimneys, front porch and windows, the dinghies pulled up on the hard below the farm and figures, sketched in with a few strokes, busying themselves in front of the boats. In the second Warfleet sketch, on a path parallel to Castle Road that you can still take today, a group with a donkey walks up the hill towards the castle. Light and shade are jotted down, including the black jacket of the man on the donkey.

The sketches show Turner's fascination with the fundamentals of the landscape – how a valley is formed, ridges are thrown up, hills fold over, and how the landscape works with the water. They show an interest in buildings – one of his earliest jobs as an adolescent, before he went to the Royal Academy school, was working on backgrounds to architectural drawings, he designed his own and other houses, and architecture remained a lifelong interest. So he draws in the detail of the old farmhouse at Warfleet and records how the settlements fit themselves along the ridges and down the cuts that fall to the river. Single lines capture outlines, dips and hard edges; light and shade are indicated with a heavier stroke, or, perhaps when he had more time, with hatching. Cyrus Redding was to say 'In his observation on the scenery, Turner seemed to command at a glance all the main points of view and all that was novel in it, and to receive the whole in his mind reflected as in a camera...'[3]

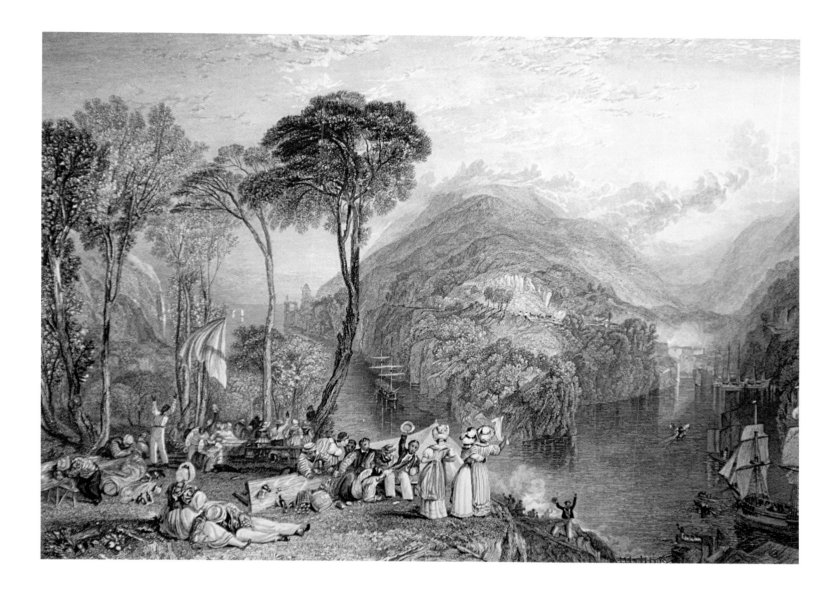

Comparing sketches with engravings shows that once Turner had got the topography right onsite, his interest changed in the studio. In two of the four engravings, his imagination dominates. Very little of the view out to sea from Kingswear is in the elaborate engraving of the sailor's wedding, which shows a largely imaginary arrangement of hill and cove around Warfleet. *Dartmouth Castle* rejigs the landscape on the other side of the river. The other two show Turner as rural recorder. In *Dartmouth on the River Dart*, an extraordinary and most interesting engraving, he combines impossible angles and proportions to show how the port worked despite its vertiginous drops; in *Dartmouth, Devon*, he has fishermen unloading barrels (of pilchards, salt, cod?) on the quay at Bayard's Cove, and pulling away in an overloaded skiff to go out to the schooner moored in the channel.

In the first two engravings Turner has bucolic scenes of frolicking peasants. These are so unimportant to him that he reproduces the same groups in work on Plymouth. The inhabitants of the other two engravings are much closer to the reality of Dartmouth then, when the cod and port trade had been destroyed by the Napoleonic wars, and banks and businesses were going bankrupt or moving away.

Dartmouth Cove and Sailor's Wedding, J.M.W. Turner, engraving, *England and Wales* series, c.1825-6. The party is a sailor's wedding in Kingswear looking at Warfleet across the river. The castle can be seen at the rivermouth.

Valerie Wills/Private collection

Dartmouth from Townstal, J.M.W. Turner, 1811. This view from Mount Boone meticulously identifies the hills and ridges defining the inclines of the valley and the houses descending to the river, a thoughtful developed landscape, with the solid tower of the church anchoring the town on the left, and the hills marking the coast on the right. 'Corfe to Dartmouth' sketchbook.   © *Tate, London 2013*

Dartmouth from Townstal, J.M.W. Turner, 1813. Here he plays with perspective by lining up St Saviour's church with St Thomas in Kingswear opposite. The castle in the middle distance is framed by Claude Lorraine-ish trees centre and to the right that take the eye out to the sea and the horizon over the houses stepping up to hide the water. 'Devon Rivers' No.2 sketchbook.   © *Tate, London 2013*

Mouth of Dart, J.M.W. Turner, 1813. Looking upriver, he focuses on the slopes of the hills coming down to the water at Old Mill Creek and beyond, catching St Clement's church on the horizon, marking the outlines of the buildings astride the ridges descending to the water. 'Devon Rivers' No.2 sketchbook.   © *Tate, London 2013*

Dartmouth Castle from Kingswear, J.M.W. Turner, 1813. Looking out to sea, he catches St Petrox church and Dartmouth Castle, the narrow cut of the entrance to the harbour, with its steep hills behind, and beyond the coastline and rocks visible at low tide. 'Devon Rivers' No.2 sketchbook.   © *Tate, London 2013*

Yet none of the fully worked-out landscapes in the sketches became engravings, while a sketch of Bayard's Cove that was hardly more than a jotting did become the watercolour, overleaf, and then the engraving called *Dartmouth, Devon*, in the *Southern Coast* series. The sketch is too faint to reproduce, but records only the essentials – the gabled house to the right, quick loops showing how the river carves out the coast and the cliffs behind and the hard point at the castle that forces it back again. Comparisons between sketch and painting show how powerful were Turner's observation and recall of light and shade and the essence of a landscape.

Colour is pivotal to Turner's imagination. It is through colour that he finds and conveys his feelings and his vision of the world around him. Turner also made colour sketches of the Dart. Rough, unfinished, and splashy, these must have been painted to remind himself of the tones.

Dartmouth, Devon, J.M.W. Turner, engraving, *Southern Coast* series, c.1811. This was based on the watercolour on p.91.

The watercolour sketch at the end of this chapter is likely to have been made in the studio – although he seems to have painted on the spot when he visited the Plymouth area, he did not usually do so – and other rough washes like this were preliminary to finished watercolours. Although this one doesn't seem to have been taken any further, it is important because it shows how Turner's imagination turned at once to colour when working in the studio. Oddly enough, this early sketch is closer to *Rain, Steam and Speed* than any of his Dartmouth watercolours.

The shift from sketch to watercolour was the big step in Turner's vision. His definition in his painting of a landscape through colour made the translation from watercolour to print a natural one. It required skill, and Turner worked on his engravings himself, but you can see that the engraving from the watercolour of *Dartmouth, Devonshire* appears to be a fairly straightforward transposition of colour into delicately differentiated tones of black and white. It is telling that Turner painted watercolours before making engravings. He had to establish what he felt, what he remembered, what he wanted to say in colour first. He then set about saying it in black and white. The medium changed the way he did it, of course. The engraving of the masterly *Sailor's Wedding* is beautifully balanced and extraordinarily fine. But the remarkable part is the vision, not the medium. Dartmouth Castle, seen through the trees in the distance, places the engraving, but otherwise the landscape has shifted, mass is added, details have disappeared. Why? This is where all the clambering and sketching comes in: he has recreated a topography that makes sense of his memory of the way the wind swirls around these last bends of the river by Warfleet. You can see it in the directions of the clouds strewn across the sky and those of the tops of the trees, and the way the tree canopies move or are suddenly still and in the excitement of the people below.

In a sketchbook, c.1808, he describes what he is trying to do – 'the greatest difficulty of a painter's art: to produce wavy air, as some call the wind...' [4] In the *Sailor's Wedding*, he has captured years later the swirl of the eddying winds that he remembered from his sketching, particularly in Warfleet. And despite the way the landscape has been changed, the feeling of the engraving is right. Winds are central to a sense of Dartmouth, and the eddies around Warfleet are well known. Autumn leaves stick to the same place on the road all winter; blown away, they always come back. Leitch Ritchie, a journalist who went with Turner on a later tour to France said he 'was frequently surprised to find what a forcible idea he conveyed of a place with scarcely a single correct detail.' [5]

So in Turner's sketches, topography and accuracy of visual detail dominate. In the watercolours and engravings it is a reality that you cannot describe in words but can in art – the play of light on water, air and movement between moments. His watercolours spring from the 'constant habit of observation' that Redding had noticed, not of the topography, which he has recorded in his sketches, but of how topography is brought alive. And this may explain why the more worked-out landscape sketches were never painted; the focus on accuracy and detail could not be taken any further and were unimportant for the later idea.

People noticing Turner walking up the steps and along the streets of Dartmouth would have seen 'an odd little mortal', a short (only five-foot), stout man, with a ruddy complexion and a great beak of a nose, a large head and low forehead, big feet and slightly bandy legs. 'He might be taken for the captain of a river steamboat at first glance' commented a friend 'but a second would find far more in his face than belongs to any ordinary mind. There was that peculiar keenness of expression in his eye that is only seen in men of constant habits of observation.' [6]

On these summer sketching tours, Turner travelled on horseback or by stagecoach, often outside to save money. He walked prodigiously, covering twenty or twenty-five miles a day, with an umbrella and fishing rod in his minimal baggage, sketching as he went. The umbrella was important, and unique. Samuel Rogers remembers Turner's anxiety when he left it behind once and saw, when it was returned, that 'It was a very shabby one, and in the handle (like a bayonet) there was a dagger quite two feet long.' [7] As for the fishing rod, Turner was a life-long fisherman; attracted to water for sketching and painting, he stayed to fish. He was happy with very basic amenities. On a trip with Redding from Plymouth, the only inn when night came had no beds. Redding – who records 'I did not mind planking it' – stayed up with Turner in the downstairs room, eating bread and cheese, drinking beer and talking until nearly midnight, 'when Turner laid his head upon the table, and was soon sound asleep'. [8]

Dartmouth, Devonshire, watercolour, J.M.W. Turner, c.1811. In the studio he adds to a very rough sketch the light and reflections in the water, the deep shadows cast by the jutting hills and the play of the sky, and the activity with the boats and the people.* *Valerie Wills/Private collection*

Determined and focused, today we would call Turner obsessive. He was notoriously secretive, rarely showing others his sketches, setting off to work by himself, often early in the morning, sometimes leaving his companions to pay the bills at the inn.

Turner's watercolours were all about 10 by 7½ inches; quite small. W.L. Leitch remembers how he worked. First he pencilled in outlines, then he 'stretched the paper on boards and, after plunging them into water, he dropped the colours onto the paper while it was wet, making marblings and gradations...His completing process was marvellously rapid, for he indicated his masses and incidents, took out half-lights, scraped out highlights and dragged, hatched and stippled until the design was finished.' This swiftness '...enabled Turner to preserve the purity and luminosity of his work and to paint at a prodigiously rapid rate.' [9] This inarticulate, secretive, blunt and difficult man could express the finest distinctions in his environment with a paintbrush and paper.

The innovativeness of Turner's artistic vision is hard to grasp fully two hundred years later, but it is illuminating to compare his work to that of contemporaries. Samuel Prout, born in Plymouth in 1783, who worked in Dartmouth at about the same time that Turner came, made the etching of the castle on the following page, which can be compared with Turner's engraving of Dartmouth Castle.

Prout was focussed on structure, emphasised by strong blocks of light and shade, with precision in the distance as well as the foreground, the hard contrasts conveying accuracy. Turner captured a fluid dynamic, of rising hills, water and land intermingling along undefined shore-

* Compare this painting with *Rain, Steam and Speed* (see the chapter 'The Long Fuse'), painted over thirty years later, and you seem to see a sequence, from realistic to abstract. But even here, while staying true to topography, Turner captures the transforming effect of light and colour. His memory of Bayard's Cove is of stillness, quiet water with soft reflections. Modulations create distance and reflection, mass and luminosity, outline and haze – a moment of serenity within a conventional scene at a busy quay.

Dartmouth Castle, on the River Dart, J.M.W. Turner, engraving, *Rivers of England* series, 1822.

Valerie Wills/Private collection

Dartmouth Castle, drawn and etched by Samuel Prout, 1811.

West Country Studies Library

lines, light modulating every outline. He reproduced a living landscape, sunlight and air redefining land and water.

Turner's watercolours, if protected from sunlight, were to survive better than his oils. It turned out that the oil pigments he used were unsafe and the ground often absorbed the colours so that tints disappeared and even fell off. When, in 1846, the painter was showing the Reverend William Kingsley his work, they saw a piece of paint 'as large as a fourpenny piece' had fallen from the sky of *Crossing the Brook*, a luminous and important painting of the Tamar outside Plymouth. 'What does it matter?' commented Turner, 'The only use of the thing is to recall the impression'.[10]

So think of this oddly shaped, red-faced, determined figure clutching his sketchbook, clambering around the hills and along the dusty roads of the lower Dart to get the view he wants. You can understand his blunt comment: 'The only secret I have got is damned hard work'.[11] But then look at his watercolours and engravings and you realise that the hard work was the sketches. It is as if he could not paint a place until he knew and understood its every angle. Once he had got the structure right, he could change it to paint his impression of the living landscape. The sketches of Dartmouth tell us what it physically looked like; his four watercolours and etchings say what it felt like. Together, they are our record of this place as he recreated it two hundred years ago.

Dartmouth, Devonshire, J.M.W. Turner, undated watercolour sketch.

© Tate, London 2013

THE WILD FREE LIFE
The Dartmouth Smugglers

Smuggling was a way of life in the south west at the turn of the 19th century. It was a time of war – the American War of Independence and endless wars with the French. International trade, the lifeblood of this area, had become difficult. The big merchant firm of Newman shifted out of Dartmouth to London, shipbuilding faltered, and merchants and even banks went bankrupt. In June 1814, to celebrate peace after the end of the Napoleonic Wars, a feast of 'hot roast beef and plum pudding and ale' was given for the poor inhabitants of Dartmouth. There were 2,300 of them; even allowing for exaggeration and outsiders it suggests a very large proportion of Dartmouth's population (3,412 in the 1801 census) was struggling.[1] But the combination of experienced and unemployed seamen and the coast, which was inaccessible and tunnelled with caves, was ideal for running contraband. And the sources of smuggled goods – France and the Channel Islands – were conveniently close. Not for nothing did the government establish the area's Customs House in Dartmouth, at Bayard's Cove, or Bearscove.

It was all about 'them' and 'us'. The town's sufferings from piracy had shown the government's inability to protect it on the high seas; smuggling during the reigns of George III, the Regency, George IV and the young Victoria was the retort. Why pay taxes to an unhelpful and distant government? Smuggling had nothing to do with wealthy merchants or captains, nor with the inventors and businessmen who were driving forward the great age of mechanisation and industrialisation in the rest of England. It had to do with ordinary coastal people making a living from the sea, and government people making a living from trying to stop them.*

Goods flowed from where they were cheap to where they were expensive – almost always from France and the Channel Islands to England. After 1792, smuggling mostly involved brandy, rum and gin, although manufactured tobacco and lace also figured. A gallon of brandy costing four shillings in Paris and the Channel Islands in 1795-98 was said to cost thirty-four in England. The incentives were obvious. As early as 1760 the collector in charge of the Exeter Custom House was telling his Board: 'The greatest part of smuggling on this coast is carried on by the Beere Boats, who generally run their goods on the Western side and shore of Torbay, within the Port of Dartmouth...'[2] By 1782, customs officials reported that twenty-five vessels of up to a hundred tons each (the tonnage of a Newfoundland fishing ship) were regularly taking contraband into the Exeter area; an astounding 90 percent of the brandy and tea consumed there between 1779-82 was said to be smuggled. 'Smuggling in the late 1700s and the early 1800s was extensively indulged in along the coast...' remarks the booklet on the parish of Stoke Fleming, talking about Blackpool Sands.[3]

* The government needed tax revenues to pay for its wars and to protect growing industries. And it had William Pitt the Younger, 'one of the most ingenious tax gatherers ever to govern England' as Prime Minister and Chancellor of the Exchequer from 1783, with one three-year break from 1801-04, until his death in 1806. (Briggs, 1999, p.108). Despite smuggling, customs revenues quadrupled from 1790 to 1815. Although Pitt reduced import tariffs on some goods – those on tea were brought down from a staggering 119 percent to some 12 percent in 1792 – those on brandy and other foreign luxuries stayed high. Confiscations from smuggling and fraud contributed a full quarter of increased revenues in Pitt's 1792 budget. Not until 1842 and Robert Peel were import tariffs reduced overall and smuggling largely disappeared.

Smuggler's Cottage, Dittisham, watercolour by John Gillo, 2007. The tidal Dart, with its steep wooded banks and rocky inlets, was a haven for smugglers.

Courtesy John Gillo

Smugglers were versatile. A notorious smuggler from Beer in Dorset who lurked along the coast to Dartmouth and beyond, John Rattenbury, crewed on a Newfoundland fishing vessel, joined privateers in the Azores, and even served in the navy. The challenge for the authorities was to catch people with the contraband. By the end of the century the structure of customs signalled desperation: there were patrols with cutters out at sea, waterguards watching the coast, people who searched moored and offshore vessels, and landguards or riding officers who tried to intercept the contraband on land. Officials had their own incentives. A seizing officer could claim an eighth of the contraband when it was sold, and at times £50 a head for smugglers impressed into the navy. The bounty shows how short the navy was of seamen. In 1776, as the American War of Independence got going, the navy had 28,000 men; by 1779 there were 70,000, and there was another major impressment in early 1793 at the start of the Napoleonic wars. Smugglers with their knowledge of seafaring were prime targets. Customs records are full of bounty claims.*

* Customs officers grew rich; smugglers mostly stayed poor. John Rattenbury was never wealthy. While in Exeter gaol in 1826 he was given an extra allowance as a poor prisoner. And he died in penury, receiving a shilling a week from Lord Rolle, the local aristocrat, and the tenancy of one of his cottages close to the beach in Beer.

The smuggler was a folk hero. A century later, Arthur Norway – father of the novelist Nevil Shute – wrote a boisterous story about a smuggling parson of Kingswear in which the exciseman is a 'picaroon', or a thief, who 'doesn't pay for the kegs he seizes...The smuggler's the honest man who pays'.[4] Smugglers are brave, resolute – and adventurous. 'Can't you see' says the parson to his preventive-minded nephew 'that men don't become smugglers for profit only? It's just as much the excitement of the wild free life...the lust for danger and the pleasure of the game.'[5] In the story, the parsons of Kingswear and Stoke Fleming, the mayor of Dartmouth, and all honest men side with the smugglers. The preventives are untrustworthy bullies and traitors. The smuggler is the peoples' hero – the little man who wins out through ingenuity, skill, endurance and courage against distant rulers, braving storms, shipwreck and dogged pursuit, with the help of the poor and the downtrodden and against a background of wild seas, high cliffs and hidden coves and tunnels. And it was in *A Smuggler's Song* to a little girl that Rudyard Kipling, with his unerring instinct for the right way to say something, captured the support of ordinary people for their 'Gentlemen':

> If you do as you've been told, 'likely there's a chance,
> You'll be given a dainty doll, all the way from France,
> With a cap of Valenciennes, and a velvet hood –
> A present from the Gentlemen, along o' being good!
> Five and twenty ponies,
> Trotting through the dark –
> Brandy for the Parson,
> 'Baccy for the Clerk;
> Them that asks no questions isn't told a lie –
> Watch the wall, my darling, while the Gentleman go by![6]

Rattenbury, who lived from 1778 to 1844, is, alongside the parson, Arthur Norway's hero. He frequently came to Dartmouth and recorded his memoirs in 1837, a rich first-hand source of information.[7] His description of an episode in Dartmouth in 1806 is the nub of Norway's book. Caught out at sea by a customs cutter in a fog he was just able to sink most of their kegs of brandy – supplied in fully waterproofed 'tubs' roped together and readily sunk in a weighted raft with a float to mark the place. However, some remained stubbornly afloat. 'The captain called us into his cabin' says Rattenbury 'and said that if we would take up the kegs for him, he would give us our boat and liberty. He gave his honour as a gentleman, and we readily agreed, pointed out where they lay, and took them up for him.' At which point the captain reneged and steered with his valuable cargo, but without his honour, for Dartmouth.

Fit for a customs official, the plaster ceiling with classical bacchanalian figures in the principal first-floor room of the Mansion House in Dartmouth. The grand house still stands, with its magnificent interior decoration largely intact, off the South Embankment, just up from the customs house at Bayard's Cove. It was built in 1736 by Captain Edward Ashe, customs officer.   © 2013 Brian Head

Bayard's Cove, Dartmouth, David Alexander, oil, 1967. There are 18th-century customs houses in the foreground.   *Private collection*

Alongside Dartmouth Castle and 'going at six knots', Rattenbury jumped overboard and made it to shore, but was recaptured 'in such a state that my own shipmates could not help laughing at me'. In Dartmouth, the magistrates sentenced them to a fine of £100 – fishing crew on vessels going to Newfoundland were paid £4 10s a month – to crew a man-of-war, or to go to gaol. After an afternoon in the gaol, a 'deplorable hole [that]...seemed to have been constructed along the lines of the Black Hole of Calcutta', they all opted for the man-of-war. When aboard, Rattenbury, noticing the captain and his officers drinking on the quarter-deck and that nobody could see the coast, jumped onto a passing fishing boat and escaped.[8]

Arthur Norway's 'Parson Peter' lived in Kingswear in 'a white house built low down on the slope of Kingswear Hill, whence a pretty garden dropped to the edge of a little cliff some ten feet above the green water of the harbour'.[9] In between preaching and visiting sick children, he facilitates Rattenbury's escape, tries to hide contraband brandy and organises Rattenbury to rescue a fugitive sailor from Slapton Sands. Parson Peter disappears at sea after delivering the sailor's girl Nance to Rattenbury's lugger in a gale 'already a hundred yards away, staggering beneath the gusts...he turned half round and waved his hand...Never again did his boat slip in beneath the castle, nor his hand moor it in the shallows underneath his garden'.[10] It was the death of a hero.

Rattenbury's memoirs have none of these heroics, but cite a few of the expedients he used to 'escape detection, baffle pursuit, and elude the vigilance of those indefatigable picaroons which everywhere line our coasts...On one occasion I had a goose on board, which the master who overhauled the vessel was very desirous of buying, but I was too well aware of the value of the stuffing to part with it, for instead of onions and sage, it consisted of fine lace. About the same time I had stowed some valuable French silks in a tin box, which was soldered to prevent the water from getting in. While an officer was searching another part of the vessel, I contrived to throw it overboard, having previously attached to it a stone and a buoy, by which means I recovered the silks perfect and uninjured.'

And then he tells a story against himself, almost the only mention of how he disposed of his goods once they were landed. 'Having landed a cargo at Seaton Hole one dark night, I was going up the cliff with a keg on my back when I had the ill-luck to stumble over an ass. It began to bray so horribly that, together with the noise occasioned by my fall, an officer who was taking a nap below awoke, in consequence of which he seized nearly forty kegs, being the whole of the cargo.'[11]

Kingswear, drawing, by the Reverend John Swete, 1793. The surprisingly empty slip is consistent with Swete's other work, which only includes token people and boats.

Devon Record Office

The slip in Kingswear, almost opposite the Customs House in Dartmouth, watercolour by Thomas Rowlandson. This painting is undated but Rowlandson was active between 1775-1817, during the peak of the smuggling period. The kegs could contain legal or contraband goods; the sailing dinghies could be going fishing, or smuggling, or both.

Valerie Wills/Private collection

Perhaps it is the excitement that Norway talks about that first draws Rattenbury to smuggling, but by the time he is middle-aged, married and with children, you sense that although fishing is 'dull and tiresome' he would have appreciated a more comfortable way to earn his living. But he had become a legend. In 1821 when he was at last arrested, his bail was set at the enormous sum of £4,500.

In an extraordinary turn of events, after this prison sentence in Exeter gaol he is called to the House of Commons in 1827 to give evidence, not on smuggling but on conditions of the sea coast around Beer, where a new harbour and canal are being considered. Who, after all, would know the coast better? 'The counsellor who examined me in the House of Commons' he says 'asked me what trade I followed. I told him sometimes fishing, sometimes piloting, and sometimes smuggling. Sir Isaac Coffin asked me several questions concerning the depth of the sea at various parts of the bay from Portland to Start Point, how I would get vessels round Portland in a gale of wind SSW, and whether I had seen a great many vessels lost through not having a harbour, to which I answered in the affirmative.' Rattenbury was told he had done well, but the harbour was never built.[12]

John Masefield, etching by William Strang, 1912.
© *National Portrait Gallery, London*

Poet Laureate from 1930 until his death in 1967, John Masefield is known for living near and in London and Boar's Hill outside Oxford. It is less well known – except by local people – that he spent time at and around the Dartmouth coast and that it inspired his writing.

Masefield came to seek psychic peace. He stayed with Jack Yeats, the brother of his friend, the poet W.B. Yeats, who had a house inland from Strete until 1909. They called it Cashlauna Shelmiddy, Irish for Snail's Castle, for reasons all gardeners around Dartmouth would understand.

Masefield's *The Captive of the Smugglers*, or *Jim Davis*, published first in 1911, is based directly on his own experience of this area. It is about a young lad kidnapped by smugglers and taken on escapades to France and Spain. He lives with an aunt and uncle just north of Strete, the smugglers' lair is at Blackpool Sands, in a hidden cave under the cliffs, and signals from the church in Stoke Fleming guide the smugglers safely home. There's a marvellous night-time chase on horseback – Jim has a keg of spirits in his saddle-bag – when sabre-wielding preventives pursue them down twisting lanes from Blackpool towards Allington, along the high road north

Smugglers: "To save their necks", 1889-1903, oil on paper on canvas, 107.9 x 213cm, Charles Hemy. Hemy, considered by many as the finest marine painter of his generation, moved to Falmouth down the coast from Dartmouth. His studio was a boat.

Art Gallery of New South Wales (purchased 1906)

from Strete (now a cycle route) and up towards the Kingsbridge road. They double back 'down the valley, along the coast-track, splashing through the little stream that makes it so boggy by the gate, and soon we were on the coach road galloping along the straight two miles towards Tor Cross. Our horses were beginning to give way, for we had done four miles at good speed, and now the preventives began to gain upon us...'[13]

Masefield's Devon is the place we know, from the stories of Spanish coins thrown up by receding storms on Blackpool Sands beach to the skeleton of an ancient Celtic king found with a circlet of gold still on his skull. And Jim running down to Blackpool from Strete, the militia taking off at a smart trot from Strete to Slapton, and the desperate smugglers thundering down the straight two-mile gallop by Slapton Sands to Tor Cross are using the roads locals now take every day.

A friend who visited Masefield and his wife in 1904 describes him as he 'sits in the chimney corner and gazes with grey-silver eyes into space, every now and then coming-to, to begin a story of a pirate...'.[14] *Jim Davis* is one of those stories. Jim's home is Snail's Castle. When

The battlemented 13th-century tower of St Peter on the cliff at Stoke Fleming was built by the Careys, concerned to command the entrance to Dartmouth harbour. Over eighty-three feet tall, it was and is a landmark.

St Peter's Parish Magazine

he stayed with Yeats, Masefield and his host floated model boats and threw pebbles at them in the nearby stream. In *Jim Davis*, Jim and his friend Hugh 'in the sunny evenings of April...used to sail our fleets, ship against ship, upon the great fresh-water lake into which the trout-brook passes on its way to the sea. Sometimes we would have a fleet of ships of the line anchored close to the shore, and then we would fire at them...till we had shattered them to bits...'[15]

When he went for his long walks with Yeats, Masefield was taking in a countryside that was to stay with him all his life. His stories of smugglers and pirates are rooted here. A ballad written about this time and published in 1916 is bylined 'Cashlauna Shelmiddy'; it includes the reference 'yonder light is Start Point', and:

> O we have been with Spaniards, and far and long on the sea;
> But there are the twisted chimneys, and the gnarled old inns on the quay.
> The wind blows keen as the day breaks, the roofs are white with rime,
> And the church-bells ring as the sun comes up to call men in to Prime.[16]

Dartmouth sailors never recorded their smuggling days. But there are many oral stories, mostly centring on Blackpool Sands and the village on the hill above at Stoke Fleming. A network of underground tunnels is said still to connect the shore with the church, the inn and the surrounding houses, as many a gardener looking down on a collapsed bit of his garden is reminded. Local legend has it that a cottage near Stoke Fleming church in a field called

SANDY COVE

Stoke Fleming from Slapton Sands, by William Payne, watercolour, c.1790.

Hilloways had a secret entrance behind the fireplace called Ketch's Hole that was reputed to be connected with Blackpool Sands.[17]

Nicholas Teage, who lived nearby as a boy, remembers his father showing him a passage behind a trap door in his house. 'If you took the passage to the left (north) it led a few yards into a circular chamber with, as I remember it, a domed roof. The passage and chamber were walled with stone. The passage to the right (south) led several more yards...before it was blocked...Presumably this is where the cottage once stood. As a child, I could stand upright in the passage; I am not sure whether an adult could. If the tunnel did ever connect with the beach, it would have had to be very long (and steep in places).'[18] Arthur Norway obviously knew these stories. The passage must have been Nance's escape route to the beach in *Parson Peter*. And the parson himself had been a curate at Stoke Fleming, where St Peter's church has a tower over eighty-three feet high, which, notes the church leaflet, has 'an unsurpassed view of Start Bay, and was long used as a landmark for shipping'.[19] The parson reputedly tolled the church's fine bells when he saw the preventives appearing out of Dartmouth.

Opposite: Sandy Cove, drawn and etched by Samuel Prout, 1812. Prout was born in Plymouth in 1783, where he periodically returned to recuperate from London life. A pre-eminent watercolourist of architecture, particularly of European subjects, his line drawing is superb.

THE LONG FUSE

The Story of Steam

Thomas Newcomen, who was born and lived in Dartmouth, was eight when King Charles II was entertained in the Butterwalk in 1671. This local preacher and ironmonger invented the first successful working steam engine. It became known as the atmospheric engine, because it relied solely on atmospheric pressure. 'The fame of this excellent pumping-engine soon spread across England and many people came to see it, both from England and from foreign nations...' wrote a Swedish engineer, Martin Triewald, in 1734.[1]

It is hard to be astonished with hindsight, but Newcomen's achievements are astonishing for his time. His engine, which some date as early as 1705, lit the long fuse of experimentation with steam power that began the transformation of economic activity in Britain.[2] It was to be another sixty years before James Watt produced a more fuel-efficient engine with a separate condenser that could be used away from the coal mines (where Newcomen engines had to be based), and another fifteen for machines to incorporate rotary motion that could drive wheels in industry. But it was Newcomen's engine that pioneered the inventions that were to make Britain the foremost industrial power of its time.

Iron and then steel were fundamental to the machines and manufactured goods that generated economic growth. Already by 1709 Abraham Darby had substituted coke for charcoal in a blast furnace at Coalbrookdale in Staffordshire, taking ironmaking out of the forests – where it depended on charcoal – and into the coalfields. Demand for coal sent mines deeper and deeper, where the problem of pumping out water became paramount, and it was in the mines of south Staffordshire that Newcomen's steam engines were first used. Tradition suggests that the first one was installed in 1712 at the Conygree Coal Works near Dudley Castle, Staffordshire. By 1733, when the patent he had used had run out and Newcomen was four years dead, there were over a hundred of his engines at work all over Britain, and more in Austria, Belgium, France, Germany, Hungary and Sweden. By the end of the 18th century more than 1,400 Newcomen engines had been built and some continued to be used into the 20th century – despite being greedy of coal, they were simpler, cheaper and more reliable than Watts' alternative. The Newcomen engine now in the Science Museum in London was built in 1791 and was working at Pentich colliery in Derbyshire until 1918.*

Like many later inventors, such as George Stephenson who started as an engineman and then a brakesman controlling the winding gear at a colliery, Newcomen's training as a blacksmith

* It is significant that the first engines were built where Newcomen had religious connections; in 1719 he is listed as a trustee of a new Baptist meeting house in Bromsgrove near the Conygree Coal Works. His religion was key to his achievements. He was a Baptist – his partner in the invention was a fellow-Baptist, John Calley – and a preacher for twenty years, as well as an ironmonger and inventor. His father, Elias, had been a Dartmouth town worthy and shipowner, but as nonconformists he and his family were barred from being freemen and participating in the town's affairs after the restoration of the monarchy. Local banking was still a century away and contemporary merchants like the Holdsworths and the Newmans financed their trade and investment using their privileges and powers as town freemen. Thomas' route to success in developing and marketing his invention had to depend on his own talents and his family and religious networks.

108

A Pit Head, British school, c.1800. This early 19th-century painting has a Newcomen engine adapted for winding and shows that the engines were being used well into the industrial revolution. The boiler is to the side of the cylinder, and the chains from the rockers some distance from a counterweight (to the left) and the pulley above the mine shaft (to the right). The man standing to the right of the cylinder is operating the valves. The engine might be raising coal rather than water.

Courtesy of National Museums Liverpool (Walker, Museum of Liverpool)

and his mechanical competence were central to his innovations and an example of the sort of imagination that went into major industrial change.

The theory of using a vacuum to drive a piston was well known at the time. Newcomen's French contemporary, Dionysius Papin, had proposed using a piston driven by steam condensation in a cylinder, and letters show that Newcomen was aware of his ideas before 1703.[3] Closer to home, Thomas Savery in Totnes patented a steam engine to pump water by creating a vacuum in 1698, but it didn't work at the depth needed.

Newcomen initially used Savery's patent to construct an engine based on a vertical cylinder with a piston, which Savery had not used. But atmospheric pressure would only plunge the piston if it could operate tightly up and down the cylinder without air leaking to the vacuum

London and by 1786 the family had left Dartmouth. Apart from pamphlets written about him by a local architect, Thomas Lidstone, in the 19th century, he was largely ignored until the 20th. His house, next to the Guildhall on a road running through from Higher to Lower Street, was demolished for road widening in about 1864, and a street was named Newcomin – incorrectly spelt. Only in 1921, a year after the Newcomen Society of London had been formed, was a granite obelisk erected in the Royal Avenue Gardens, engraved with a drawing of his engine. Dartmouth now has plaques to him, correctly spelt street names and, in the Royal Avenue Gardens, one of his engines is on display. This is largely original, dating from 1725, but has a new valve gear and a 'pickle pot' condenser allowing steam to be generated away from the main cylinder, and has been adapted to hydraulic power so that its workings can be demonstrated. The engine came from the Coventry Canal Co. and was donated by British Rail to the Newcomen Society who presented it to Dartmouth in 1963 to celebrate the 300th anniversary of Newcomen's birth. Dartmouth celebrated the 300th anniversary of the first engine in 2012 and a postage stamp was issued in commemoration.

'This is a grand day at Exeter, opening the Railway, all the world and its brother are gone to see the Show...and we shall be enabled to go to and from the great Metropolis in quick time, say Eleven Hours, what think you of this my Boy for running over Two hundred and Four miles which used to take Seven days, nothing wanted now but the aeriel carriage when I shall take a trip in it and give you all a call one morning, take dinner with you and back again to supper, it is fast approaching to it, so let nothing astonish you.'[4] So wrote a breathless John Teage from Dartmouth on 1 May, 1844, imagining himself travelling next on an aeroplane, not to London, but to his friend J.H. Carter in Newfoundland.

The Great Western Railway opened up the south west and created a whole new industry. It arrived in Exeter smack in the middle of England's railway mania when thousands of miles of countryside were being bound up in a great skein of iron track. Exeter's cloth industry was in decline, its streets were crowded with out-of-work country weavers who were healthier because the new sewerage system had reduced cholera. Travel was by stage coach, which had reduced the trip to London to only some seventeen hours from John Teage's seven days. But the railway directors on the *Orion* on that first day of May 1844 left Paddington at 7.31 am and arrived in Exeter at 12.45 pm – cutting travel time by more than two thirds. The response was dramatic. Within two years, when the South Devon Railway opened the line from Exeter to Dawlish and Teignmouth on Whitsun weekend 1846, there were 1,500 people in 22 carriages who thundered down on the morning train to bands of music and flying flags.

The Paignton to Kingswear branch should never have been built. Proposals first made in 1845 were only approved by Parliament eleven years later on the basis of a large underestimate of its costs by Isambard Kingdom Brunel and the patronage of the deep-pocketed Charles Seale-Hayne from Kingswear. But having been approved and built, the line has never stopped operating; when closed by the Western Region of British Rail in 1972, it reopened under a new company the following day and still runs with its steam engines as a tourist project.

An Incident on the Dart, oil, George Wolfe, c.1857. When Queen Victoria visited in 1856, Prince Albert went out to sea in the *Dartmouth Steamer*, while the Queen went upriver in the Royal Barge. They met here, near Sandridge. *Valerie Wills/Private collection*

Stained-glass panels at Warfleet Lodge with, at the top of the windows, the royal coat of arms in honour of Edward, Prince of Wales, far left, and the Dartmouth coat of arms (see also title page), left.

Valerie Wills by courtesy of Mr and Mrs Otto Koeppen

The idea was straightforward: running water cools hot surfaces. The engine-rooms of steamships were furnaces, with temperatures reaching 150 degrees as stokers opened stokeholes to feed fires to keep engine speeds up. Red-hot engines and funnels were surrounded by wooden bulkheads and decking, and fires were frequent. Holdsworth's water bulkheads encircled the engine room and funnel with a narrow metal casing through which water circulated, hot water flowing out and cold in. They were used, *inter alia*, by the navy, and fitted in British and Russian royal yachts, bringing engine-room temperatures down by up to 60 degrees. 'I strongly recommend' says G.T. Gordon, Commander of Her Majesty's steam vessel *Cormorant*, 'That all Her Majesty's steam-vessels, particularly those destined for a tropical climate, should be fitted with this simple but invaluable apparatus.'[2]

With the Yacht Club and the Prince of Wales came a new breed of investors. George Parker Bidder and later Francis Charles Simpson – both Yacht Club members – were among outsiders who stimulated and financed what became a remarkably modern shipbuilding industry in Dartmouth on opposite sides of the Dart at Sandquay and then Noss in the late 19th century. Like Bidder and his local partner Samuel Lake, they could be self-taught men, or like Simpson could draw on family

Warfleet Lodge, the entertainment wing of Warfleet House built in 1882-83 by the Freakes, who lived at Warfleet House until 1933. Sir Charles and his son Thomas were friends of the Prince of Wales.   *Photo: Valerie Wills; by courtesy of Mr and Mrs Otto Koeppen*

wealth, but in general they were used to success and risk. Many established inventors were drawn to Dartmouth – Sir James Douglass, builder of the Eddystone Lighthouse over 1878-92, William Froude who developed revolutionary hull designs in testing tanks in Paignton – but local self-taught inventors attracted by jobs in marine engineering were to make a substantial difference to their fields.

Bidder, a colleague and friend of George and Robert Stephenson, Brunel and Joseph Locke, and like them a celebrated engineer at a time when engineers were driving the nation's innovation and prosperity, was already a successful man in his fifties when he started to visit Dartmouth. He came in his two-masted schooner, the *May Fly*, and it is thought that it was from the yacht that he first saw Warfleet and the house Paradise, which he bought in 1860 and renamed Ravensbury. He came most summers after that, and within seven years was spending almost a third of his time there, long enough to be a town councillor and harbour commissioner.

And to get involved in the business of the town. Bidder was a man of prodigious energy and pragmatism. With the fortune he had already amassed from investments in his projects – railway shares, the Electric Telegraph Company, domestic and foreign gas companies, collieries

Near Dartmouth, by Robert Hurrell Froude, 1819, showing the new paper mill and waterwheel (the largest west of Bristol) built by Arthur Holdsworth at Warfleet. This was the romantic period, but even so you can see the poverty in the cottage on the left.

West Country Studies Library

* The *Edyth* lasted longest as a trawler, almost twelve months, and incorporated innovative features. 'I was out all day yesterday in the Edyth and had a fine haul of fish – the finest Turbot I ever saw... I should think 20lbs weight,' Bidder writes to his wife in 1872. 'Everything is done by steam' he tells his grandson later. 'The Sails are hoisted, the boat hauled on deck and the big net raised up very sharply and all by steam.' (Clark, 1983, pp. 200-01.)

and extensive property interests – he went into business with local trawler owner, Samuel Lake. The idea was to develop a steam trawler, applying to ships the principle that had transformed land transport. It was to be the 'most interesting and original work GPB did with ships'.[3]

Lake's career is particularly enlivening; Dartmouth born, by the age of ten he was at sea and came back a rich man. Forward-looking, he promoted the new north embankment and coal bunkering, both of which increased the town's prosperity. He built the first poured-concrete housing in England (still standing as Coombe Cottages, overlooking Coronation Park), a brickworks, a paintworks and slate quarry (all failed), and was finally bankrupted when he overextended himself contracting for Milford Haven Docks and the Felixstowe Docks. As a young man, he won the Albert Medal for bravery helping to rescue shipwrecked pilgrims off Calcutta, and died of fever after saving the crew of a Swedish barque off Corsica in Marseilles in 1887. He was awarded Sweden's highest honour, the Gold Bravery Medal, posthumously.

Because local fishermen believed that the noise of screw propellers would scare fish, Bidder and Lake put a small steam engine into an existing vessel, the *Thistle*, to prove that it didn't. Between 1869 and 1874 they went on to experiment with larger and larger prototype trawlers, the *Florence*, *Bertha* and *Edyth*, all named after Bidder daughters.* It was a case of an idea before its time defeated by entrenched local interests. *Edyth* could carry six times the load of a sailing trawler,[4] but Brixham, not Dartmouth, was the base for the local fishing fleet, and proceeds were shared to prevent steam trawler crews getting extra for better catches. Yet within ten to fifteen years steam trawling was to become established. The yard books of local shipbuilders Philip & Son show steady orders for steam yachts and launches from 1882. Probably the first to apply steam to humble fishing vessels and demonstrate they could be commercial, when Bidder decided they were not viable, he sold and moved on.

Enter Francis Simpson. Bidder had financed all three trawlers, two built at Sandquay on the east bank of the Dart. Simpson, who arrived in 1873, was a wealthy marine engineer from the Midlands. Rear-Commodore of the Royal Dart Yacht Club, active in local politics and mayor for ten years, he was a builder of steam launches and yachts for nigh on forty years, first near Coombe Mud, then Sandquay, and finally opposite at Noss Point, where he built Simpson, Strickland & Co., a large modern works that employed 230 men in 1897.

His coup was to attract a local Kingswear mechanic, George Kingdon. Kingdon had good credentials. He had worked on the early steam trawlers and had been chief mechanic at Froude's ship-testing tank at Paignton.

George Parker Bidder. Born in Moretonhampstead, a child prodigy for his mental calculation, George Parker Bidder summered here in middle age and always considered the Devon air good for him. His experimentation with steam trawlers in Dartmouth was pioneering. *E.F. Clark*

When Froude died in 1879, Kingdon came to Dartmouth with a patented compound engine and boiler he had invented and wanted to manufacture. Compared with rivals, it was lightweight, more reliable and a more efficient user of coal. After successfully installing one in Simpson's yacht, Kingdon was recruited in 1880 to develop his engine, which he did in the back garden of Simpson's house on Ridge Hill, 'Combecote' – which is still there.

Paradise, built in 1855 on the site of Paradise Fort damaged in the civil war. Bidder renamed it Ravensbury. It still stands in Warfleet, but is now called Paradise Point.

D.A. Gerrard/Private collection

Right: Francis Simpson.
A larger-than-life north-countryman, he was to establish a state-of-the-art marine engineering works at Noss that sent vessels all over the world and attracted and fostered local and foreign talent.

Dartmouth Town Council

Far right: Arthur Howe Holdsworth, artist, architect, and inventor, with the wealth and the connections to apply his ideas.

Dartmouth Town Council

From the 1880s, Dartmouth shipyards began churning out steam vessels, and in the market for small launches of about 23 foot needing a 4-horsepower engine to go 7 knots, the Kingdon engine was 'the ultimate in Victorian era boat engines' and his 'compounds' are among the most sought-after original steam engines today. As Simpson expanded his business, Kingdon moved from back garden to a small shipbuilding yard at Coombe, then to a larger one at Sandquay, and finally to Simpson's new modern works, which were powered by Kingdon engines. Kingdon died in 1899 and the firm supplied his last engine in 1912, three years after Simpson had retired.

Kingdon engines were used in tugs and launches, pilot boats and steam yachts, and kept their market position for a good twenty years. They were deceptively simple and, even now, hard to copy. Originals are still prized. In 1894, a 32-foot steam launch with a quadruple expansion Kingdon engine, *Flirt*, was ordered from Simpsons by Charles Busk of Salisbury, on the southern tip of the Kootenay Lake in British Columbia, Canada, to service the growing silver mining and logging industries along the

Kingdon engines were ideal for smallish motor launches; this 17-foot steam dinghy was constructed in pine and sold to a Captain Darke in October 1894.

Brixham Heritage Museum & History Society

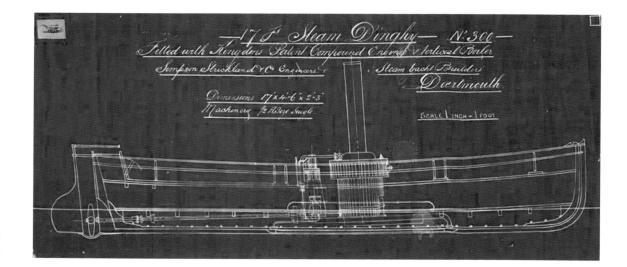

The *Flirt*, rebuilt around her Kingdon engine, on Lake Rotoiti in the Nelson Lakes National Park, South Island of New Zealand in 2012.

R.S. Hamlett

lake. She was shipped from the Noss boatyard across the Atlantic, railed over to Arrowhead, put on a barge, then back onto rail to pass the Kootenay rapids, and finally launched in Kootenay Lake. There she became the mainstay of the Balfour Steam Navigation company, delivering mail, towing timber, and carrying prospectors, surveyors and hunters on trips. She was relocated, sold, resold and by 1928 recorded as broken up. But in 1992 her Kingdon engine was discovered in a garage. In 2006, the original engine, plus some of the original *Flirt* parts, were shipped from Vancouver to Wellington, New Zealand, where a replica of the original (using teak on the deck and cabin instead of mahogany) has been lovingly built around them and the *Flirt* floats again.[5]

By the 1890s, shipyards like Simpsons and Philip & Son (who took over Simpson's Noss yard in 1916) were sending vessels all over the world. Philip's yard books show steam vessels going to Belgium, France, Norway, Cameroon, the Falkland Islands, and Brazil. They could be pilot boats, launches and steam yachts from ketches to 200-foot schooners, often with rare wood interiors. The paddle passenger steamer *Totnes Castle*, launched in 1896, was Philip's first steel vessel.

Kingdon's four-crank quadruple expansion engine, from Simpson, Strickland & Co's catalogue, 5th edition.

Brixham Heritage Museum & History Society

The reach and reputation of the works at Noss attracted entrepreneurs from far away. At Gurrow Point above Old Mill Creek on the Dart one March morning in 1894 a glider with enormous wings of handmade silk was faced into the wind. The pilot, astride a bicycle saddle in between the wings, his cap on backwards to reduce drag, hared off down the hill and the machine rose seven feet above the ground 'and flew for some distance' before a gust tipped it upside down. The pilot, Alexandre Liwentaal, a Swiss engineer at Simpsons, went back, repaired his 'Aerostat', as he called it, and tried again, this time from Bozomzeal near Dittisham, where the slope was steeper. Although the glider was bigger, with a

Liwentaal's 'Aerostat' on Bozomzeal Hill, acrylic by Gustav Butler, c.1890-1903. It's hard to see from the painting where the pilot sat.

wing-span of 70 rather than 40-odd feet, there was no 'lift off', and the glider crashed into a hedge. It was a write-off, and Liwentaal was rushed to the newly opened Dartmouth Cottage Hospital with extensive bruising and head laceration.[6]

No one seems to know by what happy chance this inventive Swiss from Lausanne arrived at the Noss works in 1892-93. But he did, and in a nearby shed owned by a small boat-builder called Lidstone, he built and rebuilt his 'Aerostat' over the next two years. The glider was shaped like a seagull and had a tubular steel fuselage and Norwegian pine spars, the broad wing in front indented to take a bicycle saddle for the pilot balanced on a bicycle wheel, and behind a small triangular wing with a skid.

Liwentaal – Levento to the locals – brought the dreams of Icarus to the Dart. 'Nothing is more common' he said 'than to see the seagulls of the Dart starting off from the roof of the *Britannia* ...sailing onwards in a rapid and effortless progression'. (*Britannia* was a naval training hulk.) His innovation was to use new materials. 'It is weight not buoyancy,' he writes 'which makes flight possible...the natural laws upon which flight has to be performed are – the law of

The Dartmouth coach going up the hill from Blackpool Sands, June 1917. Horse-drawn transport overlapped with the motor-car for many years. *Private collection*

gravitation, the resistance of the fluids, and the elasticity of the air.'[7] To a friend who commented, 'Birds' wings are alive; what can you expect from dead wings but dead failures?' he maintained he had the last word, but after his sojourn in the hospital he left Dartmouth for London. Only Sir George Cayley is known to have flown before him in England – gliding across Brompton Dale in Yorkshire in 1853 – but this flight on the Dart never achieved more than local interest.[*]

Until the Second World War, this inventive and energetic Swiss criss-crossed Europe, the Channel and the Atlantic working on all sorts of flying machines, from powered planes, to balloons and zeppelins. He even went as engineer to Walter Wellman, the American adventurer and newspaperman, on his first attempt to reach the North Pole by airship. He became a British citizen in 1914 and emigrated to Canada in 1919 where he worked on a number of engineering projects to do with shipping, mining and encryption, dying in an accident in 1940.

Just at the point when the era of the motor car was to begin, there was laughter when a lecturer to a camera club said: 'I hope as soon as possible to see the horse abolished and found only in the hunting field and parks.'[8]

That was in 1897. Hindsight tells us the laughter was misplaced, and it seems odd now that it wasn't obvious then. By 1897 the first motor-car invented in Germany was twelve years old and a British one was running on British roads. For at least thirty years Victorians had been showing their predilection for speed by joyfully mounting many different types of bicycle and riding four times faster than they could walk. Over the twenty years to the 1890s, the cost of bicycles fell threefold to some £4, even less for a second-hand one, and safety bicycles with pneumatic tyres had become the working man's transport.

But bicycles were unstable, exposed to the weather, and hard work on hills. The first petrol-engined motor-car was invented in Mannheim, in Germany, by Karl Benz, patented in 1886,

* The inventor was one of many all over Europe developing versions of balloons, airships and planes, with and without motors. Wilbur and Orville Wright were to begin their own manned glider flights in 1900, six years after Liwentaal. Liwentaal had been at the École des Arts et Métiers outside Paris, where he had been taught by Gaston Tissandier, who had made his first flight in a motorised airship in 1883-84 while Liwentaal was there. Undaunted by his disaster on the Dart, Liwentaal proceeded, like the Wright brothers, to work on designs for powered flight.

and manufactured in 1888 as the Modell 3 Benz. Six years later, Benzes were imported into England. By the end of 1895 it is thought there were 14-15 cars on the road in Britain, and by 1900 there were some 700-800. John Henry Knight of Farnham with George Parfitt, both engineers, are credited with inventing the first petrol-driven car run in Britain in 1895. Frederick Henry Royce, then making lamp-holders and light bulbs in Manchester, put his first, two-cylinder car on the road in 1904. In between the two, one night in 1900, Harry Inder, pattern-maker at Simpson's, drove his car home-made in Dartmouth at 5 miles an hour up Victoria Road, a flurry of policemen and youngsters chasing behind.

Henry James Inder was another talented inventor attracted by Simpsons. He came to Dartmouth in 1891 from Somerset for an interview when he was twenty. It was, says his family, a filthy day, and going home he decided he wouldn't take the job. But the sun was shining for his second interview – and he'd already spotted his future wife – so when an offer was made, he took it. Simpsons were interested in adapting their marine steam engines for motor-cars, and Inder worked on these. But thinking a petrol engine would be better, he began to build his own in the street-level bedroom of his house in St. Clare's Terrace on Clarence Hill in 1898. The family believes things accelerated when his wife Alice told him 'to clear his rubbish out of the spare bedroom as she was expecting their second child'.[9]

This first car looked like an old-fashioned pram. Petrol-driven and a three-wheeler, like Benz's original model, it had a wooden chassis, two wheels in the front and one at the rear, and two rows of seats with the single-cylinder engine under the front passenger seat and the driver and steering wheel at the back. Inder built his engine from scratch, and his father, a master blacksmith, made the axles and springs. The car was still on the road in 1909, when Inder sold it and bought himself a four-wheeled 'Yankee runabout'.

Henry James Inder, c.1930, engineer, family man, and mad about cars.

Private collection

Orisina Silent Night Daimler, owned by R.L. Newman, at Blackpool in 1909, with the chauffeur, S. Deller, in the driving seat. The small cars local inventors made were for the rich – Inder's car cost £100 to make – and early ones were bought by a solicitor, a doctor and local shipbuilding magnates.

Totnes Image Bank & Rural Archive

A long, varied and fruitful career with Simpsons and then Philips followed for Harry Inder. He patented a reversing gear box for internal combustion engines and a petrol capstan used at the Noss works. He travelled in 1916-17 to St Nazaire, Lorient and Brest in connection with reinforcing the hulls of vessels to deal with ice in northern seas. He was involved with starting the first garage in Dartmouth to hire out vehicles and service the growing number of cars on the roads. His family remember a hands-on, affectionate father of five, who always wore a suit, and who loved get-togethers and outings, hunting for watercress 'the finest thing you could eat' for picnics. He died in 1945.

Inder was at the crest of a long wave. The railway companies pioneered motor-cars to expand their networks. As early as 1903, the Great Western began a service from Helston to the Lizard, using five petrol cars carrying twenty-two passengers each. Two years later, it bought out a service that had already been operating from Modbury since 1904 to service Plymouth and began services from Paignton, linking Brixham, Dartmouth and Totnes.[10] At this stage, cars posed no threat to the railway system. Between 1902 and 1904, the facilities for goods and passengers at Kingswear station were vastly expanded to accommodate increased traffic.

The Inder Car, Harry driving at the back with Jack, Alice with Lily and Cecil in front. 'Everybody said these things were no good' he remembered in 1939 of his first drive. He recalled, with satisfaction, passing a Stanley Steamer, driven by George Philip who ran the shipyard at Sandquay opposite Simpsons. 'He had to stop and pump water into the boiler' he commented 'While he was doing that I was gone.'[11] *Private collection*

THE VILLAGE AND THE SEA

Hallsands

Previous Spread:
The remains of the fishing
village of Hallsands as it is
today.   © 2013 Nigel Evans

Over three days in January 1917 easterly gales combined with high spring tides hurled thirty-
and forty-foot waves over the new sea wall protecting the fishing hamlet of Hallsands to the
west of Torcross, down the coast from Dartmouth and Slapton. Gravel behind the walls was
scoured away and cottages, built tight on a low ledge above the shingle between wall and cliff,
collapsed into the gullies under the boiling waves. 'We felt like being right in the sea, the roaring
waves bouncing over us, the rafters all breaking in. We could see the white waves foaming
underneath the floors. The coal house all slipping away, no fires, the sea came down the
chimney' remembered Edith Patey, then seventeen.[1] By midnight of 26 January no house was
still intact. The villagers miraculously all scrambled up to safety as dawn brought a lull at low
tide. When the storms calmed at last, twenty-four houses were irreparable; only one, the
Prettyjohns house, towards the north end, was habitable. The village of Hallsands had gone.

These storms were the last of a series that had assaulted the villagers off and on for over
twenty years and finally broke their resolve to win out against the sea. Their story is one of
incredible courage and resilience. During three years of bad storms from 1902, the winter seas
had come up and over the old sea walls and destroyed the first cottages. The sea hurled itself
over the roofs, flooding down the chimneys, leaving shingle all over the floors as it swirled out
again. People managed as best they could. When gales threatened, children were taken in at
the cottages at the less exposed southern end of the village. The adults hung on grimly,
sweeping out the water and battening doors and windows. An elderly owner of a cottage
threatened with collapse only left when the sea was thundering over his roof and he couldn't
use the door. They hauled him up the cliff at the back by rope.[2] In 1904 the Board of Trade
inspector, Captain G.C. Frederick, found eighteen houses needed repair.

The London Inn served its last pint in the autumn of 1903. Famous for its own brew of white ale,
it had records dating back to 1784. In the winter of 1902 its front wall had slipped when a section
of the sea wall went. A year later, in September 1903, it lost its kitchen, beer cellar, conservatory
and bedroom in the first equinoctial gale of the season that coincided with a spring tide. George
Lobb, the landlord, remembered drily 'When the greenhouse collapsed two coastguardsmen and
two fishermen came to assist me to remove the things in the bedroom. While we were in the room

HALL-SANDS, DEVON.

the roof came down upon us, and we all had a narrow escape. Then the gable gave way, tearing away the stove...'[3] He and his wife left, never to return. That was when the road was washed away and the back row of village houses found itself in front. People whose cottages had gone left, but the rest stayed, putting footbridges over collapsed lanes, patching cracks, strengthening defences. The new sea wall – 23 feet high, 10 feet of it below beach level, and 6 feet 6 inches thick at its base – was built over 1903-05, in between gales, with pauses for raising the money.

Hallsands is at the southern end of the long sweep of Start Bay that faces east towards the English Channel. The Bay has six miles of shingle beach – one of the longest in Devon – from by Strete in the north to Beesands and Hallsands in the south. During the 19th century, Hallsands had been a village of thirty-seven houses and some 150 people, built in a half-moon shape on rock ledge and compacted sand between steep cliffs and a gently sloping shingle beach. At the end of the century it had a piggery, an inn with stables, a shop and a post office, a bakehouse and a Mission Room where the village met for concerts and sing-alongs. The lighthouse at Start Point just beyond was installed in 1836 to warn shipping approaching Plymouth Sound of shallow rocks.

There seems to have been no good reason why the village was below, rather than on top of the cliff, where the coastguard house and the chapel were. There was no spring there; water had to

Hallsands, Devon, oil, by W. Lidstone, 1869. The old village was tucked under the cliffs behind a wide, sloping shingle beach. The large boat in the fore-ground would be the six-man seine netting boat; the smaller ones behind, the two-man crabbers.
Kingsbridge Cookworthy Museum

135

Hallsands, c.1896, before the dredging. The main street, with the old sea wall and cottages immediately behind them were to go in the storms of 1902-5.

Kingsbridge Cookworthy Museum

be piped down from the nearest valley. But it was convenient for fishing and Hallsanders were fishermen. Fish were plentiful in the pits to landward of the long rock formation of the underwater Skerries just off Hallsands beach. The villagers fished for crab and lobster, making their distinctive dome-shaped pots from local withies in the winter. They longlined for bait – conger, ray, pollack – netted for bottom fish like plaice, sole and turbot, and inshore they caught pilchards (although less towards the end of the century), herring, mullet, bass and mackerel with seine nets.

Life was hard physical work. Crab boats could go out at 4am, depending on the tide, and fishermen were often not done until after dark. Most tackle and clothes were made by hand. During the long winters, men took labouring work on the farms. Children walked two miles to school in Huckham, their lunch-time pasties savoury at one end and sweet, with jam or apple,

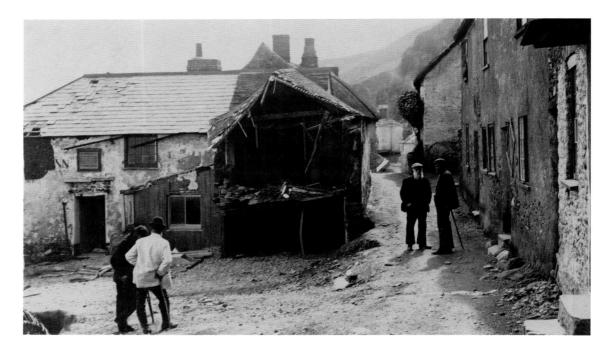

Hallsands, after the 1904 storms. Compare this with the cheerful scene, above, of c.1896.

Kingsbridge Cookworthy Museum

A View Down the Main Street of Hallsands after the 1904 Storms. The front row of cottages are now gone and great chasms split the road. Villagers strengthened, patched and put footbridges over the gullies.

Kingsbridge Cookworthy Museum

at the other. The community was strong. Villagers went to chapel on Sundays and weddings and funerals brought everyone out, often with people from neighbouring hamlets. Crabbing was done in two-man boats; in the 19th century the village had seventeen crabbers. Tuck-netting offshore needed twelve-man teams, six on shore and six in the boat. Seine-netting was a whole village affair. When the spotter on the hilltop lifted his bowler to signal sighting a shoal, the boats quietly took out the nets, still attached at either end to the shore, and dropped them where the spotter pointed. Men, women and children would haul them in, the tarred net ropes heavy and rough, yard after sodden yard, until the fish at the centre were up on the shingle, leaping and flailing, and could be caught by hand. Everyone got a share of the catch.

Hallsands had stood in its little protected corner above its high shingle beach at least since the 17th century, when an entry in the 1632 Manor Court Rolls of Stokenham referred to a 'Poke Hole' under the cliff at 'Halsande'.[4] The London Inn was already there by the end of the 18th century. Great storms in 1881 and 1891 had left it undamaged. Why did the gales of 1917, nowhere near as destructive elsewhere as the earlier storms, virtually eradicate the whole village?

There is one crucial relevant fact. The shingle beach shelving down from village to sea had, until the late 19th century, measured some eighty feet between rock ledge and high-water mark. Lidstone's painting of 1869 shows how the width and slope of the shingle shelf protects the houses. But by 1901, the first high spring tides combined with storms had brought the sea to within three feet of the closest cottages. An inspection found that the beach level had fallen by up to twelve feet. The photograph overleaf shows how far the shingle had eroded by 1917.

Why the beach had gone is the nub of a controversy that has raged since 1897. It is a drama with poor families losing everything, a cast of heroes and villains, crusading journalists and penny-pinching bureaucrats. Questions about this lost corner of a far western county were asked in the House of Parliament, official enquiries were made and reports written, some never released. Some compensation was paid, never admitting liability and always reduced by wrangling about who would pay it. Who was responsible will probably never be fully resolved.

In April 1897 dredgers had appeared off Hallsands beach. Sir John Jackson Ltd, a large civil engineering firm that had won the contract to extend the naval dockyards in nearby Devonport, had been licensed by the Board of Trade to dredge shingle needed for cement, and proceeded to dredge between the high and low water marks. The villagers were apparently never consulted about the proposal, or even informed it had been agreed. The contract was for five years, but ended abruptly on New Year's Day 1902 when the men of Hallsands and Beesands, the neighbouring village, confronted the men working the dredgers, who left for good. By then, it was estimated locally that they had taken 650,000 tons of shingle.[5]

From the beginning, the villagers believed the dredging threatened their homes. It was a 'stands to reason' position; they just had to look. The Board of Trade was unconvinced. After the first inspection in June 1897, shortly after the dredging had begun, the Board acknowledged disruption to fishing but concluded the work 'will not cause any damage to the beach or houses'. The dredging continued for another three years. By 1901 and the next report to the Board, the beach had substantially eroded and fresh winds, let alone gales, were washing the sea over the houses. The report concluded that the dredging should stop. It did, but only once the villagers took matters into their own hands.

The issue then became one of saving the village, and, once it was lost, of rehousing the villagers. The main hero of this story is Frank Mildmay, the local MP who had at the outset lobbied for the dredging to stop, and now kept the disaster on the national stage, badgering

Hallsands from the South, 1917. Comparing this with the Lidstone painting shows the ruins of the village and how the beach has narrowed and fallen, with the rocks standing high above the shingle.

The Plymouth & West Devon Record Office

the House of Parliament and the Board of Trade, and, when compensation was inadequate or delayed, making it up with personal guarantees or out of his own money. He was supported after the 1902-05 storms by Richard Hansford Worth, an engineer and authority on local archaeology who was to act, mainly unpaid, for the villagers for many years. His research on the lithology of the beach showed that the shingle was three-quarters flint, washed in as seas rose in prehistoric times, and which could therefore not be replenished once taken: 'any loss, caused by the removal of the shingle must...be permanent.' The slow destruction of the beach and then the village was, he argued, a direct result of the pit left by the shingle removed by the dredging, which allowed more to be scoured away by storms. Worth's position was never accepted by Sir John Jackson or the Board of Trade, who seem to have believed the erosion was the result of 'natural' causes.[6]

Inspections by the Board-appointed Captain G.C. Frederick in September 1901 and over 1902-05 were to confirm the role of the dredging in the disasters that befell the village, but during the

Hallsands, oil, by Frances Gynn, 2005. The Trout buildings are on top of the cliffs. The sea is breaking against the ledges at their base near the ruins of the old village. Start Point lighthouse, which Ella Trout will have watched at night as a child from the old village, is on the point (see p.141).

Courtesy Frances Gynn

long campaign to raise funds for a new sea wall many unprotected cottages were lost. The limited and late compensation that was then paid to the village recognised that the dredging had affected the fishing, but not the buildings or the beach. In the end, a village of thirty-seven homes in 1897, when the dredging began, was reduced to one of twenty-five before the ultimate storm carried it away in 1917. Eventually, in July 1924, sixteen houses were completed for the homeless families on the cliff above the old village.

Had the people of Hallsands not been who they were, there would have been tremendous injustice, but no enduring human story. They would have left after the first storms in 1902. But they owned their homes, felt strongly about their community, and were angered that a powerful company and distant government could combine to destroy what they had built. They badgered whatever authorities they had access to, demanded enquiries, and eventually took matters into their own hands and frightened off the dredgers. During the storms of 1902-05 they stayed in their crumbling houses listening to the water, patching, rebuilding, protecting their young and their elderly, fighting for compensation. Their courage and determination gathered to their cause not only Mildmay and Worth, but also local journalists and newspapers, among others, who campaigned first for the dredging to stop, then for compensation. When this was inadequate, these supporters, particularly Mildmay, paid out of their own pockets.

Elizabeth Anne Prettyjohns, who went back to the village under the cliff, repaired her damaged house and lived there until she died. The face of endurance.
Kingsbridge Cookworthy Museum

Who were these people?
Two examples tell us something...

Elizabeth Anne Prettyjohns returned with her brother to the one house still habitable after the 1917 storm. She lived on after he died until shortly before her own death in 1964 at the age of eighty. She collected driftwood, fed her cats and her chickens and climbed daily up the steep path to the cliff top to fetch her provisions, going on to collect her pension or visit relatives before coming home. Her daily newspaper was delivered by the baker, and she always had a go at finishing the crossword, peering at it through a magnifying glass. Whenever there was seine netting on the beach, she would be there, hanging onto the traditions of a village that had gone. To while away the time, she appointed herself guide to the many visitors who came to look at what had become a famous place, painting 'GUIDE' in big black letters on her cottage wall in case people didn't realise. Every Christmas she looked for the cards she had told them to send.

'I have all my memories here, but it's no good sitting down moping ' she said once. 'It was the dockyard away in Plymouth that took all our beach. It blew for four days and four nights. The sea was like mountains.'[7] Four sentences that tell everything you need to know about the people of Hallsands, why they stayed, why they finally had to leave, and who they blame.

The Trout Sisters, Ella on the left, Patience on the right, c.1930.

Kingsbridge Cookworthy Museum

A family called Trout had lived around Hallsands for at least a hundred years, and a map of the old village shows them occupying five houses in 1915.[8] William and Eliza Anne brought up a family of four girls there: Patience, Ella, Clara and Edith. The second, Ella, was to achieve remarkable things. Always the instigator of mischief as a child, when her father died in 1910 she left school at thirteen to take up fishing with her elder sister, an activity she pursued all her life whatever else she was doing. Joseph Grundy who sold fishing tackle across the area remembers Patience and Ella as the only women he knew to fish for a living, making pots, operating seine nets and crabbing alongside the men.

In September 1917, after the destruction of the village, Ella was out rowing beyond the point when she saw a ship, the *Newham*, hit a mine and go down. Without thinking about the danger of U-boats known to be cruising across the access to the Devonport naval yards, she rowed out through treacherous cross-currents for over a mile to rescue a crewman clinging to wreckage. Unable to row back because strong currents were taking them out to the Channel, they were picked up by another fishing vessel and then a navy patrol boat and eventually landed in Dartmouth. Ella was awarded the OBE (which had just been created by George V in June 1917) for war service. She was just twenty-one. She never behaved as if she had done anything remarkable; her upbringing had taught her you never questioned the need to save lives at sea. Even on the day after the old village had been destroyed and the villagers were racing to carry their possessions up the cliff before the next high tide, they had stopped to help a steamer drifting towards the rocks in the bay.[9]

Ella's next enterprise was to raise a bank loan – unheard of in her family – and buy *The Guide*, the first power-driven fishing boat in the community. 'Us got t'ave one, Paish,' she had said to her sister when they first saw a motor boat on the bay, 'Caw, no more of this B-pulling'.[10] Crabbers were heavy to row, 16 foot long and with a 5-6 foot beam, and *The Guide* changed their lives. With 'God's Wonderful Railway', the Great Western, which transported the day's catch from nearby Kingsbridge to Billingsgate fish market in London, they began to save a bit out of fishing.

141

Ella could now do what she had always wanted – build a fine house on the cliff above the old village. Prospect House rose up on land next to the coastguard station, a two-storied stone building, with Welsh slate roofs and double bay windows overlooking the views that Ella had known as a child. Building was not easy, loans were hard to get and for a year the sisters made their own concrete blocks by hand. But it became a popular place to stay, and after extensions and additions it had thirteen bedrooms and garages for cars. The sisters ran it

A Coast Scene (Hallsands),
oil, by James Clarke Hook.
Undated, but thought to be
after 1854 and certainly
before 1897. Villagers,
including women, hauling a
seine boat up the shingle.
Orchar Collection, Dundee Art
*Galleries & Museum*s

as a guest house until Ella died in 1975, at sixty-nine. Guests could relax and paint, walk and read. Or they could join Ella going out to drop crab pots in the early hours of the morning and pull on the seine nets when a shoal came in. You can still see the building on top of the cliffs above the ruins of Ella's old village. No longer a guest house, it has become apartments, but local people still know it as the Trout place. The memory of her, like that of her old village, is indomitable.

THE FRIGATE ON THE HILL

Britannia Royal Naval College stands high on a ridge running at right angles to the river and looks out over Dartmouth to the sea. It is a magnificent Edwardian building, its extended layout of weathered brick and stone finished off with low towers and cupolas echoing the wider views and soft colouring of the Townstal hills. Close to, its height enhances its scale, yet from a distance it fits into, without dominating, the landscape. Nikolaus Pevsner disliked its scale – he called the side cupolas 'niggling' – but Dartmothians and all right-minded people disagree with him.[1] From the College, there is a view of the town and the river where cadets row, sail and set off for sea training; from the town you see the clock on its 120-foot tower, hear the bugles, the drills, the helicopters and the music and fireworks of the end-of-training celebrations.

The architect was Aston Webb, later Sir Aston. His brief was to project an image of British sea power at a time when this was unsurpassed, and simultaneously build a school to train officer cadets, with dormitories and classrooms, dining rooms and halls. His 'masterpiece of Edwardian architecture' as it has been called, finished in 1905, combines presence and utility. The magnificent façade of red brick and creamy Portland stone has a central tower with extensive wings, terraces and sweeping driveways set in parkland. Inside, the building rises via a series of steps to a long corridor connecting chapel and dining areas at either end and a great vaulted central hall reminiscent of a Tudor mansion.

Webb's appointment was based on a reputation for sticking to his estimates and being responsive to his clients. Before the Naval College, he had been responsible for the Victorian law courts in Birmingham and was working on the University of Birmingham and the Royal Colleges of Science in London and Dublin as well as the main section of the Victoria and Albert Museum in London. He was President of the Architectural Association and the Royal Institute of British Architects and his skills of charm, courtesy and common sense were crucial in bringing together the best contemporary artists and craftspeople to create the integrated aesthetic of the College.

As one of a new breed of architect/artists, Webb also oversaw the interior work. The cream stone and red brick exterior is echoed in the Bath stone and brick facings inside. Webb's preference for local materials is in the green Delabole Cornish slate on the roofs, the Torquay limestone on the terrace walls, and in the chapel the Torquay limestone columns and the Ashburton limestone chancel, altar rail steps and plinths. There is a naval theme throughout, from the hulls of warships on the façade to the models on the light fittings, some of which Webb designed himself. Much of this work is extremely fine. Edward Bankart of the Bromsgrove Guild, who specialised in heavily foliated designs, made the enriched plaster mouldings on the ceilings, and the Guild did much of

College Occasions, drawing, by Bryan de Grineau. The quarter deck, or great hall, is the heart of the College, with its Bath stone pillars and arches, brick facings, trussed beam ceiling and elaborate iron-work.
Valerie Wills/BRNC

the wrought ironwork. The altar cross in the chapel, given in 1925, is by Sir Ninian Comper, a contemporary architect and often considered the greatest church furnisher since Wren.

Why Dartmouth? The Admiralty had several reasons. The first was probably that cadets had been trained on large hulks – successive *Britannias* and the *Hindostan* – moored in the river since 1863-64, so Dartmouth was a known entity. The site on the ridge was sheltered, the water good, and it did not have the distractions of a larger town. At the crucial early planning stages, the Captain of *Britannia* walked the ridge and 'came back to the cricket field with its magnificent outlook. Standing there for a few minutes, I was convinced that the site could not be improved upon...' and there stands the Naval College today.[2]

> *It is on the Navy, under the good providence of God, that our wealth, prosperity and peace depend*

These words are carved on the front of the College, paraphrasing the Naval Discipline Act of 1661 that founded the modern Royal Navy. Naval officers have been trained in leadership to meet these responsibilities in Dartmouth for 150 years. Before the Second World War, the College was essentially a public school, taking cadets at thirteen, but its curriculum was revolutionary for its

148

HMS Britannia, lithograph, by John Ward. The *Britannia*, before she was reduced to a training hulk, was the flagship at Portsmouth between 1836-51. Ward's lithographs of the ship have been called 'amongst the most accomplished marine lithographs ever made.'[3]

Hull Museums and Art Galleries

time. In December 1879, at the world première of the *Pirates of Penzance* by W.S Gilbert and Arthur Sullivan in the Royal Bijou theatre in Paignton, Richard Mansfield had belted out 'I am the very model of a modern major general', satirising the military education – ancient history, mathematics, elegaics and Greek drama, hieroglyphics and out-of-date military knowledge – then given to the officer class. (The song was thought to have been based on Gilbert's own experience of instruction at the Wellington Barracks when he was in the Civil Service Rifle Volunteers as a

The Battle of Trafalgar, oil, by William Lionel Wyllie, 1905, one of the College's most treasured paintings.   *BRNC*

young man. See the chapter 'Mansions of the Entertainers' for more on the Bijou production.) Admiral Sir John Fisher is generally credited with changing the navy: introducing modern engineering and science into the education of naval officers before the First World War. Since, the College has trained older students, now mostly graduates, in leadership, navigation, seamanship and relevant academic studies, such as naval history, strategic studies, meteorology and oceanography, engineering and naval weapons and sensors. Generations of naval officers who formed lifelong friendships there remember times of manic haste, exhaustion, wet and frantic sea deployments, and periods of intense professional development.

The College opened in 1905, the centenary year of the Battle of Trafalgar and the death of Admiral Horatio Nelson, whose ethos and heroism have inspired generations of naval officers. W.L. Wyllie's painting for the centenary of Nelson's death is one of the College's finest works of art. People in the College know of another link with Nelson. At 4.15 pm on 21 October, the time when Nelson is dying but victory clear, the sun shines through the small top west window of the chapel and casts a shaft of bright light on the raised right hand of Christ in the reredos.

Three British kings were educated at Dartmouth: George V, who was a cadet on the river in 1877-79; and his two sons who became Edward VIII and George VI and were cadets onshore

Stoke Gabriel, pencil and wash, by Robert Hurrell Froude, 1826. For relaxation, Princes Edward and George would row up the Dart to Stoke Gabriel to have cream tea at the forge.

West Country Studies Library

Britannia Royal Naval College, watercolour by Frank Wood, 1908, shows the College seen from the town.   *The Britannia Museum and Archive*

over 1909-12. The Duke of Edinburgh was a cadet as Prince Philip of Greece and Denmark in 1939. Prince Charles and Prince Andrew, his sons, were here more briefly in the 1970s. Prince William is the latest son of royalty to have been, when he came during a two-month detachment with the Royal Navy in 2008. He ended his time at Dartmouth 'continuing a family tradition, signing the ceiling of the Wardroom atop a human pyramid, before completing the even more impressive challenge of circumnavigating the Wardroom without touching the ground.'[4]

Edward, Prince of Wales, later Edward VII, was enthusiastic about the Naval College (as he was about Dartmouth generally), sending his sons for two years, believing that the education and discipline would be good for them, despite Queen Victoria's reservations about 'the very rough sort of life' and the risk it would 'encourage national prejudices'. The boys themselves were treated pretty much like the other cadets, and George V was to remember 'It never did me any good to be a Prince, I can tell you, and...the other boys made a point of taking it out on us on the grounds that they'd never be able to do it later on...' He was particularly exercised by his meagre but standard shilling-a-week pocket money, and after he had vainly begged his grandmother Queen Victoria for a sovereign to tide him over, he turned the tables on her by selling her kindly refusal letter for three pounds. Her response to this enterprising solution is unknown. His elder brother Edward was to die young, but George was to be a naval officer for almost twenty-two years before he was crowned in 1910.[5]

The Prince of Wales came regularly to race in the regatta at Dartmouth as well as to visit his sons, and one of his first public duties as Edward VII was to lay the foundation stone of the onshore Naval College in March 1902. He arrived with his family by train, the engine renamed *Britannia* for the occasion, travelling non-stop from Paddington to Kingswear in an astounding four hours twenty-three minutes,[6] and was brought across the river in a refurbished ferry, the aging *Dolphin*, to a

Christ's hand in reredos of BRNC chapel, lit up at the time when Nelson died.
Richard Porter/BRNC

The Dartmouth Encounter.
Prince Philip and Princess
Elizabeth with the Dart in
the background when she
was visiting the College in
July 1939. It was not the
first time they had met, but
probably the longest they
had been together. *BRNC*

rapturous welcome. The king and his party were met by the mayor and other dignitaries, the foundation stone was laid with its two time capsules (a bronze and silver casket made by Bromsgrove and a casket of timber and bronze from the hulk of the *Britannia*), and the party then returned to the *Dolphin* and the train, the whole event lasting just one hour and fifteen minutes.

Princess Elizabeth met her future husband, then Prince Philip of Greece, at the College in 1939. The legend that it was their first meeting is not true, but over the two days that the royal family was there she and the Prince were certainly together a great deal. He was with them for tea and dinner, church, elevenses and lunch – sitting between Elizabeth and the Queen – and he taught croquet to the two princesses. He was then eighteen and had a war to fight and Elizabeth was five years younger, but much later Lord Mountbatten was to write to Prince Charles: 'After all [your] Mummy never seriously thought of anyone else after the Dartmouth encounter when she was 13.'[7]

Many able administrators and leaders and many courageous men came from the College. Since 1900, the Victoria Cross – the highest military decoration for valour in the face of the enemy – has been awarded to twenty-eight cadets. Examples give an idea of degrees of determination and courage. In November 1940, Captain Fegen commanding the armed escort of a convoy of thirty-seven ships was attacked by a better-equipped German battleship in the Atlantic. He engaged the enemy head-on in a three-hour battle to give the convoy time to scatter. His right arm was shattered, the bridge destroyed beneath him, and he went down with his ship, but thirty-one ships of the convoy escaped. Lieutenant Place was twenty-two when he and another officer commanding two midget submarines carried out a daring attack on the German battleship *Tirpitz* that disabled her for months. It involved travelling at least 1,000 miles from their base in England to northern Norway, through minefields, patrols, gun defences and listening posts to place charges under the ship. Unable to escape under a heavy counter-attack, they scuttled their craft and were taken prisoner.

Events made heroes of ordinary cadets. On 1 August, 1914, three days before war was declared, the entire College was mobilised, some cadets as young as fifteen; only civilians remained behind. Less than two months later, Midshipman Riley had died when serving on HMS

Aboukir, pulled under water by the drowning man he was trying to save. A few weeks later Midshipman Boulton went down with HMS *Monmouth* at the Battle of Coronel, off the coast of Chile. Both were just fifteen. The *Monmouth* also carried a number of naval reservists from Dartmouth who died at the same time and there is a memorial to them in St Petrox Church at Dartmouth Castle. Within five months, 41 of the 434 cadets who had been applauded on the Dartmouth embankments on their way to the trains had been killed.

Of all the war heroes connected with the College, Fred Wilkes is among the most remarkable. He joined the navy at fifteen, and was Petty Officer Torpedo Gunners Mate in 1939. He received the Conspicuous Gallantry Medal for 'leadership, coolness and splendid example' in the Battle of North Cape in December 1943 when he kept torpedoes firing on the enemy while his ship was burning and despite spray from splinters and the loss of several of his team. He was never a cadet, but came from Dartmouth, and when he left the navy in 1948 he returned to work as an electrician at the College until he retired. On his death, his family discovered that of all the medals he was awarded for many other acts of courage during the war, only the CGM had been mounted and formally presented to him; he had avoided all other public presentations.

Dartmouth residents have always felt part of the life of the College. When cadets were mobilised in 1914, the history of the College describes their departure from the railway station at Kingswear: 'Three trains were standing by in Kingswear...the line of vehicles loaded with luggage almost the entire length of the northern embankment. Cadets marched to the *Mew*...cheered on by large crowds of residents.' Shortly afterwards, notices appeared around the town inviting the locals to be drilled in rifle practice at the College, since 'every man should be able to defend his home and use a rifle'. The response was tremendous; everyone wanted to learn.[8]

Her Majesty the Queen inspecting Lord High Admiral's Divisions with Commodore Martin Alabaster in 2008. *BRNC*

The Prince of Wales Bringing his two Sons to the Naval College on the River in Dartmouth in October 1877, from a contemporary illustration in *The Illustrated London News*. They are being welcomed at Kingswear with the *Britannia* and *Hindostan* on the river in the background.

Private collection

The royal connection is a source of local pride, and crowds turned out for royal visits, from the Prince of Wales bringing his two sons to the College in 1877 to the two-day visit of King George VI and his family in July 1939, when over 20,000 people are said to have arrived to see the royal party. When King Edward VII came to lay the foundation stone of the College in 1902 the visit might only have lasted a little over an hour, but Dartmothians talked for many months about the details of his ferry trip and his landau and horses. The *Dolphin* was a specially built steam ferry introduced in 1869, pointed at both ends so she could go in either direction, and was thirty-three years old when called on to carry the monarch. For her fifteen minutes of royal occupation she was repainted with a gold stripe on the hull and a bright red and black funnel, and her saloon transformed with curtains, carpet and new furniture (later sold in Torquay for

THIS WINDOW IS DEDICATED
TO THE GLORY OF GOD AND IN MEMORY OF
CAPTAIN ROBERT F. SCOTT, C.V.O., R.N.,
CAPTAIN L.E.G. OATES, 6TH INNISKILLING DRAGOONS,
DOCTOR E.A. WILSON,
LIEUTENANT H.R. BOWERS, R.I.M.,
AND
PETTY OFFICER EDGAR EVANS, ROYAL NAVY,
WHO PERISHED IN THE ANTARCTIC, MARCH 1912,
ON THEIR RETURN FROM THE SOUTH POLE.

"But for my own sake I do not regret this journey, which has shewn us that Englishmen can endure hardship, help one another, and meet death with as great a fortitude as ever in the past."

CAPTAIN SCOTT.

Memorial plaque in the chapel to Robert Falcon Scott and his team who died returning from the South Pole in 1912. Scott was a cadet from 1881-83, and until 1901 when he weighed anchor in *Discovery* for New Zealand and the Antarctic he was a serving naval officer. His college records show no sign of his exceptional qualities. He passed out seventh in a class of twenty-six.

Valerie Wills/BRNC

Dartmouth Regatta, watercolour, by John Donaldson, mid-1990s. Since 1864, when the Admiralty started to send gun-brigs, naval vessels like this frigate have been a highpoint on the river at the August regattas.

Courtesy John Donaldson

£100). But it was the landau with its seven horses, four coachmen and two mounted postillions brought from Windsor that caused most comment. They had travelled by train to Churston, then by road and over the Dart on the *Floating Bridge* to take the King to and from the College. For the next two weeks, to everyone's delight, they drove out daily from Lady Freake's Warfleet House.[9]

Today, cadets – like townspeople – are always on the river. At the College's Sandquay facilities they learn seamanship and navigation and are regularly out in rigid inflatables, sailing dinghies, motor whalers, picket boats and Cornish pilot gigs. They race with townspeople at regattas and in gig events on the Dart and at international events, often sharing crews. A ferry collision is one of their maritime leadership scenarios. Cadets help in fire and rescue emergencies; at the 2011 regatta a cadet was one of the four who rescued a paraplegic sailor trapped beneath a capsized keelboat. Calls can be disconcerting, like the one for a cow that fell from a cliff between Kingswear and Coleton Fishacre.

The Naval College means more than a building on a hill. The long association of the navy with Dartmouth brought royalty and the interest of the outside world to enliven and enrich the town and expand its horizons. The Admiralty, making successive decisions to choose Dartmouth for various practical reasons, changed it, and it has become more than a quiet place with a magnificent outlook. Countless cadets trained there develop an affinity that constantly brings them back.

Altar cross in the chapel by Sir Ninian Comper.

Richard Porter/BRNC

The Dart, Dartmouth Regatta, August, oil by Lucien
Pissarro, 1922.   *Courtesy of Richard Green Gallery, London*

The Mill Vale (or Blackpool Sands), oil, by Lucien Pissarro, 1921. This was the lane he would walk so many times in early spring to catch the right moment to paint Riversbridge.

Valerie Wills/Private collection

Touching Nature

Lucien Pissarro in Dartmouth

On the way from Stoke Fleming to Strete, at Blackpool Sands, there is a small road off to the right that wanders inland up the narrow valley made by a spring-fed stream. It is sided by high banks, copses and a hill on the right for most of the way, and it turns with the chuckling water round corners, past a mill or two and the junction at Embridge until it reaches Riversbridge.

For locals living in the valley, it is the way back from the beach. But it is also the way taken by Lucien Pissarro, eldest son of Camille, when he was staying in Blackpool for the second time in 1921. When he walked it in April and May, the banks will have been dense, as they are today at that time of year, with bluebells, primroses, campions – red and white – and stars of Bethlehem. Lucien always painted out of doors, and had written in 1914 to the collector Blackwell that he always tried 'to render the feeling that the subject gives me...It is the colour and tone which specially attract me, and to me an atmospheric effect cannot be truly rendered by a bold sweep of paint but by touches of subtle difference which suggest the delicate variety of nature'.[1]

Lucien Pissarro, pastel, by Clara Klinghoffer, 1928, some seven years after his second visit to Blackpool Vale. He is wearing one of his beloved hats and you can see why his ties were never visible.

© *National Portrait Gallery, London*

Going over the bridge at Blackpool Vale at about the time that Lucien Pissarro was there. *Private collection*

Pissarro will have been wearing his usual greenish tweeds, his green cloth cap – 'where is my nice green hat?' was a refrain – and, hidden under his long black beard, a carefully chosen tie, often yellow. A nephew once asked him if he wore a tie. With a sweet smile, Lucien lifted his beard to show him. He was fifty-eight in 1921, his left hand still clinched after a number of strokes in 1897, rosy cheeked – someone described him as well-soaped – and his long black beard streaked with white, although his powerful eyebrows were still black.[2]

His easel tucked under his arm, Pissarro is on a mission on those walks. The weather had been bad and slowed him down but he is determined to paint a landscape with apple trees in bloom. 'There is a very poor amount of flowers on the few trees which show sign of blooming' he complains to his wife, Esther, in a letter in April.[3] At the place where you first see Riversbridge from the south, there is an orchard on the other side of the stream, with the farmhouse tucked down into the hills and the trees in the middle distance. Here, Pissarro found the subject for his painting, and he kept going back there until he had sun on the early blossoming trees.

Pissarro had been in Blackpool in 1913 and came back twice in 1921, from mid-January to mid-February and then for another month from mid-April, staying with a Mrs Cole at The Mill. The letters he wrote to his wife describe the effect he was trying to capture in the nine paintings he made while he was there. They mix French and a strangely spelt English; although he lived in England from the age of twenty-seven, Pissarro was never fluent. On his arrival in January, he wrote: 'This Valley is like Switzerland, the sun remains only a few ours [sic] as the hill takes it very soon...' And in a following letter, on 21 January 'I have two...*en train*, gorgious [sic] *motifs* and effect, if only I can manage to go on with them without spoiling them – I started one this morning, a *temps gris*, with little drizzling of rain..'. But he wants the combination of shade and sun. 'This morning' he wrote four days later 'I had a go at my *temps gris* and I believe it is out of the wood [but] the poor sunny effect is backward...'. And a day later 'I have just finish my *temps*

Apple Blossom, Riversbridge Farm, Blackpool, oil, by Lucien Pissarro, 1921. This view up the valley in early spring is the same today.

Royal Albert Memorial Museum & Art Gallery, Exeter

gris – Or at any rate I have decided not to return to it – The place where I stand now is plunged in a slipery [sic] morass '*et en pente*' so that I have to think all the time of my feet in order not to tumble down, with palette, easel and canvas!' He complains so much that Esther (doing her best) sends him his snow boots.

Finally, a triumphant letter from his second visit in April that year: 'I have two pictures in hand...One is the one I have drawn in with the mill – late afternoon (after tea) nearly half the picture "foreground in the shade" with the sun lighting the background with a red light over the new green and budding trees – Gorgious [sic] effect...' The painting of the Mill Vale (at the start of this chapter) has the combination of shade and sunlight and the colour he was talking about.

163

But he wanted the atmosphere of early spring, and summer was already advancing. On 29 April he wrote 'The weather so far is gorgious [sic]. I have two things in hand and am trembling for fear that the leaves will all be out before I manage to finish them...' Then, in a letter on 5 May: '...for two days I have not been able to work at the pictures I started – I am very distressed because everything is turning green and less beautiful!' By 12 May he was saying sadly 'Now the green has invaded everything'; twelve days later he left.

These 'little blossom pictures' of Pissarro were highly prized from the first time he exhibited them. His friend J.B. Manson, artist and Director of the Tate Gallery in London, wrote to Esther in May that he had seen in an exhibition 'His little blossom picture' and that it '...is beautiful – very exquisite in colour. It is wonderful to come across it in that extraordinary *mélange*.' Even from reproductions you can see why. With their beautifully balanced tones, artless structure and restraint these Blackpool paintings capture perfectly the charm of the countryside in early spring in this part of Devon.

With the dreaded green invading the summer countryside the following year, Pissarro chose to come to Dartmouth to paint. He had already been there in 1921 to visit his friends, the Campbells. In his letter to Esther of 13 January he described, in his inimitable style, 'the *vue* on the right the sea with the ground round the old castle and [on] the left the Dart disapearing in the distance amongst the hills, with a cascade of houses on the foreground – Opposite Kingswear pearched on the hill are its pink and white houses stuck on it like cardboard construction on a lampshade – lovely.'

So he came, from April until late September in 1922, staying first with Mrs Major at Channel View, Above Town, and then at Rose Bank. His standards for comfort seemed to be met. 'The Majors are very nice people' he wrote to Esther 'and the place is spotlessly clean – the cooking is very good so far.' He painted twenty pictures this time, going back to Blackpool Vale to paint four. 'I am...simply bewildered by the drawing of mass of houses!' he told Esther in early May. His painting of Waterhead Creek shows how he decided to do it: delicate touches of tones and shades reflected in the water to produce the impression he sought. This was painted in August and you can see him trying to avoid the uniform greens of summer. The painting from Mount Boone is from a position taken by many artists over the centuries, from Schellinks in the 17th century and Turner in the 19th to the present day. But Pissarro's interpretation is entirely his own, a painting with the early tones of autumn.

Pissarro's letters from Dartmouth in 1922 are fixated on money. 'You imagine I can produce pictures by the dozen!' he tells Esther, who must have been

Waterhead Creek, Kingswear, oil, by Lucien Pissarro, 1922. An unusual view, looking down on the station with the Royal Dart Hotel next to it and church behind, the colours and tones minimise the 'terrible green' of summer. The glowing grey light is the light of early morning.

Valerie Wills/Private collection

worrying him 'I have been working hard evening and morning...But I cannot manage more than ...two *séances* per day! I must not put the quantity foremost or else I shall go under!' Manson in London – 'My dear old Bag' – is the honest broker, talking to potential buyers, advising on prices and negotiations over them. Pissarro writes despondently to Esther at the end of September about his receding vision of affording a winter in the south of France '...if I don't do enough at my show to warrant such an exorbitant expenditure that a stay in the South would require – I could go to Paris... mother could ...let a *chambre meublé* and do our little *popotte* ourselves. I would do the shoping [sic] and I could do some engraving...' and then, as if this was altogether too depressing a thought, 'Do try to read *Candide* it is fine French.'

'...Nobody thinks of buying pictures, only of motoring, tennis and polo'. So wrote Brown, the exhibitor of Pissarro's paintings, to Esther that summer. But the exhibition of the Dartmouth work was a success, Brown sent them a cheque of £742, with more promised, and Pissarro was able to go south to Le Lavandou for the winter, staying six months.

Pissarro's Blackpool and Dartmouth paintings have always been prized. Manson, ever the true friend, wrote to Lucien on 9 August 1924, 'Passing 122 Harley Street this morning, the window of the front room was open; on the wall facing the street was one of your Dartmouth pictures unless I am very much mistaken...I don't know which of [the residents] is the person of taste and enlightenment.' (The person is believed to have been a Dr Jane Walker.) In 1929, his painting of *Embridge in Blackpool Vale* was exhibited at the Venice Exhibition and sold for 90 guineas, and his 1922 painting *Garden at Dartmouth* was bought for the Luxembourg by the French state.

Pissarro, although a member of many groups of painters, never fitted any of them well. He grew up, always drawing, in the heart of the Impressionist movement at the side of Camille Pissarro, his father, and among paintings of Manet, Dégas, Monet, Cézanne, Gauguin, Morisot and Seurat. He and van Gogh exchanged works and he had close relations with Monet before and after Camille died, giving him seeds for the garden at Giverny and discussing their ongoing work. But he was the next generation. Frank Rutter, the art critic of the *Sunday Times*, who had called Lucien the 'most exquisite landscape painter from whom I have learnt all that I know of the science of colour'[4] wrote in 1919 of an exhibition that showed Lucien with Impressionists including Camille, 'Great as the qualities of the first Impressionists were...the work of the second generation is closer knit in structure, firmer and stronger in design, and it gains accordingly.'[5]

Perhaps the best-known association that Pissarro had was with the Camden Town Group, named after the London area where some of the members lived, which lasted from 1911-13. (An exhibition of the Group at the Tate Gallery in 2008 had 88,000 visitors.) It was a reaction against the conservatism of the Royal Academy and the New English Art Club. Its President was 'the tactful' Spencer Gore and included, among others, Walter Sickert, Robert Bevan, Harold Gilman, Charles Ginner, J.D. Innes, Malcolm Drummond, William Ratcliffe and J.B. Manson.[6] These were Post-Impressionists, painting colours and light effects, and they had a great respect for Pissarro, who had lived French impressionism and understood it in a way that nobody else did. These paintings of Blackpool and Dartmouth show Pissarro at his best, capturing precise effects of light and shade, trying to stay true to the atmosphere of the view before his easel.

Mount Boone and the Dart Estuary (or *Tunstal, the Estuary*), oil, by Lucien Pissarro, 1922. From Willem Schellinks in the 17th century and J.M.W. Turner in the 19th, many artists have painted this view from a ridge above the town. Pissarro's painting of an Edwardian garden overlooking the water is all subtle harmony.

Valerie Wills/Private collection

LOST WORLDS

Flora Thompson and Children of Dartmouth in the 1930s

It was in Dartmouth, sitting in her study at The Outlook high over the Dart in Above Town, that Flora Thompson began to write the books that were to survive her and will probably survive the rest of us for generations.

Flora came to Dartmouth, reluctantly, in 1928, from Liphook in Hampshire where she had lived happily for twelve years. She had stayed behind for almost a year after her husband John moved there to become postmaster. She was to live in Dartmouth until March 1940, when she and John, now retired, moved to Brixham to a more manageable house away from the dangers of wartime Dartmouth, whose Naval College and shipbuilding works made it vulnerable to attack. She was to die in Brixham seven years later, just outlasting the war. During her time in Dartmouth, she published preliminary sketches of her childhood in Juniper, Oxfordshire – *Old Queenie* and *May Day* – in 1937, and *Lark Rise*, the first of her well-known trilogy, two years later. She was working on its sequel, *Over to Candleford*, when she left. It was written, she told a friend, 'under difficulties, several of the passages to the sound of bombs falling...the typescript already looks worn through being taken in and out of the Morrison shelter.'[1] *Candleford Green* and *Still Glides the Stream* were yet to come, works of a now assured writer who had found her voice.

Dartmouth, watercolour, by F. Walters, 1910. Flora's view up the river from the hill beyond her house, The Outlook, will have been similar to this. The Naval College dominating the left-hand ridge had just been built when this was painted.   *Valerie Wills/Dartmouth Museum*

We have little idea of what she looked like; her daughter could only find two faded photographs after her death. The one here must have been taken when she was in her twenties. But her friend Arthur Ball wrote a vivid description when he saw her in 1946, only a few months before she died. 'My first impression' he wrote 'was quite unlike what I expected.' He had probably seen the photograph reproduced here, because he goes on that he anticipated someone 'dark and willowy...very graceful and feminine. I saw a Flora Thompson who was sturdy and resolute, and, with her features chiselled to an expression of remarkable strength, more like the portraits of Marie Curie than anyone else I can think of. Of course the winning, gentle side was there all right, but she seemed to have attained a remarkable independence in her character... And there was that underlying simplicity which the very best natures usually seem to acquire or have as a matter of birthright. When I think of the terrible time she must have had with her illness I am struck too by her remarkable freedom from absorption in self or self-pity – it was all in the other direction, a vital and eager interest in the people she was talking to.'[2] Flora had been frail since recovering from pneumonia in the winter of 1941 and had developed angina, often having to force herself to write.

It had taken Flora more than forty years to find her tone of integrity, simplicity and unsentimental observation. She had been 'a great spoiler of paper', as she put it, since her childhood, but was sixty-three when she began to make her name with *Lark Rise*. In 1951 her daughter Winifred, or

Diana as she was known, was to write after her death 'Unfortunately her success came really too late for her to...appreciate it, although she had been writing all her life and had had many minor successes.'[3]

In Dartmouth, with Dyer's Hill rising behind her house and the river angling its way to the sea in front, Flora took pen to paper. 'The hamlet stood on a gentle rise in the flat, wheat-growing north-east corner of Oxfordshire. We will call it Lark Rise because of the great number of skylarks which made the surrounding fields their springboard and nested on the bare earth between the rows of green corn.'[4] She was back in the 1880s, in the end-house of the rural hamlet where she was born, among people whose beliefs and hopes, habits and eccentricities she had never forgotten, although she left them when she was fourteen. *Lark Rise* was called after the big field of corn that came almost to her door, and she was to write that 'every one of the characters lived at Juniper and were just as described, with only the names altered'.[5]

Oldreive Brothers, Poulterers and Butchers in Fairfax Place in Dartmouth at Christmas 1927 with their stunning display of game. It could have been this shop that so horrified Flora.

Dartmouth Museum

She wrote little about Dartmouth. A letter to Arthur Ball dated 22 December 1931 gives a rare glimpse of how she saw the town, with the same combination of intense awareness of nature and wry observation of people that made her writing about her childhood so effective. 'I look out of my bedroom window' she wrote 'on deep silence and star-reflecting waters, the harbour lights burning red and often a lighted ship passing across the mouth of the river...Then the night winds – soothing or exciting – and white night-blooming flowers in summer, frost-sparkle in winter and, best of all, just the mysterious darkness and soft wandering winds.' Then, in the same letter 'I have just been down to the town – such shop-windows! Poor birds slaughtered in thousands and cakes and crackers enough to set up a thousand parties. I thought of the Frenchman's "The English are a nation which celebrates the birth of its God with a pudding and His death with a bun" but of course there is another side to it – there is to everything –.'[6]

But in the little she did write about the area, Flora mostly turned away from the Dart, looking for country scenes that had resonance for her. 'From my seat on the hill-top a week ago' she wrote in 1930 'the distant cornfields showed like lakes of sober gold between dark shores of copse and hedgerow...The wide stretches of gold seemed as much part of the landscape as the hills or the woods or the still blue eye of the little round pond on the heath yonder...There are sails too; the long red revolving sails of the mechanical reaper. Harvest has begun.'[7] Eight years later she was to remember harvest home in *Lark Rise*, when 'Laura would make little dashes into the corn for poppies, or pull trails of the lesser bindweed with its pink-striped trumpets, like clean cotton frocks'. The mechanical reaper was new then, and 'while the red sails revolved in one field and the youth on the driver's seat of the machine called cheerily to his horses and women followed behind to bind the corn into sheaves, in the next field a band of men would be whetting their scythes and mowing by hand as their fathers had done before them.'[8]

Dartmouth, oil, by James Bolivar Manson, c.1921, showing the hills where Flora walked behind her house, from which the town is practically invisible. Manson came to Dartmouth with Lucien and Esther Pissarro. On one car trip they took together, Esther – an erratic driver – stalled on a hill. Lucien was deeply asleep in the back, so Manson wedged two large stones, kept in the car especially for the purpose, under the back tyres. Esther started up and roared off. Manson had to trudge the three-and-a-half miles home carrying the stones, which he didn't dare leave behind.[9]

Royal Albert Memorial Museum & Art Gallery, Exeter

Two years later, she wrote 'To the night-watcher at the upper window comes the scent wafted from the flowers below – stocks and prinks and roses – all the cottage garden flowers. Then, borne on the breezes, comes the breath of the hayfields.'[10] Flora, now in her mid-fifties, leaning out of her back window, was looking out towards Dyer's Hill, but the memory it evoked of summer at Juniper Hill was eventually relived in *Lark Rise* with that intense observation of a child. 'Against the billowing gold of the fields the hedges stood dark, solid and dew-sleeked; dewdrops beaded the gossamer webs, and the children's feet left long, dark trails on the dewy turf. There were night scents of wheat-straw and flowers and moist earth on the air...'[11]

Flora had gone back to a way of life truncated by the First World War. Machines were beginning to come in, but the farm people worked mostly by hand, carthorses pulling the heavy equipment. The year was punctuated by May Day processions, harvest festivals, bonfire nights at Hallowe'en, dates from ancient agricultural cycles. Children walked to single-room schools down roads empty save for an occasional farmer's gig. By the age of ten, most village girls were in service and boys in the fields. Entertainment was singing and story-telling and the occasional fair. People believed in endurance, not 'flinching' from difficulties, they had pride in their work, thought appearances important – admiring cleanliness, nice clothes and possessions – and rallied to neighbours in need with spoons of tea or sugar on the days before wages were paid, soup for the elderly, and help for the sick. 'Poverty's no disgrace' says one of her characters 'but 'tis a great inconvenience.'

So Flora wrote on, immersed in her memories, producing small masterpieces about a lost rural countryside and its kindly, solid way of life.

Around Flora was another way of life, modern for her, with its shops and glitz, but this was to go as well, truncated in its turn by another world war. Those who were children in Dartmouth in the 1930s as Flora had been a child in the 1880s have memories too of that time. They are oral, not polished and written, and of a town, not a rural hamlet, but they bring the place alive and tell us about the daily lives of people around Flora as she wrote.

Dartmouth people who were young when Flora was there remember above all the river...

All the important activities happened along it – the coal-lumping, jobs at the gas and the paint-works next to the incinerator by Coombe Mud, now Coronation Park, the ship-building at Sandquay and Noss and the fishing. By the 1930s, the era of the large fishing fleets sailing the Atlantic was over, but small trawlers were still plying the local coasts. The distinctive Brixham trawlers were still being built on the Dart, and although the fleet had fallen from the 213 registered by the Mutual Insurance Company in 1910, there were still 58 when Flora arrived in Dartmouth.[12] Coal bunkering was also in decline and was to peter out by 1950, but many fathers and brothers were still coal-lumpers, offloading the coal from the coal-ships from south Wales onto small boats, taking these across to the Embankment and then carrying the sacks over planks and along to the coal piles at the gasometer. Children used to go out to the Castle to watch for the coal-ships, going around the seat three times for luck, while mothers signalled back to the coal-lumpers to be ready as the ships appeared on the horizon.

There were always boats; every family in Dartmouth passed through the Rowing Club at some time or another between the wars. Everyone fished. The lucky children with access to motor boats went feathering for mackerel and felt 'posh and snooty' about the rowing-boats as they roared past. Others would row the heavy coal boats from the gas works up the river for picnics at weekends. They would go to Noss Point, Galmpton, or Old Mill Creek, winkling and cockling. The children who could would swim. There was acute embarrassment if you hadn't any shorts and had to wear the swimsuit your mother had knitted, which was heavy, sagged, and threatened to fall off. The treat was lettuce or sugar sandwiches.

On the Dart, watercolour, by Wilfred Knox, 1920. Knox was an engineer and musician as well as an artist and was with the Royal Flying Corps in the First World War. He worked mainly in watercolours and often in the West Country, and here has captured a peaceful scene up the Dart between the wars when Flora knew it.

Elford Fine Art, Tavistock

Between the wars, sheep and cows used to be ferried over the river on the *Mew* – the local name for seagull – and driven down to the Friday market, the farmer shouting and whistling to the dogs. The animals were penned in the market square, and once a girl fell off a plank into a herd of calves in the pen. Men took hold of either arm and hauled her out, all mucky.

Mrs Farmer, who lived next to the incinerator, sold home-made boiled sweets at the market – all sorts, aniseed, lemon, citrus, and red-striped ones. Children ate carob bars, seeds from the carob tree, chewy, with a lovely liquoricy taste. (Carobs, from India or the Levant, are still used, grated, as a healthy substitute for chocolate.) A soup kitchen was run by two spinsters in the market, with great big urns of soup on long tables. You paid a penny to have bread with it, but the bread was stale. Mostly just children went (adults were reluctant to be seen there), carrying a tin can for the soup with a lid to keep it hot. It always tasted like pea soup, with bits of mutton thrown in. There was a man there with a wooden leg, and the children thought he stirred the soup with it, making them wary of eating it when he appeared.

The Palladium cinema was on Anzac Street, then called Hanover Street, opposite Pillars. (The earliest medieval guildhall was here, next to some priests' houses.) The screen was the wall painted white and someone played the piano. Another cinema, the Cinedrome, opened later on Zion Street where the clinic is now. It cost 2d to go to the pictures on a Saturday afternoon, and you shared a seat. There were fairs. The Regatta Fair was held on the Dirty New Ground where the car park next to the Royal Avenue Gardens is today. It was called Dirty after the cinders underfoot. On Bonfire Night different groups had fires on the Dirty New Ground; part of the fun was stealing wood, chairs, carpets and mattresses from the others. There was a carnival in June or July, when people danced.

Just like the people at Lark Rise, Dartmouth families had sing-songs. People still remember some:

Where be that blackbird to?
Us knows where 'ee be,
'Ee be up the worzel tree
And us be adder 'ee.
'Ee knows I
And I knows 'ee
And 'ee knows I be adder 'ee
With a bloody gret stick us'll knock
'ee on the 'ead
Blackbird I'll 'ave 'ee.

Another is:

'Alf a pound of flour and lard
Makes a lovely claker
Just enuff for you 'n me
cor bugger jacker.

Ooh 'ow 'appy us will be
When us gets back to the west country
Where the 'oggies grows on trees
cor bugger jacker.

(A *Worzel* is a turnip; *claker* is a sort of porridge; and *'oggies* are pasties.)

The Market Square, Dartmouth, woodcut, by Enid Wise. This shows the square on a non-market day and a photograph of the same place today would look very much the same.

Courtesy Enid Wise

Fishing Boat on Old Mill Creek, acrylic by Andras Kaldor, 1983. Old Mill Creek, just upriver from Dartmouth, was a favourite picnic and swimming place and many fishing boats were kept there.

Courtesy Andras Kaldor

Houses were often two-bedroomed and, where there were gardens, people grew vegetables and had chickens in the back yard. Chicken food – leftovers, corn and potato peelings – would be cooked in the copper boiler in the kitchen and the smell turned your stomach while you ate. The men used to wash in a tin bath in front of the fire, and the children would scrub their backs. There were wash places outside, often shared between adjoining houses. One family had a monkey in the loft, which one of the men had brought home from the First World War. The children fed it bananas (they ate no such fruit themselves) and it was smelly and frighteningly fast. The children were called monkeys and wondered why, although as adults they think it was with affection. Mothers were called birds. In large families, children could be farmed out to grandparents at weekends. They often had happy memories of new friends in these homes away from home, buying ice for a penny from the ice-works if grandparents lived in Brixham, getting sunburnt, and trying to lick off the clotted cream Gran put on the sunburn. This Gran was always dressed in black with a brooch at a lace collar, and made her grandchild clean the brass stair rods.

Coal was delivered to the houses in a trolley or a wheelbarrow – "coal-ee-ee coal-ee-ee" shouted the coalman as he went up the road. Milk came in a churn carried by a man with a yoke on his shoulders or in a wheelbarrow and was ladled out with a dipper. The fourteen-year-old boys used to do the milk rounds in the morning and after school and bring the bread at lunchtime. Horse and donkey carts used to carry the milk and vegetables into Dartmouth from the farms. The blacksmith was always a Middleton, and the forge was on the corner of Zion Place, next door to the anchorsmith. The last Middleton blacksmith sold up from Zion Place in 2010.

In spring, the children went out to Compass Cove to pick primroses, tie them in bunches on a stick and walk home selling them for a penny a bunch. A popular place to play was Coombe Mud, now Coronation Park, where wrecks of ships and all sorts of relics of building sites lay half-covered in mud. But it was perilous; children cut themselves on bits of glass and metal and one little girl who cut her leg there died of blood poisoning. Her sister didn't know what had happened – her parents kept saying she had gone away – but remembers marking her name on a wooden cross for the grave.

In the 1930s you went to school until you were fourteen, walking there and coming back for lunch. There was little traffic on the roads then, and anyway, you went 'up steps' to school. If you were a small and timid girl, you worried about being bullied on the way, by girls as well as boys, and had to go a long way round to avoid them. There were two schools, the Catholic and the National (or Board) School. The Catholic School, gentler than the Board School, had two classrooms and boys and girls had separate playgrounds.

When they left school, girls could be apprentices. Miss Prout, who had a draper's shop on the corner of Fairfax Place and Hauley Road, used to employ them at 2s 6d a week. The shop was on the ground floor, the toilet out in the back yard. Miss Prout lived on the first floor, and the stores – a good place to fool around – were in the attic. You wore a black satin dress made up on the dull side with a little white lace collar, heavy stockings and black shoes. Miss Prout sold materials, Liberty bodices in white paper packages, and thick blankets, striped swimsuits, stockings and nightdresses among other things.

Miss Prout was very strict, and had an equally strict housekeeper, Miss Mann. If apprentices were there all day Miss Mann would lay out tea and buns in the back in the afternoons. Every time they went for tea, the apprentices had to recite poetry by Patience Strong – a sharp cultural contrast to the sing-along songs.

STAY AT
DARTMOUTH

DEVON'S BEAUTY SPOT

FREE GUIDE
FROM SECRETARY
'DEPT. P'
COMMERCIAL-
ASSOCIATION
DARTMOUTH
OR
FROM THE TOWN CLERK 'DEPT. R' DARTMOUTH

G.W.R

Herring Fishing off Lighthouse Cove, Kingswear, 1930s. Photographs tell you what was really happening and what things really looked like.

Dartmouth Museum

Wartime Dartmouth was active, noisy and dangerous – not conducive to creative thought and Flora was trying to write *Over to Candleford*. In 1940, when she and John moved across the river to Brixham, it was to Lauriston, a secluded house, with no view of the town centre or the sea. It was in Brixham that she finished *Over to Candleford*, *Candleford Green* and *Still Glides the Stream*, and here that the trilogy *Lark Rise to Candleford* was published. And it was whilst here that Flora, whose closest brother Edwin had been killed at Ypres in 1916, heard of the loss of her youngest son Peter in the merchant navy at sea in the autumn of 1941. In 1942, she wrote to Arthur Ball 'His ship was torpedoed

Last paragraph of the letter from Flora Thompson to Arthur Ball, 16 August 1942, in which she talks about Peter's death.

Courtesy of Special Collections, University of Exeter

His ship was torpedoed nearly a year ago in the night and went down in just over one minute. There were only six survivors of whom he was not one. It was a terrible blow to me and a loss I shall never get over and yet the world is in such a state today that I sometimes feel that he, being at rest, is better off than those still at sea. But it is not rest one would wish for a boy of his age, but life, and life abundantly. It is a mad world.

    With all my best wishes for everything,

        your old friend,

                    Flora Thompson

nearly a year ago in the night and went down in just over one minute. There were only six survivors of whom he was not one. It was a terrible blow to me and a loss I shall never get over.' [13] Her words speak for everyone who lost family and friends then.

There are no coal-lumpers in Dartmouth now, and the paintworks and gasworks have gone, with the incinerator. The children who played in Coombe Mud in the 1930s married, went off to war, and those who came back had children who are now nurses, builders and sailors. When Flora, who struggled to write after Peter's death, died in Brixham in May 1947, her funeral service was held at St Barnabas Church below her Dartmouth home. She is buried in Longcross cemetery on the hill above the town. There are two plain headstones in her memory, shaped like an open book, one side for Flora and one side for Peter.

Above: Flora Thompson wrote a charming short story called *How Warrior came to Windwhistle*. Set on the cliffs above Compass Cove, she renamed Dartmouth as 'Britmouth'. You can still pass Flora's solitary cottage on your way to Little Dartmouth today.

Right: The gravestone of Flora and Peter Thompson in Longcross cemetery, Dartmouth.
                                                                    Valerie Wills

AT WAR

An American M7 'Priest' self-propelled gun of the 4th Armored Division east of Coronation Park. The medieval Ship in Dock pub watches, as it still does today, from the foot of Ridge Hill. *Dartmouth Museum*

Previous Spread:
Boats drawn up at Torcross, at the southern end of Slapton Sands, where the D-Day exercises took place and where the memorials stand. *© 2013 Nigel Evans*

* The archives of the Britannia Royal Naval College have a copy of a Luftwaffe reconnaissance photograph showing the College, shipyards at Noss, the railway station and the surrounding area in some detail. (Harrold and Porter, 2005, p.124.)

Once again, after the fall of northern Europe in the Second World War, Dartmouth's deep, secluded harbour was to become its destiny. Just as sailors and merchantmen had, centuries before, hidden in the estuary in between piracy or privateering raids, so the navy and the Free French hid here between raids on the Norman and Breton coasts. Just as vessels for the crusades and the Armada had gathered in the safe haven of the mouth of the Dart, so it became a preparation point for part of the largest invasion force ever combined that was to turn the tide of the Second World War. Where our ancestors had a protective chain between the castles at the river mouth, our parents and grandparents installed an anti-submarine boom in virtually the same place.

Because of the Naval College and the Noss shipbuilding works, which built some 230 war vessels during the conflict, Dartmouth might have expected to be an enemy target.* In fact, despite heavy raids on Exeter and Plymouth, and nearer at hand in Torbay, there were only two serious attacks on the town. In September 1942, six Focke-Wulf 190s came down the river, paired off, and bombed and machine-gunned the Naval College, Noss, and coal bunkering vessels on the river, killing some twenty-five people – just one at the college, because the cadets were still on leave – and injuring about twice that number. (Cadets were moved to Bristol and eventually Cheshire.) Then in February 1943 there were sixteen deaths in an air attack on the town. But there were many casual 'tip-and-run' raids on the area, and local people remember being surprised by aircraft as they sunbathed on the rocks, watching dog-fights over the Kingswear hills and flight after flight of aircraft making for Plymouth or Exeter.

Motor Launches, Dartmouth, oil, by Charles Ernest Cundall, 1940.

In June 1940, Dartmouth provisioned and sent off a collection of small boats to rescue soldiers from Dunkirk. Douglas Reed, a journalist living in Dartmouth, recalls seeing 'the elderly owner of an elderly yacht, one of the relics of...[the] great regatta days' busily getting ready to go, and the ancient railway ferry, the *Mew*, built in 1908, steaming off.[1] No-one knows how many boats from Dartmouth actually crossed the Channel; the *Mew* was only used for ferrying work in Dover and returned ten days later. But evacuees from Dunkirk came; cadets remember the smell of 'unwashed human bodies, particularly feet' pervading the college.[2]

Motor Gun Boat, photograph taken from the stern of the one ahead.

H. Lloyd Bott/Dartmouth Museum

War littered the river with ships. As Belgium, Holland and France fell, so refugees sailed in, the Belgians bringing trawlers – records vary from 77 to 200 of these – and two French tugs, the *Aube* and the *Isère*, arrived from le Havre. They joined the congregation of local fishing boats, private yachts and navy vessels used for minesweeping, patrols at sea and along the coasts and other, more clandestine, operations. At night, convoys of merchant ships with their escorts came in through a gap in the boom for refuelling and to take on provisions while they sheltered from German submarines and E-boats operating only ninety miles away out of Brest. As the convoys came in, out went the motor torpedo boats and motor gun boats of the navy and the FNFL – *Forces Navales Françaises Libres* – or the Free French. In 1940, police reports on a fight at a dance hall and drunk and disorderly charges record English, French, Belgian and Danish sailors in Dartmouth, 'with other aliens', which could have included the Free Poles.[3] Wartime Dartmouth was an international place.

Dunkirk, oil, by Charles Ernest Cundall, 1940s. On 4 June, 1940, Winston Churchill announced that nearly a thousand ships of all sorts, shapes and sizes, had brought 'over 335,000 men, French and British, out of the jaws of death and shame'. Many small boats set off from Dartmouth, but are unlikely to have made the crossing.   *BRNC*

One memorable refugee was Denis Vibert who arrived from Jersey in September 1941. He had rowed his eight-foot *Ragamuffin* the first few miles out to sea to avoid detection, used his outboard until the petrol ran out (an extra tank was contaminated with salt water), and then rowed on, adjusting his course for the tides until, off Start Point, he was picked up by the 'Hunt' Class destroyer HMS *Brocklesby* and brought in to Dartmouth. He had travelled an estimated 150 miles. When he returned to Dartmouth after being debriefed he had to pay ten shillings duty to have his boat back. He spent the rest of the war in the RAF.

MTB 777, oil, by H.E. Beavis. This motor torpedo boat is thought to have operated from the east coast, but vessels stationed at Kingswear during the Second World War were very similar.

Dartmouth Museum

The Local Defence Volunteers, almost immediately renamed the Home Guard, recruited men aged between seventeen and sixty-five early in the war when invasion seemed imminent, especially after Dunkirk. That meant setting up a 24-hour coastal watch in Dartmouth, manning positions around the estuary, such as the guns at the Castle, usually at night. The defence capacity of the Strete Section of the Guard was vastly improved when they got hold of rifles and ammunition from the impounded Belgian trawlers.[4] As coastal defences strengthened, the threat of invasion receded.

Seamen from the Dart on secret naval exercises made up some of the most effective small units of the war. From the Royal Dart Hotel by the Kingswear ferry slip, the hotel renamed HMS *Cicala*, missions went out nightly on patrol or taking agents or explosives across the channel, and bringing back agents, combatants, refugees and secret information. These missions were manned by special units of the Royal Navy and the Free French. Their gun and torpedo boats, heavily armed and fast, left at nightfall, without lights and without radar. Engines were cut off near the French coast and the last few miles were rowed with muffled oars. Countless lives were saved by these men. A German helmet on a hook in the pub might have been all local people would know of their achievements.[5]

Opposite: The Home Guard, a cadet's-eye view. The cadet's cartoon is typical of the many jokes made about its military muscle, and Douglas Reed, recruited into the group, confirms its early lack of arms and uniforms (made up for, he says, by enthusiasm), but records the arrival later of ancient rifles and an even more ancient Boer War Hotchkiss. From dusk to dawn Reed would man this antique gun on the cliffs waiting for German aircraft to come into its rather limited line of fire – which they never did while he was there. (Reed, 1941, pp. 289-94.)

Valerie Wills/Britannia Museum and Archive

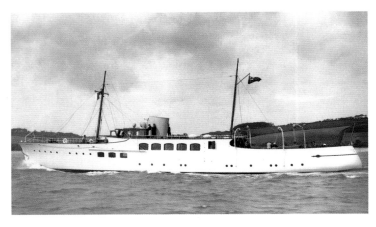

Campeador V, 126-foot motor yacht built at Philip's in Dartmouth in 1938, was offered to the Admiralty by the owner, Vernon McAndrew of Dartmouth, and used for sea patrols, commanded by the owner and his friends, all aged between 58 and 67. She was blown up off the Isle of Wight in June 1940. Two of the twenty-two crew survived, but not McAndrew or his friends.

Royal Dart Yacht Club

Brookhill, a twenty minute walk from Kingswear, where the crew from the Free French Flotilla stayed during the Second World War and a sailor stood guard at the door beside the cross of Lorraine. This view from the river is from a 1908 postcard, but the house changed little until after the wars (see opposite).

Michael Stevens

Kingswear was awarded the *Médaille d'Argent* by the French Government for its assistance to the Free French in the war. The cross was part of the arms of Lorraine, annexed to Germany for much of the war, a symbol of French patriotism and the Free French.

Michael Stevens/Kingswear Historians

The Free French spent most of the war in Kingswear, first with the 20th and then the 23rd Flotilla of motor torpedo boats. There were some 200 of them after 1942, under the overall command of English coastal forces. The officers, including Philippe de Gaulle, the son of Charles, were housed at the '*petit hôtel délicieux*' of Longford, opposite the Royal Dart Hotel, and the crew down the coast road at Brookhill and on HMS *Belfort*, the base ship on the Dart.

The French remember nights out at sea off the French coast, periods of tense watching and then the roar of engines and deafening explosions, followed by a return to an idyllic sunlit Devon coast.[6] Locals still remember Captain Léon Coquerel who escaped with the tugs from le Havre in 1940. In a wild storm in 1942 he went to the rescue of local sailors trying to stabilise a yacht at the Dart harbour mouth and saved the life of one by jumping overboard in raging seas. The 23rd Flotilla Association still meets annually in France, and contacts with Kingswear continue, often through members who, like Coquerel, married local girls.

Operation Overlord was the biggest event of the war. Although it involved the area intensively for only about seven months, it disrupted many lives and is what people most remember. The Naval College in Dartmouth became one of the headquarters of the USNAAB (US Naval Advanced Amphibious Base) responsible for training US forces for the Normandy invasions – called the U forces in Devon and Cornwall after their target, 'Utah' beach. By early 1944, more than 4,000 US navy personnel plus army units, British liaison staff and others were billeted in the Dartmouth area. Apart from the training, the main task was to ready the fleet of ships and landing craft. From the estuary almost up to Stoke Gabriel, 110 landing craft were moored in the Dart, and concrete slipways were constructed to load them at Sandridge, Waddeton and Dartmouth.

Modern Brookhill, which was home to the Free French Flotilla during WWII. This photograph was taken on 4 June 2012 during the Dartmouth Jubilee Flotilla. The queen sailed past here in July 1939 when, as princess, she spent time with her future husband, Prince Philip.   *Richard Webb*

Life before the evacuation; ploughing above Lancombe valley, Strete, thought to be 1930s. *Courtesy Nick Teage*

The US army seems to have had an unforgettable style. The advance guard steamed past the blacked-out castle in a blaze of light and with music blaring late one December evening in 1943. At their new headquarters, the Naval College, they dumped their stores of cigarettes on the quarterdeck, the commander's pride and joy, where a soldier was seen to put a cigar in the mouth of the statue of King George V 'and lit it with a match which he struck on the statue of His late Britannic Majesty'.[7] When a convoy of US vehicles driving down a narrow lane met a car driven by a woman who wouldn't reverse, they attached car (complete with driver) to chains and lifted it with a crane over the hedge into the next-door field before moving right along.[8] Children remember the soldiers for their friendliness, their endless supply of sweets and food and readiness to let them 'have a go' at the equipment.

A Landing Craft on the Library Ceiling at Greenway on the Dart, where Lieutenant Marshal L. Lee of the US Coastal Reserve painted a frieze of the journey of his landing craft from the time she was built in Orange, Texas in 1942/43 to the time she was decommissioned in April 1946.

This section above the door shows her just off the boathouse at Greenway where she stayed from January until June 1944, when she joined the convoy headed for Normandy.

Agatha Christie, asked whether the frieze should be painted out when Greenway reverted to her, said no, although she had the sketches of Churchill, Roosevelt and Stalin covered.

Courtesy National Trust

192

It was at Slapton that the U forces of the US First Army trained between late 1943 and D-Day in June 1944, when they set out to join the US forces headed for 'Omaha' beach and those of the British Second Army leaving from further east for the 'Gold', 'Juno' and 'Sword' beaches.[9] Training exercises had to recreate real battle conditions using cruisers and destroyers pitted against heavy coastal defences, with both sides using live artillery. Although firing was meant to be overhead, there were mistakes and, consequently, fatalities. To isolate Slapton beach, the major practice area, the government evacuated the entire population from Blackpool Sands to just south of Torcross along the coast and a stretch of about ten miles inland. People were put out of their homes from December 1943 until the autumn of 1944. Some 3,000 people had to be re-housed, and 30,000 acres of good farming land cleared of stock, crops and equipment. And all in about six weeks; people were told on 12 November that they had to be gone by 20 December. The massive effort mounted by different services to help was proof of the government's determination. And, indeed, the villages were virtually deserted by the deadline, houses locked and keys deposited with the authorities.

People went to friends or relations, found places to rent, or were billeted. One problem was the livestock – most families found homes for chickens and some bullocks or cows, but the rest had to be sold at giveaway prices because so many came onto the market at once. Another problem was money; many farmers or businessmen became farm labourers, some were called up, some left the area. There were transitional hiccoughs: relatives who promised to take families in and refused when they arrived, doors shut on families with children, pets that disappeared on the day of the move... And it rained.

At first, some US troops didn't realize that the area would be resettled. A participant was to describe how they blew up houses and walls, threw grenades through windows and triggered

St Columba's window in the chapel at the Naval College, given in April 1945 on behalf of the members of the United States Navy resident there during the war.

Richard Porter/BRNC

Dainty Afternoon Teas by Emett, published by *Punch* in 1944, was contemporary to the arrival of US troops for the Normandy landings, and could easily have been inspired by experiences in Devon.

Reproduced with permission of Punch Ltd., www.punch.co.uk

"They say, can we do two hundred and eighty-seven Dainty Afternoon Teas?"

The statue of King George V survives with some minor damage from the destruction of the Quarterdeck.
Photograph by John Barlee

booby traps until, after two weeks, they were told to take it easy because the place was going to have to be restored. That, says this serviceman, stimulated renewed bombardments; 'don't knock the doors off the hinges...we're going to knock the houses off the doors.'[10]

They left behind considerable destruction; a large hotel in the middle of Slapton Sands was essentially demolished, several houses in Blackawton were roofless, and Slapton, Stokenham and Blackawton churches were damaged. In general, there was more damage to roads, walls and buildings along the coast, except at Blackawton where an exercise must have taken place. But there were shell holes and unexploded material everywhere – 270 shell holes were counted in one fourteen-acre field – as well as contaminated wells, outbuildings that had simply disappeared, and damaged houses; handing the keys over had been futile. Lucky owners came back to dirty but undamaged homes. Others found shell holes in roofs, lawns and fields, boxes of dynamite and ammunition in the barns and hedges and roads covered with glass. One family who had left their Rover car behind found it submerged in Slapton Ley.

But not all the destruction was military. Some people braved the threat of shells and sneaked home before D-Day to snare rabbits, collect fruit and see how things were going. They found fields and villages deserted and overgrown, church bells silent, and no birds singing. But when they finally returned officially in the autumn, they found much more damage had been done to their properties after the troops had left. Brass window catches, door knobs and knockers – unobtainable at this time – had been stolen, even when hidden, doors had gone and windows smashed. Blackawton church had almost no glass left, the organ had been dismantled and the oil lamps gone. Although the area had been patrolled after the exodus while it was being made safe from explodable devices, 'repair men' had come in and filled lorries with removable goods and vandals had simply smashed what they could not take.

Field Marshal Montgomery, oil, by William Balkham, 1970s. Balkham, a Dartmothian who served in France during the war, was a designer at the Dartmouth Pottery and an artist.

Private collection

Map of Operation Overlord, showing how the troops from this area joined others from along the southern coast of England for the Normandy invasions. The force involved 1,213 warships, 4,126 landing craft, 11,500 aircraft as well as other ships and gliders, and an allied army of 3½ million, of which 1½ million were American.[11]

From Arthur L. Clamp, Orchard Publications

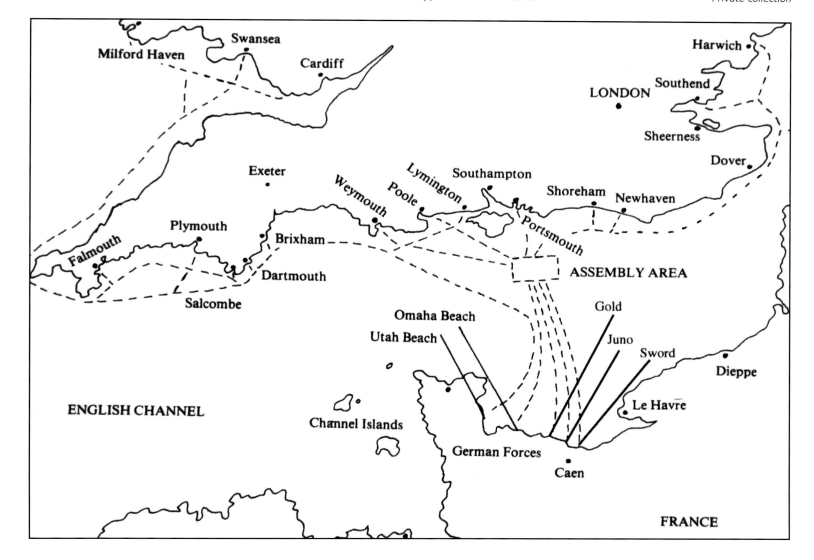

Locals had little information on the details of events. Civilian cars needed a permit to be on the road and, as D-Day approached, had to have a second permit to go anywhere near the coast. The coast watcher who leapt over a hedge into the evacuation area to find himself confronting Field Marshal Montgomery and General Eisenhower must have realised this was serious, but ubiquitous posters saying 'Careless Talk Costs Lives' would have dampened his report to the pub.

On Sunday 4 June 1944 thousands of troops and hundreds of tanks converged on the Dart and Dartmouth, and a day later some 485 vessels set off, taking all day to sail out to sea past the ancient castle. People around the Dart had been told to stay indoors when they left, but waved from balconies, signalling 'Good luck' in semaphore, and played Vera Lynn singing 'We'll Meet Again' on record players audible through open windows. One observer walked, against orders, to the top of a hill above Kingswear that evening and wrote: 'The ocean was just crammed with long low craft as far as one could see. It is as if someone had emptied many boxes of matches into a bowl of water, almost as if one could have walked on them, so close together were they'.[13] They attacked the northern French coast at dawn the next morning, 6 June. 'Utah'

The Lighthouse, charcoal sketch, by Sarah Gillespie, 2005.

Courtesy Sarah Gillespie

The sketch is from Slapton Ley with the beach behind and the lighthouse at Start Bay in the distance, and shows the flat *bocage*-like topography similar to that behind 'Utah' beach in Normandy. The tranquillity of the scene hides a terrible history. (See 'Pictures Writers Paint' for an account.) Men from here were part of 'Exercise Tiger', one of six exercises that simulated a night-time Channel crossing and assault on Normandy beaches between 22 and 29 April 1944. But as local historian Ray Freeman describes, 'In the dark, some German 'E' boats...sank two LSTs and seriously damaged a third. Over 700 Americans were drowned...The rest of the exercise involving landing on Slapton beach went ahead, with more casualties because the supporting naval vessels fired too low and killed their own men. The damage which would be caused to morale, if this became known, led to threats of court-martial to anyone who revealed anything of this tragedy. Controversy has raged ever since as to what happened to the bodies of the almost 1,000 killed...'[12]

The Coast Inhabitants Wondered, watercolour, Dwight C. Shepler, 1944. The departure for the Normandy invasions.

beach was taken with only some 200 losses, far fewer than the number killed during training, but on the neighbouring 'Omaha' beach about 3,000 died. Local people could hear the concussion of the bombardment when the invasion started.

Faced with disruption and discomfort, and for many the destruction of property and land their families had held for generations, the war was traumatic, particularly for the elderly. But memories of great events are often the funny local incident. Odd, comforting things happened to those returning to the evacuated area: an old hen left behind, and still there; cows, scattered by the move, going back into their customary stalls on their return. Even theft had its entertaining side. A family that had locked away two precious sets of antlers later saw them adorning the front of two American tank transporters, painted red and festooned with roses.[14] And nothing was as strange as some realities. One woman remembers cycling home down a Devon lane with a can of petrol for the farm machinery and meeting 'a pack of mules with their Gurkha handlers'.[15]

In the end, people managed. The policeman who drove away an unexploded bomb from the evacuation area in the back of his Morris Seven showed the same pragmatism and courage as others caught up by bigger events. The many memorials in this area record the debt we owe them all.

MYSTIC RIVER

Robert Graves moved to Vale House in Galmpton by the south bank of the Dart beyond Greenway with his new wife Beryl Hodge in 1940. He was forty-five, an established poet, and with several popular books to his name, including *I Claudius* and *Goodbye to All That*. Until the Spanish Civil War in 1936, he had been in voluntary exile in Mallorca, and before he came to the Dart 'to avoid being bombed unnecessarily' he had been wandering Europe and the United States.

Turned down for the infantry in Devon, Graves applied for the special constabulary, but 'our village policeman declined to forward my application. His reasons, as I found out by discreet enquiry, were that my German second name made him suspicious; that I had been heard talking a foreign language to two disreputable foreigners (Spanish refugee friends, as it happened, one a major, the other a staff colonel); and that the words HEIL HITLER! had been found scratched on a vegetable marrow in my garden.' Graves' second name was indeed German – von Ranke, after his mother's father, to whom he owed his 'clumsy largeness,...endurance, energy, seriousness,

200

and …thick hair'.[1] But the tribute on the marrow was never explained. So Graves became an air raid warden. But he got his own back. When he was called to Exeter for his medical and the same policeman bought him a third-class railway warrant, he would only travel first class, to which he was entitled as a pensioned officer from World War I.[2]

One of Graves' eight children was to be killed while he lived in Galmpton – David, in the First Royal Welch, on the Arakan peninsula in March 1943 – and two were to be born, William in 1940 and Lucia in 1943. The Graves made friends with their Greenway neighbours, Agatha Christie and her husband Max Mallowan. Colourful and exuberant, there were bound to be stories about him, as well as those he told himself, and one legend has it that in 1944, during the D-Day preparations, he would swim out to the American ships on the river to pick up tins of food thrown overboard because their labels had gone. Beryl complained that she never knew whether they were going to have tinned stew or tinned prunes for supper.

In Galmpton, Graves worked, as he normally did, on several books simultaneously. He was to produce more than 140 works during his lifetime. Among his Dart books were two on the American civil war, *Sergeant Lamb of the Ninth* and *Proceed Sergeant Lamb*, published in 1940 and 1941, the *Story of Mary Powell, Wife to Mr Milton*, published in 1943 and the *Golden Fleece* in 1944, as well as poetry and other works. But perhaps the most demanding, important and most substantial book he wrote while he was there was *The White Goddess*.

Robert Graves, oil, by John Arthur Malcolm Aldridge, 1968. © *National Portrait Gallery, London*

Here is Graves' own description of how it happened: 'In 1944, at a Devonshire village called Galmpton, I was working against time on a historical novel about the Argonauts and the Golden Fleece, when a sudden overwhelming obsession interrupted me…I stopped marking across my big Admiralty chart of the Black Sea the course which…the *Argo* had taken…Instead I began speculating on a mysterious 'Battle of the Trees' allegedly fought in pre-historic Britain, and my mind worked at such a furious rate all night, as well as all the next day, that my pen found it difficult to keep pace with the flow of thought…. Well,' he goes on, 'within three weeks, I had written a 70,000-word book about the ancient Mediterranean Moon-goddess…'[3] There had never been a lunatic in his family, he points out, so he 'was just being inspired'.

The *White Goddess* is dense. At one level a reference book – Graves subtitles it *A Historical Grammar of Poetic Myth* – it covers an enormous range of history and knowledge, with what Ted Hughes called 'some kind of witty dry distance'.[4] At another level, it is a modern poet's rediscovery of the ancient source of poetry and knowledge, the White Goddess, non-rational, wild, cruel and capricious who was destroyed by a combination of Christianity, classical Greece and rational man.

Small Leaf, Frances Gynn, 2010. Ancient birches tie the Dart to pre-Christian mythology.

Cover illustration for *The White Goddess*, by Karl Gay. In the book the Goddess gives man an eye – the gift of poetry. 'Imagine' says Graves in the book 'the pictures on a vase. First, a naked young man cautiously approaches three shrouded women of whom the central one presents him with an eye and a tooth; the other two point upwards to three cranes flying in a V-formation from right to left.'[5] The cranes bring the understanding of omens and the alphabet.

The book, which first appeared as *The Roebuck in the Thorn* in 1946, is Graves' journey to find this prehistoric source of poetry, the White Goddess. It explores the connections between pre-classical matriarchal cultures and myths and our own, through migrations starting in the second millennium BC linking Celtic Britain with Egypt, Jerusalem, north Africa and Armenia. Ted Hughes, given a copy by his English master before going to Cambridge in 1951, had the book beside him for three years. It was to have a big effect on him.[6]

Graves links the Dart to this ancient mythology. When 'Brut the Trojan' invaded Britain at the end of the second millennium BC, Graves notes that he defeated the giant Gogmagog (Gog, son of Gog) at Totnes. Magog was the grandson of Noah and the son of Japhet, who reappears in Greek myth as Iapetus the Titan, father of Prometheus and Atlas. So the wandering tribes of the ancient Black Sea and their beliefs and stories appear and reappear in Hebrew and Greek myth that wash up on the shore of the Dart at Totnes.[7] And all around the poet were symbols connecting Graves with his ancient muse. In the woods grew the sacred trees of Irish myth: the birch, willow, holly, hazel, oak, apple and alder. Among examples from Crete, Palestine and the Nile, he notes: 'The blackthorn (bellicum in Latin) is an unlucky tree; villagers in Galmpton and Dittisham, south Devon, still fear "the black rod" carried as a walking stick by local witches, which has the effect of causing miscarriages.'[8] Along the river swooped the birds of prey of Celtic and Greek lore – the eagle, hawk and falcon. Stalking the water and echoing in the skies above him he would see the ibises and herons, our Western versions of the sacred Greek crane, source of learning.*

Some forty years after Graves was writing *The White Goddess*, and on the other side of the river where it is still wide and tidal, with large sweeps as it scythes away the softer banks, Bridget McCrum came into her own as a sculptor. Travels to Egypt, Sudan, Syria, Algeria and

* The Dart, once you have negotiated the tight, fast outlet at Dartmouth, has always given a ready entrance into the South Hams, and there are traces around the river of settlements and trading here from the Mesolithic period, and particularly from the second millennium BC when people came for the tin on Dartmoor.

In a Bronze Age barrow excavated at Brownstone near Kingswear, a polished axe-head of green jadeite from Brittany was found – physical evidence of migrations that will have brought the beliefs and cultures Graves studied.

Somalia, as well as the southern Mediterranean, had brought her into contact with the pre-Christian cultures that Graves wrote about and these were to form the bedrock of her work. At the same time, the contours of the hills sweeping down to the Dart and the clefts of the valleys come out in the chiselled lines of her sculpture.

At the age of six, McCrum saw two photographs. One was of some Greek columns with rams' heads' capitals, the colonnade at Baalbeck, and the other of the enormous figure of Rameses dominating the west bank of the Nile at Luxor. Her immediate thought had been 'I want to see those'. From the same very young age, she was drawn to stone and ancient things.

While bringing up a family with a peripatetic naval husband, McCrum's fascination with ancient cultures, combined with a love of travelling, was a line that was always taut. When her husband's ship docked in Beirut it was an opportunity to go to Baalbek; when a friend in Mogadishu was asked to survey Arabic coastal settlements in Somalia, McCrum accepted an invitation to work with her and got to know that part of the East African coast. And everywhere, museums and archaeological sites. But not to see sculptures, to look at the artefacts, the axes and the ladles, the votive figurines from graves, the hoes and the picks and the tools that worked stone,

Bridget McCrum in her garden above the Dart, 2011. © 2013 Steve Russell

203

Tiny ancient Cycladic head that inspired McCrum's much larger version.
Courtesy Bridget McCrum

Cycladic Head, Clipsham stone, by Bridget McCrum, 1993.   *Courtesy Bridget McCrum*

the little ignored objects that are only there because they are old and, because they are thought uninteresting, are usually jumbled together in some unlit dirty heap.

Although McCrum admired the sculpture of classical Greece and Rome, she was drawn much more toward the earlier carving of the Phoenicians and Greeks. When she finally came to sculpture in her forties, her mind was full of these pre-Christian carvings and the odd magnetic shapes of ancient artefacts with their deeply buried mythical associations. 'They give you a feeling. The whole point is to put it over.'

The way she puts it over is unique. Her sculpture is large, and most of the artefacts that inspire them are small. Her talent is to combine their symbolism with her own interpretation, while staying true to the artistic punch of the original. When she magnifies an object, the proportions change and meanings are added, not lost – an axe-head becoming a bird gathering for flight embodies the fall of the heavy head of the axe with the lift of the bird. The other lesson learned from these ancient pieces was about minimalism; an image that has always stayed with her is a Berber artefact in the Musée Nationale d'Algérie, a smoothly washed pebble, the single line incising a horn on it suddenly showing a sheep.

The wing of the small Damascus bird opposite was scribbled, a technique she replicates on the softer stones with an air hammer. The irregular impact of hammer on stone breaks up hard contrasts and moulds flat surfaces. On hard stones, like marble, she textures with the hammer first and then uses different grades of sand paper to manipulate and graduate contrasts. Carving and texturing, McCrum creates deeply massed shapes with flowing contours out of sometimes relatively thin slabs, constantly walking around the sculpture to ensure there are no dead flat places.

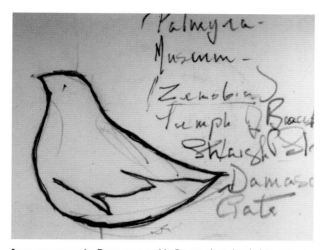

In a museum in Damascus, McCrum sketched this minute bird from Palmyra. She amplified it and combined it with the shape of a Congolese knife seen in a museum in Paris, making the small bird the handle of the blade plunged into a base. She calls the sculpture *Conflict*, the powerful dark knife visually offset by the white bird of peace counterbalancing the angle of its thrust.

Courtesy Bridget McCrum

Stone was the draw, but not exotic stone. McCrum uses stone that can be honed and textured, both mass and surface must be worked. So she takes Portland, Ancaster and Kilkenny stone and carefully chosen Carrara marble. Marble, she says, is very 'in your face', and has to be used wisely, always in an enclosed space. She learnt her lesson when she placed a new marble sculpture in the garden and a friend across the river said "Bridget, what's that big white plastic bag doing in your place?"

Some of McCrum's bronzes are cast from stone sculptures adapted to the different medium, but most are made directly first in plaster. To give texture, she works with the skeletons of prickly pear leaves dipped in plaster. Patina, like texture, is very important, and she works with a blow-gun and acids to achieve the effect she wants.

Conflict, by Bridget McCrum, 2011. *© 2013 Steve Russell/ Messum's*

Figures were an early development. *Cycladic Head* is based on the half-finished figure shown next to it. It was tiny – 7 centimetres high – probably a votive head placed in a grave. Magnification has produced a sculpture in which the minimal outlines, the tilt of the head and the carving away of undulations together give an expression of gentle, watchful pensiveness. Working in Clipsham stone, McCrum could use hand tools and work with the natural grain to produce this magical head, which seems to move as you turn around it. This was to be her last sculpture of a head; in her own words, she had taken the human figure as far as she could.

Mythical Horses, Portland stone, by Bridget McCrum, 2010. *Courtesy Bridget McCrum*

These *Mythical Horses* stand six feet out of the ground. They are separate, one head raised, the other lowered and turned, but seem, from their angles, to come from the same stone. The placement of these heads is key; the empty space between them is as much a mass as the heads themselves. Scribbling makes reflections of waves along their necks as if they they are rising from the sea, and accentuates their cheek-bones and the deeply drilled eyes.* A tiny pair of horses' heads in a museum in Palermo gave McCrum the idea for these ancient shapes.

From her windows high on a slope above the Dart, birds swooping, soaring, hovering, have always been a fascination. Their moving shapes are easily abstracted and carry the potential for drive, ferocity and watchfulness, qualities that spark McCrum's imagination and memories of ancient shapes. *Spirit Bird* was inspired by a Chinese axe-head. 'I liked the idea of combining the fall of the axe with the bird rising' she says. So, one edge of the axe cuts deep into the base while the head soars up and out in the opposite direction, the energy of the lift punching out great curves in the bird's body. The texturing is crucial, and not only to soften the visual impact of the marble; the stone is only 4 inches wide, yet the sculpture has body, weight and muscle.

* In Orphic legend the horse is pure, associated with heroes. Hercules rode the wild horse Arion, Bellerophon rode Pegasus, and the Celtic Llew Llaw had magic power over horses. Graves has it that the horse was sacred in Britain from prehistory, venerated by the Saxons and Danes as much as by the Celts. While Poseidon and his Roman counterpart Neptune rose from the sea in a chariot drawn by mythical creatures that were half-horse and half-serpent, McCrum's are not classical Greek horses. Minimalist, heavy, symbolic, they rise from the waves of earlier waters.

Spirit Bird, Carrara marble, by Bridget McCrum, 2001. With the title of this piece, McCrum has gone to the heart of ancient symbolism. Inhabitants of the air, birds stand for the soul, spirit and transcendence. In Egyptian legend, the bird with a human head shows the power of the soul to leave the body. As with all nature, and indeed, Grave's own *White Goddess*, birds are not necessarily beneficent. Later Christian symbolism can make birds kindly – the dove is peaceful – but in earlier mythology they have power for good *or* malevolence, both qualities McCrum carves into her birds. Even her doves have a rapacious edge.
Courtesy Bridget McCrum

Herons are solar birds in antiquity with the same symbolism as the crane. In Egyptian legend, the heron, Bennu, is the first transformation of the soul after death. Flying away from the Nile when the river floods, it symbolises regeneration, the renewal of life. In pre-Christian mythology it is the messenger of the gods. According to Graves, Hermes invented the alphabet after watching the flight of the cranes in their dramatic twice-yearly migrations from the Arctic Circle to the Tropic of Cancer and back, flying at a great height in wide V-formations. The birds are associated with poetry by the Greeks and wisdom by the Irish. The last breeding crane in England was shot in Anglesey in 1908, but herons still come to the Dart. In his poem, *The Return of the Goddess*, Graves describes her as a 'gaunt red-legged crane' lunging for frogs along the banks of a river. It could have been written looking out over the mud-banks of the Dart at low water.[9] McCrum, as she carved *Bennu*, could have been watching the same scene. *Bennu* stands heavy-footed, head turned, waiting, a wading bird like the herons that nest on the banks of the Dart opposite McCrum's house. She first saw the shape in a small Slovenian ladle. The curves are deeply scribbled, making a lighter grain flow with the contours.

The largest bird sculpture McCrum has created so far is *Merlin*. Commissioned by Rolls Royce and named after their iconic engine, its proportions are based on the *Spitfire,* which has a 'merlin' engine. Standing 4 metres high, and in its first position on a mound of 2.5 metres, it is a giant of stainless steel. The inspiration came from a story the sculptor heard about soldiers on the Somme in the First World War reporting they had seen a cross in the sky. 'I bet that was a gliding bird', she had thought, and watching the birds below and above her on the Dart as they hovered and then wheeled against the wind, she began to plan how she could sculpt one.

It was an enormous undertaking. Starting with a guess at the right size and a small model, structural engineers had to estimate how it needed to be supported to stand up to weather and winds before a full-scale polystyrene model was made, cast into resin and then stainless steel. It was cast into a single piece, weighing nearly three tons. The mould was made, the metal poured, the piece finished and angles checked before it was taken on a flat-bed truck to the Rolls Royce factory at Filton in Bristol to be installed.

This bird, enormous, steely, angled, is a bird of prey, like a kite or a buzzard. Birds of prey are common on the Dart; the medieval name for the place in nearby Kingswear called Kittery today is

Bennu, Kilkenny limestone, by Bridget McCrum, 2011.
© 2013 Steve Russell/Messum's

thought to have been Kite-Tor, or Kite Hill.[10] Such large birds are associated with the sun, thunder and wind in mythology, and a bird on a pillar, as *Merlin* is mounted on its mound, symbolises the spirit held back by the earth. In Celtic legend, birds can be messengers of the gods, and perhaps the soldiers looking up from their war trenches and believing that they saw a cross were seeing a symbol of something much more ancient.

So a legendary, mythical Dart flows through the work of both Graves and McCrum. Both are concentrated on ideas, Graves verbal, McCrum visual. Both are conceptual; taking an idea and creating their version of it. Graves collects detail, cramming it into shape so it fits, or just; McCrum hones detail away to create minimal forms that capture the essence of individuality. Both turn back to pre-classical Greece and ancient mythologies to understand their world and the creative and destructive force of nature.

Opposite: Merlin, steel, by Bridget McCrum, 2007.
© 2013 Steve Russell/Messum's

208

CAPTAIN'S GOLD

It was May, 1762. George III was newly on the throne, the Seven Years' War with France was ending, and England was declaring war on Spain. Off Cape St Vincent, Philemon Parnoll, a young shipwright's son from Plymouth, was commanding his first naval sloop when he and a frigate captained by a Herbert Sawyer met up with the *Hermione*. Sailing home to Spain from Peru 'she was the richest prize of the entire war. Her holds were filled with 653 chests of treasure containing 28 bags of gold coin, trinkets set with semi-precious stones, 1,896 bars of tin as well as a large cargo of cocoa, wool, saddlecloth and gunpowder... her contents were sold for the then staggering sum of £519,705 10s. Let us not forget the shillings! Philemon's share was £64,872 [Pevsner has £64,963, equivalent to appoximately £11.7 million today]. Overnight both he and Sawyer became multi-millionaires. The gold is said to have been carried from Plymouth to the Bank of England in 24 wagons with flags flying and a band playing.'[1]

Philemon, then twenty-seven or twenty-eight, commissioned a painting of himself leaning against a massive anchor by the society artist Joshua Reynolds, who came from outside Plymouth. Reynolds was a painter of the new school who 'drew not only the face, but the life, the soul, the mind, the temper, the habits of the man'.[2] And Philemon commissioned himself a house on the Dart from a fashionable London architect.

Sharpham House, outside Ashprington, Nikolaus Pevsner's 'tautly designed neo-classical mansion by Sir Robert Taylor', has a stunning position on a promontory high above the west bank of the Dart where the river creates a great meander on its final tidal reach towards Totnes. There had been a house here since at least the 15th century, but Taylor created a Palladian villa by adding a neo-classical building, at first only one room deep, overlooking the river.

In 1841, when Parnoll's direct line at Sharpham came to an end with his grandson John Bastard, the notice of the sale[3] describes the completed estate. It is interesting not just for a picture of what Parnoll had started, but because it shows what contemporary buyers of such trophy houses looked for. Among many references to the beauty of the Dart, the 'luxuriant woods' and the extensive views to Totnes and Torquay, it describes an imposing mansion of Portland stone with a Doric porch, and a drive of almost two miles through parkland along the Dart. Outside was stabling, a conservatory, 'hot and succession houses' for exotic plants, a pinery for growing pineapples over compost, a 'French' garden and extensive fruit and kitchen gardens. The park included a rhododendron walk 'through the fields of Elysium' and salmon and trout fisheries renewed every tide. In all, the estate encompassed 1,250 acres, including property in Ashprington, and was worth £3,000 a year. The description notes that the railway brought London within nine hours' travel and that the area would no longer 'be annoyed by the perpetual

Captain Philemon Parnoll, copy of a portrait by Joshua Reynolds, c.1765, some three years after the capture of the *Hermione*. The painting is in the contemporary romantic style. However, the ships in the background and the anchor Parnoll has chosen to lean against are, unlike his dress, not fashionable adjuncts to a society portrait, but show his individual character and preferences. Instead of enjoying his wealth on land, Parnoll continued in the navy, and died at sea in 1780.

Valerie Wills/Sharpham Trust

turmoil of politics' since one local seat had been secured for a good conservative and another for a liberal. The agents were targeting a man of taste but with a nose for business, alongside country interests, but who liked to keep in touch with London, and of a conservative bent.

Inside, the neo-classical design of Sharpham, which cannot have changed a great deal, is all restrained geometry, with an octagonal hall and drawing room above it imaginatively fitted into the exterior canted bay. But when you go through the hall, to resort again to Pevsner, 'the staircase hall comes as a shock of high order. It is an elongated oval, top-lit, around which the stairs rise up to the second floor in a dizzy and alarming cantilever...It is one of the most spectacular and daring later C18 staircase designs anywhere in England'.[4]

Built from prize money, Sharpham became a prize. Parnoll almost certainly never lived there, killed at Ostend in a sea battle with a French privateer in 1780. His wife had pre-deceased him by two years, and their daughter Jane, then sixteen, inherited the estate. Parnoll's will and the 1753 Marriage Act made her marriage before she was twenty-one subject to the approval of the executors.

The staircase at Sharpham, which came as such a shock to Pevsner. After the Second World War, before it was sold, small boys from the village played here, darting in and out of the doors at every level.

Brian Head/Sharpham Trust

Reality outclasses fiction in what happened next.[5] Edmund Bastard, also a naval officer and the younger son of an ancient local family, had visited Sharpham and had been 'so struck by the beauty of the place he was impelled to walk three times round a very large old wych elm in the park devoutly wishing that he might marry the heiress of this desirable property and that all he saw could be his.' It was. Three years after Jane was orphaned, when she was only nineteen, and despite Parnoll's will that attempted to protect her from just such an assault, Edmund bore her off to Gretna Green where the English Marriage Act didn't apply. It was a long flight, and well planned, and Edmund took the time first to hire all the post-horses in the district to forestall pursuit. Once married, and the bride was truly compromised, the couple went on to a second, society wedding at St. George's, Hanover Square. Jarrold notes Jane's shaky signature on her will after the completion of the documents transferring her fortune to her enterprising husband. But the couple were to live long and happy lives at Sharpham with their four surviving children.

Richard Durant, a wealthy silk merchant, bought Sharpham in 1841, reputedly for £110,000. He was to inherit another large estate in Hertfordshire, but lived for almost forty years at Sharpham, an energetic squire who upgraded Ashprington, restoring the church and rebuilding the school. The Durant family were to hold the estate for about a century, but only the first Richard and his spinster daughter Elizabeth Jane lived there for any length of time. Elizabeth inherited at her brother Richard's death only nine years after his father's and stayed another twenty years, dying in 1906. Censuses show conditions at the estate in her day a far cry from her father's pineries and French gardens; in 1891, she had a butler, housemaid and kitchen maid, and ten years

Sharpham House and Estate, showing Parnoll's new house in front of the older and the estate surrounded by the wide meanders of the Dart below the weir at Totnes. Copy of a painting by John Lewis.

Valerie Wills/Sharpham Trust

later just two servants. The descendants who inherited from her came periodically or lived there briefly, until Sharpham passed out of Durant hands in the war days of 1940. The estate was broken up and sold off, the house being withdrawn from sale when the price fell to its reserve of £1,900.

Times were bad for large houses. But Sharpham, requisitioned during the war, and then passing through a number of hands, became a home again in 1962 when Ruth and Maurice Ash bought the house and home farm. There they raised their family, ran the farm, and entertained a wide network of writers and artists, following the tradition of nearby Dartington Hall outside Totnes, where Ruth had grown up as the daughter of Dorothy and Leonard Elmhirst. Sharpham is now a Trust, which has managed the estate since Maurice's death in 2003. The house still stands magnificent on its hill, a neo-classical frontage with its more ancient lineage behind and its rolling parkland encased in the meanders of the Dart, still much as Parnoll must have envisaged it.

Coming downriver from Sharpham to Dartmouth, Captain Ashe, customs officer, had grand ideas too when he came into money, but not with the landed pretensions of Captain Philemon Parnoll, naval commander. Ashe put his Mansion House on a fishing slip: filthy, smelly, crowded with moored vessels, baskets of fish and shouting, working humanity.

Bacchus with a chained leopard, detail from the drawing room ceiling, Mansion House.   © 2013 Brian Head

Zeus and Penelope, detail from the drawing room ceiling, Mansion House.
© 2013 Brian Head

Now hidden in a side street off the South Embankment, Ashe's Mansion House was built in 1736 when he was commander of the customs sloop *Princess Royal*. The house has miraculously survived almost intact, and Pevsner calls it 'Dartmouth's best C18 house'.

The origins of the Mansion House are guesswork. The quality of the building and interior work shows Ashe was wealthy. The 18th century saw high days for smuggling and the 1730s seem to have been a peak.[6] In 1733 Walpole's Excise Bill was designed explicitly to prevent it. Interference with smuggling was unpopular: Walpole's bill was withdrawn after violent opposition and in 1736 there were fatal riots in Edinburgh when a smuggler called Wilson was executed. The south coast was an active smuggling area and Dartmouth customs covered all the coast from Torquay and Brixham down to Salcombe. Officers were on low salaries but shared in seizures of contraband. It seems Ashe was paid £50 a year, but would have supplemented his income with takings from the tea, tobacco and spirits that were the backbone of local smuggling. The focus of smuggling seems to have been varied; there is a record of an Edward Ashe, customs officer of Dartmouth, being due 'a moiety of the seizure of English Coin from the "Prosperity" sloop' in November 1733, for example.[7]

Very little is known about Ashe, who appears to have left Dartmouth by 1743 and is referred to as deceased when his leases are surrendered in 1773. As a customs official, he was part of the prosperous middle class and seems to have been well-connected with local gentry. He chose to build himself a house near his work – the customs offices were just round the corner at Bayard's Cove, and a new customs house was built there in 1739. He must have cared about architecture and design. The Mansion House belongs squarely to the aesthetics of the Renaissance, reflecting contemporary ideals of elegance and a focus on order and classical learning. Within thirty years, Philemon Parnoll of Sharpham was being painted in front of scudding clouds and choppy seas, but there is no hint of the romantic in Ashe's house. The road along the main elevation is still very narrow and the house hard to see, but it was built in brick with three storeys and five bays, and a Venetian-style entrance with a ten-panelled door. The interior is constructed with the main Palladian inter-connecting reception rooms on the first floor where the ten-panelled doors were, unusually, repeated internally.

The house has magnificent interior decoration and exceptional craftsmanship. A fine hall leads through an arch with Corinthian columns towards a splendid Spanish mahogany staircase lit by a skylight three floors above. The stairwell is lined with plasterwork wall panels showing the twelve labours of Hercules surmounted on the top floor with the twelve signs of the zodiac. The main first-floor room has 'an accomplished ceiling in low relief...with some rather light-hearted classical gods surrounded by bacchic figures and chained leopards.'[8] It is a triumph of 18th-century classical restraint with charmingly provincial touches. The use of plasterwork, a Dartmouth tradition, in the latest low-relief style with simple classical subjects and restrained detail is a style used on a much grander scale in the new mansion with its Adam interiors that the Parkers were to build at Saltram outside Plymouth some ten years later.

Ashe may have built the Mansion House as a mayoralty house, anticipating high office. We know he had pretensions because he called himself captain without ever holding the rank of a naval captain. Although he was never mayor, the house was used for mayoral functions in the 18th and 19th centuries. The town accounts show that the great merchants of Dartmouth met to drink and

The Paul de Lamérie punch bowl, engraved in c.1720, is known locally as the Holdsworth bowl and was given to Arthur Holdsworth, the fishing admiral, sometime before 1727. The quality of the bowl reflects the wealth of the Dartmouth merchants; de Lamérie is thought to have been the greatest silversmith working in England in the 18th century. He was goldsmith to George I, and had important commissions from Peter the Great of Russia and John V of Portugal, as well as the British aristocracy.

Ashmolean Museum, University of Oxford

converse as 'The Corporation of Bramble Tor' (the membership was largely the same as that of the Dartmouth Corporation), consuming quantities of lobsters, mutton and cheese. They met not in the Guildhall, known for its stench, but at a 'mayoralty house', and the Mansion House was one of these. George Treby, MP for Dartmouth from 1722-47, presented Arthur Holdsworth (the fishing admiral, see 'Their Day in the Sun') with a magnificent silver punch bowl. On one side, it is engraved with what is thought to be a mayoral procession along a quay very like that at Dartmouth – Arthur was three times mayor of Dartmouth – with a boat offshore. On the other side of the bowl, under the appropriate inscription 'Prosperity to hooks and lines', these men face outwards, tricornes off, seated at a finely swagged table, drinking toasts, with dogs at the ready for scraps below. The panelled walls behind them might well be those of the grand drawing room of the Mansion House.

The Mansion House, still an elaborate 18th-century town house. © *2013 Brian Head*

Although later building work hides its side and back elevations, the survival of this house and its interior decoration is due to the care of many people down the centuries. This is despite its being put to many uses. In the 19th century it was for a time a hospital for the naval cadet training ships, and a Masonic Meeting House. In the 20th century it was a furniture shop, and in 1942 was taken over as an annexe to the cottage hospital, dealing with casualties from the bomb that fell on the Butterwalk in February 1943. A photograph taken in 1946, when war damage and some demolition opposite allowed you to see its full front elevation, shows this too to have been war-damaged and dilapidated. Since then, repaired and refurbished, the Mansion House has been used commercially, and after the turn of the century it has returned to private hands.

Sir Walter Raleigh's Greenway [sic], watercolour, by William Payne, c. 1790, just after Roope's rebuilding. The house still rises as it does here above woodland descending to the river, but the lower semi-derelict buildings to the left of the taller building are gone.

West Country Studies Library

Previous spread: Coleton Fishacre, three miles from Kingswear, designed by Oswald Milne for Rupert D'Oyly Carte, son of Richard, impresario of the Gilbert and Sullivan operas that were the craze of the late Victorian and Edwardian years. The planting here would have pleased Rupert; in Hyde Park one day he saw red, orange and yellow zinnias and told his designer to match them in the seating at the Savoy Theatre. *© 2013 Nigel Evans with kind permission of the National Trust*

Opposite: Kwan Yin, by Nicholas Dimbleby, looks down on a pond in the garden. Agatha's son-in-law, Anthony Hicks, was a Buddhist, and Nicholas took the idea from a figurine of Kwan Yin collected by Agatha, adding a carp in a basket, an element of the myth associated with Kwan Yin. A subsequent cast of the statue was bought by the owner of Kadoorie National Park in mainland China, where it was installed on the top of Kuan Yin Sham (Kwan Yin's mountain). 'She is now a shrine visited by thousands of Chinese' says Nicholas.[1] *© Nicholas Dimbleby/National Trust Images/Andrew Butler*

THE MANSIONS OF THE ENTERTAINERS

Greenway, for most people, first and foremost belonged to Agatha Christie. High on a promontory, it stands in its woods above the east bank of the river near Dittisham, upstream from Dartmouth, a Georgian house overlaying a Tudor mansion. There are 400 years of history in its stones and trees, but it is famous today for the forty-odd years it was the holiday home of the world's most successful crime writer.

Agatha bought the house with her second husband, the archaeologist Max Mallowan, just before the Second World War and her daughter and son-in-law, Rosalind and Anthony Hicks, stayed on after her death. From 1946 she came with family and friends to this 'ideal house, a dream house', as she calls it in her autobiography, for summers and at Christmas, playing croquet and clock golf on the flat ground above the woods, walking the grounds and taking tea at the boathouse on the river.[2] A hidden retreat for a very private person.

The garden at Greenway tapped into the sources of enchantment the writer had found at Ashfield, her beloved childhood home in Torquay. The park and its ancient trees and copses had the mystery, terror and secret delight of the woods she had explored then. Coming back to the house with Max after the war, she remembers 'How beautiful Greenway looked in its tangled splendour'.[3] Agatha, an astonishingly inventive story-teller, began making up stories for herself in the garden at Ashfield, making 'my own world and my own playmates'.[4] As an adult, at Greenway, she could do the same. The privacy and wildness of its gardens replenished the imagination of this most imaginative of writers.

The position of the house, with its slanting views of the river and hills beyond, and the wandering drives and walks, which now open up the vistas and then close them down, matched her need for the thrill of discovery. ' "Views" can be dull, too' she says. 'You climb up a path to a hill top – and there! A panorama is spread before you. *But it is all there.*

* The *Rosario*, flagship of the Andalusian squadron, was towed by Raleigh's 300-ton privateer, the *Roebuck*, into Torbay as the main fleet of the Armada continued east down the Channel. A plaque on the floor of the 'Spanish barn' at Torre Abbey in Torquay records that 397 prisoners from the *Rosario* were held there in July 1588. (Russell, 1950, p.74.)

There is nothing further.'[5] Walking through the house looking out of the windows, strolling down the garden at Greenway, there is always something further.

But it's the house that brings you closest to this very secret person. The grandeur is made almost homely by the clutter of the collections that fill its wall cabinets, cover its furniture, spill out onto the floor, into the corners and even onto the statuary. You see Agatha pursuing the thrill of discovery as she hunted auctions, antique shops and classified advertisements for objects that said more than they appeared to – boxes hiding secret compartments, little useful objects that told of the lives of Napoleonic prisoners-of-war. Collecting was a family passion. Agatha inherited furniture and china from her parents; to be different, she says, 'I have accumulated quite a nice stock of papier-mâché furniture and small objects which had not figured in my parents' collections.'[6] So her boxes are in the hall, papier-mâché pieces in the bedroom, mauchlinware and silver round and about. Max's bargeware is in the library, the Hickses' pottery, botanical porcelain, watches, snuff boxes and portrait miniatures and, particularly, Anthony's hats are everywhere. Furniture and paintings from Ashfield dominate; Agatha's happy childhood lived on through her own life and that of her daughter.

Greenway's successive owners mark changing economic and social times. The Gilberts, well-established seafarers and landowners from nearby Compton Castle, built a Tudor mansion here in the 16th century and owned it until 1700. Mariners and explorers sailed from here then, notably Sir Humphrey Gilbert, born at Greenway, who claimed Newfoundland, his half-brother Sir Walter Raleigh, and the doughty John Davis, who came from a farm on nearby Sandridge, and explored the north-west passage, discovered the Falklands and piloted the early East India Company voyages to Indonesia.[7] The 18th century brought in the self-made Roopes, one of the early merchant dynasties of Dartmouth. They were followed by four families with wealth from new industrial sources, none of whom held it for as long as the Gilberts and the Roopes – a merchant adventurer from Bristol, and from Cornwall a tin miner, a copper magnate and, finally, a banker-cum-smelter. Agatha, a woman who earned her money from her writing talents, brought in the 20th century, buying the house in 1938. During the Second World War, Greenway was requisitioned, and houses a frieze painted by Lieutenant Marshall Lee of his war, including a section showing Greenway and his landing craft by the boathouse. (See the chapter 'At War'.) The National Trust arrived in 2000.

The Gilberts had their heyday when Dartmouth had national importance. Educated at Eton and Oxford, they became sheriffs of Devon, knights,

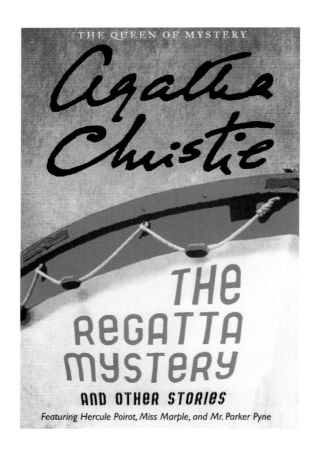

The cover of *The Regatta Mystery and Other Stories* by Agatha Christie, which includes a short story featuring Hercule Poirot set at the 'Royal George' hotel in Dartmouth (so no doubt based on the Royal Castle Hotel). The story was first published in the *Chicago Tribune* in the USA on 3 May 1936 and then in the *Strand Magazine* in June 1936. It first appeared in book form in the USA in June 1939 (Dodd, Mead & Co) and only later appeared in collections of short stories published in the UK in the 1960s. This paperback edition was published in 2012 by William Morrow, an imprint of HarperCollins Publishers.

courtiers and explorers with national as well as local achievements. Little remains of what they did at Greenway, then called Greenway Court, but the cobbles of a Tudor courtyard lie beneath the flagstones of a back hall and the buildings to the left of the taller house in Payne's painting may have been part of their mansion. But we do know that they laid out the garden: Sir John Gilbert, Humphrey's elder brother and Vice-Admiral of Devon during the Spanish Armada, used the crew of the captured *Nuestra Señora del Rosario* to build terraces there.* Around 1700, the family returned to Compton Castle, and Greenway Court was sold.

Greenway Looking out towards the Dart. Below, the gardens fall steeply to the river in what Agatha Christie described as 'tangled splendour'.

The Roopes owned Greenway for most of the 18th century. Their wealth was from trade. A Nicholas Roope sent to the Amazon in 1617 'a cargo of knives, hatchets and spades, and 54,000 glass beads for the ladies, to receive in return 175 ends of "red and peckled wood" '.[8] The inscription on a Roope memorial in St Clement's church, Dartmouth, records their well-travelled lives:

> William Roope of Little Dartmouth
> died in Bilbao 30 January 1666
> in the sixth year of his abode there,
> being embalmed and put into a leaden coffin
> was after ten weekes tossing on the seas
> here below interred.
> Ao Dom 1667 aetatis suis 35.[9]

It was a Roope who built the central Georgian section of the house we see today. Roope Harris Roope was a shipowner and merchant adventurer of Dartmouth involved in the cod/port business.

Plaster Overmantel at Greenway showing Daniel's three friends being thrown into the fiery furnace for refusing idolatry. A similar overmantel in the Butterwalk, Dartmouth, dated 1635-40, shows the Pentecost, with Moses and King David.   © *National Trust Images/Nick Guttridge*

He is thought to have built in front of the Gilbert mansion, leaving, if Payne's painting is accurate, Tudor wings. But he may have left more; the elaborate 16th-century plaster overmantel in what is now the winter dining room is said to have come from the Gilbert house, and has a similar style and Puritan message to a plaster overmantel and ceilings in the Butterwalk in Duke Street in Dartmouth. Overstretched by the building, and his trade virtually destroyed by the Napoleonic wars, Roope was bankrupt by 1800, and sold. He moved back to Kingswear, apparently taking the overmantel with him, because the Mallowans brought it back in 1964.

Ownership passed out of local hands during Dartmouth's long decline. The merchant adventurer's family, the Eltons, lasted three generations, leaving the Regency wings on either side with the dining room and drawing room. The next families came from estates in Cornwall and brought with them an excitement about landscape and plants, transforming the gardens and modernising the estate, which then included the nearby village of Galmpton. But their stays were relatively brief before they inherited other estates or, like the Harveys, died childless.

If Greenway is still a Roope house, its gardens belong mostly to the 19th century and the Cornish tradition. The Eltons brought in the picturesque, flowing landscapes of Humphry Repton then influencing the gardens at Antony, Caerhays and Lanhydrock. Parkland came up to the house and fell away between swathes of beeches opening for glimpses of the river. Elton's great vista along his new driveway, his beeches, and his camellia garden are still there, but successive Cornishmen and women overlaid the lines of the Elton structure with new planting. You still see plants from the same distributors and seed-hunters used in the Cornish gardens, the east rockery planted by Veitch, and rhododendrons and magnolias from seed brought back from China by George Forrest, who was also supplying Caerhays and Trewithin.

The gardens still carry the imprint of their history. Agatha Christie, walking down to the boathouse where she liked to take tea, would have passed the 19th-century vinery, fig standards, and the peach house, which grew peaches and nectarines until 2000. She may have passed under a sweet chestnut planted 300 years before and through woodlands that Roope would have recognised. The camellia gardens that were the pride of the Cornish owners may still have contained camellias planted by the Roopes, who brought seeds back from Oporto. And the terraces bordering the river walks could have been built by the prisoners from the Armada.

The boathouse links its owners across the centuries. Raleigh is said to have smoked his pipe there and, according to local legend, been deluged under a bucket of water (or perhaps ale, versions differ). And it is there that Agatha has Marlene Tucker strangled in *Dead Man's Folly*. Was that what she was thinking about as she drank her cream there on summer afternoons, idly watching the boats passing on the tide?

Follow the east bank of the Dart from Greenway and out of the estuary, hugging the rocky coastline as far as you can, and you come to Coleton Fishacre.

This house, restrained, small and beautifully proportioned, is unusual, but it takes a while to identify why. Generally, mansions grow from their soil. The rich who own them are local, wealthy from local activities, and often they build near these. They might move a bit from town to country – Roope Harris Roope went upriver from Dartmouth to Greenway – but not far. Their roots hold them, as roots hold the houses they build, which often grow out of earlier buildings to give us a heritage of domestic architecture with longer and longer histories in the same places. But Coleton Fishacre is an exotic.

Rupert and Lady Dorothy D'Oyly Carte were Londoners, wealthy not from trade or privateering but from the entertainment industry. Although they called the house after the medieval name for the area, they had no family bond with this headland and its deep inlets between Brixham and the Dart estuary. They first planned Coleton Fishacre in the early 1920s when they were sailing along the coast and discovered its cove and then its hidden, steep valley. Landing and clambering up the hill, they decided to build where the valley opened onto the plateau above. The result is an isolated house, designed by Oswald Milne, in a glorious position that is purely of its time and has changed little since. It did not grow out of the land or communities around it. There is no visual history in the building – no odd back dining-room to remind you of a Tudor foundation as at Greenway, nor even a converted stable, because the house was built in the time of the motor car. It stands where no building was before, set up against a ridge, looking down the valley with a garden tumbling down beside a stream that falls towards the sea.

The library at Coleton Fishacre.

Rupert was the son of Richard D'Oyly Carte, the opera manager who, with W.S. Gilbert and Arthur Sullivan, made the music-hall respectable by staging comical operettas with absurd plots, witty dialogue ("What never? Well, hardly ever") and good tunes. They were enormously successful; HMS *Pinafore* had a 700-night run when it was first produced in 1878. High society in the 19th century had disliked culture, but the 20th brought it 'home to roost among the duchesses'.[10] The comic operas, modelled on the *opéra-bouffe* that Jacques Offenbach was turning out in Paris, were modern enough to delight the Edwardians as well as the post-war flappers with their ingenuity, Wildeian irony, and good-humoured mockery of almost anything and everyone. The D'Oyly Carte copyright only ran out in 1961, and the operas are still performed all over the world.

Rupert took over the business after his father died in 1901, marrying Lady Dorothy in 1907. Coleton Fishacre was built in eighteen months, starting in January 1925. Virtually all the contractors and suppliers were from outside Devon, and most from London.

Photographs like that opposite tell us that Lady Dorothy dressed up as Ruth in *The Pirates of Penzance*, although there is no record of her ever performing the role. In an odd twist of circumstance, the world première of *Pirates* had been performed near Coleton Fishacre, in the Bijou, a lavish little theatre in the Gerston Hotel in Paignton, on 30 December 1879. Both hotel and theatre, built for the fashionable crowds arriving by railway from mid-century, have sadly since been demolished.

It was a rushed and unscheduled matinée. Gilbert and Sullivan were then in New York, where Sullivan had completed most of the music for *Pirates* on 28 December, just three days before the opera was to open there. To secure the English copyright, the 'second *Pinafore* company' then appearing in Torquay, hurried to Paignton after one rehearsal on the morning of the performance. There was no overture (Sullivan had not finished it), and the scenery and costumes were makeshift. Nobody seemed to mind. One review commented that 'the libretto is exceedingly funny, and the airs are catching, and...we congratulate the talented author and composer on another brilliant success.' 'Thanks to the energetic manager...and the clever conductor...the performance went off without a hitch' said another, and a third pointed out that the opera was 'produced...in presence of a most aristocratic audience'.[11] Among the onlookers was the Prime Minister, Benjamin Disraeli

Left: Lady Dorothy as Ruth, the pirate maid, in *The Pirates of Penzance*. One of the most popular Gilbert and Sullivan comic operas, the world première was performed in Paignton to secure the English copyright, a reason and result that would not be out of place in a Gilbertian plot.   *Courtesy National Trust/Peter Parker collection*

Right: Rupert D'Oyly Carte, cartoon by Autori.   *Courtesy National Trust Images/Peter Parker collection*

1930s D'Oyly Carte programme showing characters from Gilbert & Sullivan's *Patience* and *Iolanthe*. Reproductions from original designs by George Sheringham (d.1937) at Coleton Fishacre.

© *National Trust Images/ John Hammond*

(visiting his mistress), who reported the next day to the House of Commons that after seeing *Pirates*, he had gone on to Paignton Pier, where he had won a penny and a coconut.

Architectural styles proliferated in the 1920s. Osbert Lancaster, in a book published in 1939, describes with some hilarity at least six, from the rustic Aldwych farcical (galleries and sporting prints) to Modernistic (hideous woods, chromium plate and gramophones hidden in cocktail cabinets).[12] Not far from Coleton Fishacre, Edwin Lutyens was then 'finishing' (after fifteen years) Castle Drogo in yet another style – medieval – for Julius Drewe. And within six years at nearby Dartington Hall, one of England's few Modern Movement houses now open to the public was to be built, High Cross House, all concrete, Bauhaus curves and steel.

At Coleton Fishacre, Oswald Milne seems to have avoided the excesses in all these styles. A contemporary reviewer describing this house noted 'the happy and tactful way in which it has been spliced into its lovely setting'. Letting this dominate, the house backs into the west side of the valley, hinged at the north end so the sea could be seen from the big rooms inside (sadly, trees now block these views). Devon shale, grey, blue and red, was quarried from below the gazebo for the walls, and the roof-tiles are Delabole slate, so the tones of the building and the sweep of the gabled roofs with their small chimneys fit the colour and planes of their surroundings. The house 'lies low and says nuffin', as Hussey put it in his article in 1930.[13] The simplicity and integrity of the materials echo the Arts and Crafts movement, but with none of the self-conscious rusticity. Milne had been an assistant to Lutyens in 1902-05, and displays at Coleton Fishacre his master's attention to materials and craftsmanship, unity and flair.

The interior is designed for entertaining. Corridors flank the valley side on the east, leaving space on the ground floor for two large rooms, the magnificent 'saloon' and the dining room, and two smaller ones to the west. While the house has an Arts and Crafts feel outside, inside it is restrained Art Deco. Spaces have clean 'modern' lines, whitewashed walls merging with coved ceilings, sharp black skirtings and beautifully balanced proportions. Little remains of the original movable furnishings, but photographs show sparse yet striking furniture. What remains of this and the fixtures are top quality. There are Lalique lights, Art Deco stepped mirrors and door surrounds, grand semi-circular steps down to the saloon, which has a fine Italian marble fire surround, a magnificent overmantel in the library and a blue scagliola table in the dining room that echoes the colour of the sea. These are a world away from 'William Morris...hand-woven linens, vegetable dyed, and plain unstained oak furniture by 'good workmen wel ywrought''.[14]

Like Lutyens, Milne designed the house and garden as an entity. His hard structure of the gardens – terraces, rills, ponds and paths – are still there. The well-known firm of Milner-White were responsible for the plantings; Edward Milner had worked with Joseph Paxton at Chatsworth, and the firm he founded continued after his death in 1894, to survive as the oldest garden design practice in Britain until 1995. The planting has evolved a bit since Lady Dorothy's day. Her roses in the rill garden, difficult to keep healthy in Devon, have been replaced by salvias and other herbacious perennials, but the stream still chuckles along the rills, through the bog garden, down over two ponds to the sea. Coleton Fishacre, with its unique combination of tender trees and plants in a range of situations, is a Royal Horticultural Society Garden. The gardeners, planning to open the old vistas from the house to the sea have a constraint: the D'Oyly Cartes' beloved Dalmation 'Patch' is buried beneath the now-gigantic tulip tree just outside the house.

Man Fishing, tile in back bathroom of Coleton Fishacre, designed by Edward Bawden, manufactured by Carter's of Poole, 1920s.
© National Trust Images/ John Hammond/ The estate of Edward Bawden

The 1920s were caught in a bubble between the horrors of the First World War and the depression of the 1930s. Beauty, according to Aldous Huxley, had shifted from the 19th-century countess to the soubrette and 'the face has broadened and shortened, the profile is less noble'.[15] Gone was the du Maurier damsel, making way for 'the Fish girl and other kindred flat-faced species'. Fish girls do fish girl things – it was the jazz age, a time of bright young people who danced the Charleston in amazingly short skirts, of suffragettes chained to railings in longer ones. A bathroom at Coleton Fishacre displays the wit of the times. Here, tiles show six different Edward Bawden designs for Carter's of Poole with chic young people invading traditional country pursuits, hunting and fishing with abandon, scarves flying in the back seat of a motor car, playing golf or punting or, as flat-faced beauties, just smiling.

Lady Dorothy would stay at Coleton Fishacre full-time – she was a passionate gardener – Rupert joining her at weekends. They entertained, played tennis, sailed and gardened here, bringing down the young and the clever, artists and writers, including Sir Malcolm Sargent and the artist Charles Ricketts. But after their son, Michael, died in a road accident in Switzerland in 1932, the marriage collapsed, and they separated four years later. Rupert and their daughter Bridget continued to come to Coleton Fishacre and fill it with people until the end of the war. The daughter of the tenant farmers at Coleton Fishacre Farm remembers Rupert as 'a gentleman's gentleman' who rode around on his horse, and so disliked rabbit traps and rabbits that he put rabbit-proof fencing along the entire cliff-top perimeter of his property.[16] Bridget inherited the house when Rupert died in 1948, but she sold in 1949 to devote her energies to running the D'Oyly Carte opera company and the Savoy Hotel (she was still a director at her death in 1985). The National Trust came in 1982. It is a time capsule from between the wars, a memory of heady days before things got serious, an exotic plant on a stunningly beautiful Devon combe.

RIVERSONG

Alice Oswald

Who's this moving alive over the moor?
An old man seeking and finding a difficulty.

So begins Alice Oswald's story of the Dart, up on Dartmoor.[1] A single poem, it's the song of the river as it eases itself out of moorland swamps and ledges, moving down past the junction at Dartmeet of the east and west Darts, on beyond Totnes where the water spools over the weir, and still onwards, tidal now, and broader, to the estuary at Dartmouth and the sea. Alice has received many awards for her poetry since her first collection in 1996, and *Dart* won the T.S. Eliot prize in 2002.

The song is sung by the people along the river, real and imagined; a walker on the moor, a naturalist and an eel watcher on the upper reaches, a canoeist who drowns, town boys, and John Edmunds washed away in 1840 at Staverton. Then, where the river goes slow and meandering, a dreamer, dairy workers and stone wallers, boatbuilders and salmon fishers, until it reaches the ferryman, the sea cadets, crabbers and sealwatchers of the town here at its mouth, and the Mewstone just out to sea 'where the shag stands criticising the weather'.

You are forced to imagine as you read. The rhythms move you along, quick short lines interspersed with prose and then something in between, with sudden leaps, hesitations and breaks. You can hear the early uncertain streams in the differing lengths of the lines, sentences stopping in the middle as an incipient rush of water encounters an obstacle. You halt at the silence of the one-page gap where John Edmunds drowns. You struggle with the boatbuilder as he tries to make a go of it – short lines, broken lines, long hopeful paragraphs of prose – and then swing along with him when he talks about his boats. The lark's cry is 'splitting and mending'; 'spickety leaves' cling to 'knee-nappered trees'; you feel the 'rush of gold to the head' as the swimmer jumps into cold water.

Each has its own voice. The walker: 'What I love is one foot in front of another'. The fisherman has paid to fish and 'I fish like hell'. The worker at Buckfast Woollen Mills describes 'A fully

On the Dart, watercolour by Peter de Wint, c.1848. The river above Totnes as it tumbles down from Dartmoor, seen in the distance.

© *The Fitzwilliam Museum, Cambridge*

vertical operation'. The dreamer below the weir at Totnes sees 'the river's dream-self walk' where the salt water meets the sweet. 'It's a rush, a sploosh of sewage' says the sewage worker; 'every roll of fibre glass two hundred quid' says the boatbuilder; and while the salmon netsman and poacher remembers 'the days when I was handsome', the naval cadet announces 'I've got serious equipment in my head'.

The river sings of the dead as well as the living, the mythical as well as the real. Above Totnes, dead tin miners speak of friends who have gone and of the east and west Darts 'smashing' into each other at Dartmeet, a water nymph sings, and the King of the Oakwoods, who had to be sacrificed to a goddess, laments the passing of a drowned canoeist. Below Totnes, where the river is navigable, the boats chatter of yachts and powerboats, rowers and dinghies and the lad off to New Zealand to find his girlfriend, while at the river's mouth a rememberer sings of

river pilots, sisters rowing plums over from Dittisham and within the same phrase crusader ships and Humphrey Gilbert going down.

'I work the car ferry', 'I go like hell and there's the sea', 'Ten years of that you pay for it with your body', the poem is a sequence of phrases from chance encounters and remembered conversations. Alice says it's 'a scavenging poem', finding its way like the river, picking up people, images, stories and memories as it travels by. At first, she took a tape recorder as she met people, but to be less intrusive, she held it behind her, and most of the tapes became inarticulate noise. Then she tried a notebook, but her notes were partial and often indecipherable. Finally, she relied on memory. So the voices are filtered through imagination, pegged to phrases that came through the tapes, the notes or her memory.

The voices tag along, one after the other, talking for their stretch of the river, telling a story that is not Alice's, but that of the river. *Dart* was a new type of poem for her, and she says she found it exciting not to be in charge, to have other voices, real, misheard and imagined, driving it. These 'mutterings of the river' as she calls them, became an epic, a song of other people's doings. The poem begins with a wake-up question, bustles along and then pauses to think and reminisce a bit, rolls helter-skelter

Above. Random Order, acrylic castings of found objects, oil, tar on canvas, by Francis Gynn, 2010. Gynn scavenges like Oswald, each object she paints has its own story. The large stone could be the 'slate as flat as a round pool' picked up by Oswald's dreamer. *Courtesy Frances Gynn*

Cottonwood, oil and charcoal on canvas, by Francis Gynn, 2006. Dusk, when all things are preparing to sleep, and birds dart in and out of the frame. 'The only light's the lichen tinselling the trees' say the oyster gatherers. *Courtesy Frances Gynn*

Bird in the Wood, cast olive-stone (from original wood carving) on stainless steel, by Jilly Sutton, 2008.

through steep shallow rapids, and dreams along slow-moving reaches. Instead of a tale of heroes and kings, battles and dragons, the succession of modern river people and people from the past churned up by the water are all the action.

We people of the Dart know them all. We know about the drownings and the crusader ships and the stories of Trojans and water nymphs that make the river's past. We know the walkers with maps in their mac pockets, the naturalists with their noses in the earth, the chambermaid who does room cleaning with her rubber gloves (please do not leave toenails under the rugs), and the fifteen-year-old crabbers who smash up the town a bit when they come in after a week out at sea. Some of them, like the boatbuilder and the stonewaller are still at it, some like the dairy workers stopped when the company went out of business. Alice sometimes bumps into people from the poem in the shops. Alice's Dart; our river.

people, tee-shirts and road theft, growing up and dying, things that make him happy and those that make him angry.

Here he remembers Joyce Gundry's fruit cake:

Twas black as a Saint's cape
Yet tender as the light
As it rose like the sunlight
which filled the bay...[3]

And talking about a row on the river:

Rowing my boat down the quayside
The water's like mercury
It's thick and silver
And the town so silent
I can hear the water talk to me...[4]

Here he's sailing into the wind, urging his boat on to get a bit closer and make a bit more way in choppy water:

Hold in the wind Elizabeth Mary
And steal another knot
From the wind's purse
As you dance the gaffer's dance
On this a new clear spring morning...[5]

And here he's out in a light wind:

Only one day of brightness
Between bookends of grey and wet
The river was as empty as Christmas day
Our red sails like the red cows
Were set, then made no hurry in the light wind.[6]

Kevin Pyne

Lost at Sea, acrylic, by Andras Kaldor, 1983. One bad-weather day a local fisherman, Paul Goddard, took his boat, laden down with pots, out to sea and never returned. 'A little ship never found' writes Kevin Pyne in his poem 'Paul Goddard'.[2]

Courtesy Andras Kaldor

Kevin Pyne is a poet from the West Country. He has always lived on and around the Dart at Dartmouth. He has worked on ferries and boats for forty years – he is Alice Oswald's ferryman in *Dart* – and he has rowed it, sailed it, fished it and generally messed about on it all his life. The river and its people inform his poetry and have done so since he began writing it at the age of fourteen.

'My subjects seem to pop up for me to take a shot at,' he says in his introduction to *First Across the Line*, where he writes of places and

Kevin's wife Lyzie died young, and when he nearly died himself in 2002, he wrote:

I almost came to meet you
I saw you in my dreams
Standing where the warm green waters
Touch the bowing oaks at autumn time
At first I didn't see you there
Your so so long red hair
Still hides you in the autumn foliage...[7]

In the introduction to *First Across the Line*, Kevin writes 'At first I thought, foolishly, I could try to write a book of poems that made no reference to my late wife Lyzie. It's now six years or so since her death and I thought that I could move on. In truth I can't.'

Kevin peoples his poetry with local characters:

> Joe Mugford
> Was madder than a rabid dog
> As thick around as a floating log[8]

And writes to a friend:

> A round turn and two half hitches
> Ties my life to you
> Yes, there have been many glitches
> But the rope stayed strong and true...[9]

Kevin finds himself a curiosity, a poet who couldn't write, and different from the others:

> I'm the kid from the back of the class
> Grubby shirt and muddy ass.[10]

And too sensitive:

> We work the river all the time
> My old dog and me
> We don't much mix with others
> They only hurt you see...[11]

Kevin's verse, original and powerful, tells us what he thinks about. 'I do wonder' he says, in *First Across the Line*, 'what actually makes a poet...What I have to say is simple, sometimes at either extremes of my thoughts.' At the heart of this verse is the river:

> Bright water light mark
> Spring a tide through my mind
> I'm away up the river
> To see what I can find...[12]

Brian Patten

Brian Patten writes poetry in his garden under lichened ancient trees overlooking the Dart as the tides swing it past. His deeply felt verse talks in everyday language about death, love and loss, and the magic and dreams of a remembered childhood. The poems are placeless, but breathe our rivers and countryside.

The Castle Ferry, acrylic, by Andras Kaldor, 1986.   *Courtesy Andras Kaldor*

Brian Patten, quill and ink, by Paul Riley.   *Courtesy Paul Riley*

A poet from fifteen, Patten first came to the area as a guest of Maurice and Ruth Ash at Sharpham on the west bank of the Dart below Totnes in the 1970s. Still in his early twenties, he had helped make poetry new and popular. By then, he had published *The Mersey Sound* with fellow-Liverpudlians Roger McGough and Adrian Henri, and *Little Johnny's Confession* and *Notes to the Hurrying Man*, solo anthologies recognised early on as modern masterpieces. After four or five years at Sharpham he left, but returned often to visit, settling permanently nearby in 1999. Another link was his friendship with Robert Graves and his wife Beryl. Patten's poem about them was read at Beryl's memorial service in 2004, and he remembers later taking their daughter Lucia across the Dart to Galmpton on a nostalgic visit to the house where she was born.

Patten is a craftsman, his simplicity disarming. Images have a thump. Ambulances are 'alert with pain', orange blossom 'fierce on dead branches', boats coming into the quay have sails 'stained as if time's pissed up against them', and a tiny bird sings 'a lament as small as a seed'. A few words tell you about the worlds his people carry with them – children going to Batman films are 'sucked from tiny terraces on Saturday mornings', package holidaymakers 'blamed each other for the clouds'. And intricate ideas are precise and vital – something beneath the corrugated iron in the corner of the orchard 'shuffles about, just beyond the corner of my eye', between mismatched couples 'something grotesque migrates hourly between our different needs', and 'if you found the perfect love it would scald your hands'.

Rivers, the sea and the people that use them have been a constant in Patten's life. The holiday ing Dart below his orchard jogs a memory of the working Mersey and its merchant seamen. He writes of 'a boat down on the quay come home at last':

> I knew its crew once,
> Those boys manacled to freedom
> Who set sail over half a century ago,
> And were like giants to me.
> A solitary child in awe of oceans
> I saw them peel their shadows from
>   the land
> And watched as they departed.[13]

238

Solstice, oil, by Sarah Gillespie, 2009-10, a painting of Slapton along the coast from the Dart estuary. *Courtesy Sarah Gillespie*

Opposite: View of the River Dart, Zdzisław Ruszkowski, c.1960s. The artist stayed at the boat house in Sharpham during the mid-sixties, so Patten missed him by only a few years. The horizontal layering in his paintings of the Dart follow the structure of the river flowing between the Sharpham lawns, flower beds and trees and the wooded hills on the other bank but turn the view into a harmony where the colours take on the solidity of the landscape. *Valerie Wills/The Sharpham Trust*

The First to Land, oil, by
James Stewart, 2005.
Courtesy James Stewart

A sketch transformed by the vision that the birds have waited to sing for the tired traveller, turning the hopelessness of nothing ahead into relief that nothing matters.

These two poems come from memories of a child's awe of the magic and soothing power of nature, but Patten has a sharp edge, particularly in his poetry to do with relationships. In 'The Cynic's Only Love Poem' he comments:

> Love comes and goes
> And often it has paused,
> Then comes back to see
> The damage it has caused.[15]

Here, he distances himself by putting the words in someone else's mouth and by adding a neat rhyme. Other poems have a similar edge but are in the first person and have no neat rhymes; these are deeply felt. In one, he is asked for a poem, and told his offered blade of grass is not good enough:

> And so I write you a tragedy about
> How a blade of grass
> Becomes more and more difficult to offer,
>
> And about how as you grow older
> A blade of grass
> Becomes more difficult to accept.[16]

Masks and delusions are a theme for Patten. Are they bad? Are they good? Is he a jester who knows he jests? He is enigmatic. The poet rejects masks demanded by a poem wanting to be written – the lyrical one is old, the troubadour's awkward – until finally he tries on the right one, his own face. But delusions bring magic. In 'Drunk', 'People are sober as cemetery stones',

> And the best monsters are drunken
>   monsters,
> Trembling and dreaming of beanstalks
> Too high for sober Jack to climb;
> And the best tightrope walkers are
>   drunken tightrope walkers,

The language is straightforward, the pictures striking, the emotional charge tangible.

Even as a city child, Patten haunted the parks that relieved the mass of urban housing. In 'Travelling between places' he writes about what it means to a traveller to come back to places like the woods around his riverside home in Devon:

> Leaving nothing and nothing ahead;
> when you stop for the evening
> the sky will be in ruins.
>
> When you hear late birds
> with tired throats singing
> think how good it is that they,
>
> knowing you were coming,
> stayed up late to greet you,
> who travel between places
>
> when the late afternoon
> drifts into the woods, when
> nothing matters specially.[14]

The Jester, oil, by John Wimbush, 1854-1914.

Dartmouth Museum

A bottle in each hand they stagger
  above the net made
Of the audience's wish for them to fall.[17]

Drifts from the deep wood.
  A medicine for the soul,
  It rinses out the clogged up world.[18]

We leave Patten, 'scribbling', as he describes it, in his orchard above our river:

  The encoded message of birdsong

The songs of tired birds are singing to him still, a thread to his past, and telling us what our place is saying to this poet on his journey.

241

The Pictures Writers Paint

A place can inspire by events, or by triggering the imagination. Other chapters show French monks recording medieval battles, Arthur Norway and John Masefield inspired by smuggling, and Robert Graves and Flora Thompson turning away from the Dart to pre-Christian myth and rural idylls. Later 20th-century writers are less nostalgic. For Agatha Christie, Dartmouth inspires inventive stories about ordinary people from houses and villages she knows, caught up in crimes she may have read about in the newspapers. Nevil Shute and Leslie Thomas go back to the war.[1] Shute wrote *Most Secret*[2] in 1942, describing commando operations out of Dartmouth he would have known about from his work at the Admiralty; the book was so close to reality that security precluded publication until 1945. And in 1981, almost as soon as secret papers were released, Thomas wrote about Exercise Tiger. Christopher Milne turns inward, writing about how in Dartmouth he comes to terms with being a literary celebrity[3] – Christopher Robin in the *Winnie the Pooh* books written by his father, A.A. Milne.[4]

Previous Spread:
The Estuary of the Dart, oil, by David Alexander, 1996.
Private collection

Nevil Shute's 1942 novel about commandos in Dartmouth, *Most Secret*, is clearly based on very accurate local knowledge...

'It was a warm afternoon of late spring, with a gentle southerly breeze. He went upriver on the flood from the trawler anchorage off Kingswear, in between the wooded hills beyond the town...past the Naval College, past Mill Creek. He skirted by the Anchor Stone, and so came to Dittisham, with its whitewashed and thatched cottages straggling down to the creek.'[5] The 'he', Oliver Boden, is going to see the boat he is to take on secret commando missions to northern France during the Second World War. She was a 'very large, black fishing boat, perhaps seventy feet in length. She had an enormously high, straight bow and a great sweeping sheer down to the stern...'[6] It was the *Geneviève*, a sardine boat from Douarnenez, which was to mingle with the local fishing fleet across the Channel to supply arms and spies to the resistance and attack German *Raumboote* until she went down in a blaze of glory.

Shute is not a writer's writer. Before becoming a successful novelist after the Second World War he was an engineer and industrial entrepreneur. He was addicted to risk, as a sailor, a pilot – he flew his own small plane to Australia and back in 1948-49 – and a racing driver, a passion

French Crabbers, oil, by Harold Harvey, 1930. These boats are thought to be from Douarnenez where Shute's commandos went, and whence *Geneviève* came.
Private collection, on loan to Peulee House Gallery and Museum, Penzance

245

that began after his first heart attack in his mid-fifties. His work reflects both the engineer and the love of danger, the first giving it credibility, and the second, excitement. War work for the Admiralty on weapon development would have told Shute how combined operations in Dartmouth functioned with clandestine operations against northern France.[7] His descriptions in *Most Secret* are consistent with information that became available some thirty years after it was written. 'At War' describes the exploits of the Free French and naval commandos that operated out of the river, and local people remember a raid on St. Nazaire. Most accounts of Breton fishing boats, like Shute's *Geneviève*, have them working from the Helford river, west of Falmouth, but these did sometimes come to the Dart before crossing the Channel, and there is a local account of a secret French vessel painted black that went to France from Kingswear. The crew of the *Geneviève* included Bretons, and we know that at least two Breton tugs came into the river after the fall of France. There are more memories of Belgian fishing trawlers arriving with refugees, particularly at Dittisham.*

So although the seclusion of Dartmouth and its proximity to northern France make it an obvious place to set a fictional story of commandos, *Most Secret* was based on fact. Shute was famous for his detailed research. An acquaintance who visited him when he was working on his last book, *Trustee from the Toolroom*, saw 'a large navigation chart on his wall – Shute was not only working out the routes of his character but plotting the currents so he would have various boats at the right place at the right time'.[8] To go back to the quotation at the beginning, from a map he could certainly have found the detail in the description of the journey upriver from Dartmouth, and perhaps he might have worked out you could only sail easily up to Dittisham on the flood with a southerly breeze, but he would have known that anchorages were off Kingswear rather than Dartmouth from his pre-war visits to the area.

Shute was prolific, writing on average a novel a year from 1938 until his death in 1960. He was top of best-seller lists for more than twenty years and his novels are still in print. The day before he died, he wrote to a friend, 'From the strictly technical point of view, I think *Most Secret* is the best-formed book I ever wrote'.[9]

The house at the Greenway ferry in the 1930s where Marlene Tucker from *Dead Man's Folly* lived. The ferry was called across the river from Dittisham by the bell in the left-hand corner. Shute's *Geneviève* was moored close by.

Postcard, Carolyn Hayward

Agatha Christie knew this area well

Born in Torquay, Christie lived in the same house, Ashfield, until the end of the First World War, when, in her late twenties, she moved to London with her then husband Archie. She always kept her ties, holding onto Ashfield after her mother died eight years later, and then, when she sold it, buying Greenway. She came to Greenway as Mrs Mallowan, generally in summer, with her second husband, Max.

Three of Christie's sixty-six books are set on the Dart – *Five Little Pigs*, *Dead Man's Folly*, and *Ordeal by Innocence* – as is one of her short stories, *The Regatta Mystery*, about Dartmouth.[10] Christie has a flamboyant artist poisoned by his model in *Five Little Pigs* while he paints her on the Battery, the gun emplacement above the boathouse in the garden at Greenway, alias Alderbury, up the river from Dartmouth. In the same boathouse, in *Dead Man's Folly*, Marlene Tucker is garrotted during a garden fête; this time Greenway's alias is Nasse House. In a comfortable sitting room in a nice suburban house overlooking the same swing of the river but on the Dittisham side, a kind mother of five is bludgeoned to death with a poker in *Ordeal by Innocence*.

The houses that are the props for Christie's crimes stand in the great wooded banks above the Dart. An exotic foreigner sails up the river from Dartmouth into her stories, the ferrymen take the crime-busters and the criminals to and fro, the London train and the drive from the station bring the sleuth, Hercule Poirot, face-to-face with a member of the criminal Italian underworld masquerading as a hitchhiker. Places are disguised, but often thinly; Gitsham is Dittisham, Danemouth is Dartmouth, the Dart is the river Helm.

Agatha Miller, later Agatha Christie (1890-1976), as a young woman in pink, Nathanial Hughes John Baird, 1910. The portrait hangs at Greenway House and captures her quiet inquisitiveness.
Courtesy National Trust; photograph by Christopher Woodman

Christie's enduring appeal is the extraordinary inventiveness and timing of her plots. She left exercise books in which she worked them out, making lists of possible victims and culprits and picking combinations.[11] She engages the reader by giving the detective a confidante with whom he or she helpfully summarises the state of play. But the help is a mirage; the author confuses the trail at every step. Red herrings masquerade as clues, and Christie cannily keeps crucial information to herself until the end. Despite the complex action, Christie's drama arises from the fairly simple idea that evil, recalcitrant and without conscience, is inborn. The interest is on its impact. Crimes separate those affected into the seekers after truth, those who turn aside, and the victim. Only a little step, Christie tells us, and ordinary people make crime inevitable.

One of the pleasures of reading Christie is the picture she gives of her time. Her writing career spanned 1920-76, and her three Dart books were published over 1943-58. She writes about middle-

Mr and Mrs Mallowan, or
Agatha Christie, on
Blackpool Beach.

*Totnes Image Bank &
Rural Archive*

6769. PIER CAFE TEA GARDENS. DITTISHAM. NR. DARTMOUTH.

The café on the pier at
Dittisham in the 1930s,
opposite the Greenway
ferry. In the background are
laid-up boats, a sign of
recession.

Postcard, Carolyn Hayward

and upper-class people in big houses, who give fêtes in their gardens, bicker with trespassers, and
are horrified at the intrusion of uncompromising youth. Some are in straitened circumstances but
hold onto appearances; in *Dead Man's Folly* Amy Folliat in the lodge with her fine china and Meredith
Blake in his dilapidated house. There are competent women in servile positions, unsung, but without
whom nothing would function. The bitterness of one, Kirsty Lindstrom, makes her a murderer in

Ordeal by Innocence. Christie's descriptions are often pure social satire. Poirot, going to meet Blake, a country squire, prepares his way with introductions from Lady Mary Leveson-Gore and an Admiral. So when he arrives with his odd accent, button boots and enormous moustache, clearly never having hunted or shot in his life, Meredith will forgive him for being foreign. He does, just.

Though we know that the Dart was the scene for these books, we have no idea whether the people in them were local. In her autobiography, Christie says that at one point she decided not to write about real people.[12] But then she says that the idea of a Belgian sleuth came from the Belgian refugees in Torquay during the war. And she mentions that when working in a dispensary there and thinking about writing, she was struck when the pharmacist showed her a piece of curare (a paralysing poison from Latin American plants) he carried around with him because 'it makes me feel powerful'.[13] The pharmacist and his latent threat, she tells us, was part of the inspiration for the *The Pale Horse* some fifty years later. So which is the right clue? Did she truly not use real people? Our experience with Christie tells us we should not always trust what she says. Real local people could be all over her books.

The Magic Army by Leslie Thomas is one of the earliest accounts of Exercise Tiger, published in 1981...

Like many places on the south coast, the Dartmouth area was host to armies preparing for the D-Day landings in early June 1944 (see 'At War'). During the 1970s, the British thirty-year rule and the Freedom of Information Act in the United States disclosed secret information on Exercise Tiger,

Side view of the almost unrecognizable landing craft crippled by the E-boat attack of April 1944, in Dartmouth harbour.

Dartmouth Museum

Not the traction engine Doey Bidgood drives, but a combination of tractor and threshing machine that would have stopped the lanes just as effectively.

Dartmouth Museum

in which hundreds of American servicemen were killed here by E-boats, new, lethal and tremendously fast German vessels. The first book to cover this topic was *Bodyguard of Lies* on secrets of the Second World War, published in 1975 by Anthony Cave Brown.[14] It was followed by others, using American and British, national and local sources.[15] There is no dispute about the E-boat attack on the convoy out on a training exercise in the early hours of a late April morning, moving towards Slapton from Plymouth, and that two landing craft were sunk and one crippled. Most agree that bad communications, life-jackets that were faulty or wrongly used, an inadequate escort and slow reactions to the attack were to blame. But there is still debate, particularly locally, about how many died and where they lie buried. So the books continue to appear.

Leslie Thomas tells the story of the American army – the 'magic army' – over their five-month training period around Slapton, their arrival, what they found, what they did, and their departure on the invasion. The narrative lies between fact and fiction. The Author's Note says that the evacuation and the E-boat episode 'are widely based on fact' but that the characters are not. Like Christie and Shute, Thomas knew the area. He came first at thirteen from late summer 1943 to March 1944 to a reception home for Dr Barnado's in Kingsbridge after his father had been killed at sea and when his mother was dying of cancer. He remembers 'Teatimes at Lower Knowle [the home] were redolent with peanut butter, a gift from American soldiers; many years later those same Americans provided me with the basis of *The Magic Army*, a book which revealed for the first time the bungling tragedy of more than seven hundred young men who died by German action in one night while they were only practising invasion landings off Slapton Sands, Devon.'[16] After the book was published he was invited to the Pentagon to receive an award for his part in telling the terrible story.

Thomas' book is written from the American side. It shows two very different cultures. Accents are mutually incomprehensible. US servicemen chew gum, wear smooth clean uniforms and leather shoes, chat with their colonel, don't salute very often and can't march. Most have crossed the Atlantic for the first time and ask how far away the Germans are. Worse, they are a magnet for the local women, outclassing the British in their clumsy boots and with their meagre pay. And 'How did they get medals' wonders a British soldier 'When they had not done any fighting yet?'[17]

Much of the humour in the book comes from this tension between the two sides. The visitors often find local behaviour inexplicable. On their first daylight exercise as the landing craft come up to the beach under live bombardment, the Americans see right in their assault path Old Daffy and his dog digging for bait. Daffy has avoided the barricades by simply coming in on his dinghy. As the shells explode, landing craft swerve to avoid him and wave after wave of soldiers rush past, he 'glanced up, reached out to his bucket and brought it disdainfully closer to him'. Then, seeing his dog cavorting along the beach, he says 'Silas, you come 'ere boy. You be getting in the way'.[18]

Early on, in a narrow high-banked lane, a convoy of American soliders with 500 new troops meets a parade of farm vehicles going in the opposite direction, led by 'a monster motor traction engine, great-wheeled, high-chimneyed...[which] soared above the landing jeeps'. It has, inevitably, no reverse. Doey Bidgood, the driver of the towering monstrosity, certain of victory, kindly advises the long convoy of soldiers to reverse into a nearby field. But cows advance when the gate is finally opened. A small boy clutching a new-born lamb is delegated to move the cattle back. It takes an hour to get the convoy into the field. 'Thankee Yank!' shouts Doey as he triumphantly huffs by.[19]

A fine example of the competition between the sides comes when a stray German fighter is hit – amazingly – by the British gun outside the evacuation area ('My God' said the captain in command 'Whatever have we done?'). The plane crashes in a field north of the village, and the British soldiers, a convoy of American vehicles and all the villagers rush up the hill. With great foresight the British lieutenant quells the headlong race by shouting 'They'll turn the machine guns on you!' at which everyone falls flat. Then comes 'Police Constable Lethbridge...as thin as the bicycle upon which he creaked up the lane', who, with 'a distrustful look at the American soldiers in the ditch', said 'Zur,...oi think this be a matter for the civil power.' So it is the policeman who walks over to the figure that has emerged from the plane, with whom, to everyone's astonishment, he shakes hands. 'Jesus Christ' mutters the American colonel 'Now I've seen every goddam thing.'[20]

But the exercise was not for fun. The to-and-fro between evacuees and evacuers finally ends when the survivors from Exercise Tiger straggle back. The quay of the village just outside the evacuation zone is lined with villagers, 'all the population of Wilcoombe staring at their blackened, bloodied and defeated faces'. As the ambulances arrive, one of the survivors, to reassure those who might think they had come back from the actual invasion, sobs at them 'It's okay...We was just practising.'[21] It is at this point, just before the Americans leave on the invasion of Normandy, that the local people fully realise what the evacuation has been all about.

The Shambles, drawing by Helen Hunt. This is the Dartmouth that Milne worked to preserve. The drawing shows the 17th-century buildings behind the quays, where Higher Street is today.   *Private collection*

Christopher Milne first came to Dartmouth on 10 May 1951...

The town was sparkling in the sunshine. 'I cross on the car ferry,' he said in his autobiography, *The Path through the Trees*, almost thirty years later 'walk along a narrow street – and there on the corner facing me is the very place I have come to see.'[22] It was the Fairfax Sports Shop, an old building of lath and plaster. He buys it on the spot and creates a Dartmouth institution – the Harbour Bookshop.

Milne was to become deeply engaged in Dartmouth. He co-founded the Dartmouth & Kingswear Society (with John Smith and Lt Colonel Richard Webb), which was run from the bookshop and is still important. A mathematician and an engineer, his description of the 'townscape' is analytical. 'Most towns grow out from the centre,' he writes 'adding a succession of annual rings rather as a tree does. But though Dartmouth eventually got the better of its mud, it has never got the better of its hills.'[23] Milne seems particularly adapted to the small scale of Dartmouth and his life here. 'So I live at the bottom of a valley. I have a small bookshop in a small town; and I seldom venture far afield,' he writes in the prologue to his autobiography.

Christopher Milne was not just Christopher Milne. He was Christopher Robin Milne, and his father was the A.A. Milne who, over seven years while his son was growing up, wrote books of poetry and children's stories about him, using his name and the names of his toys. Christopher Robin, with his long hair and smock that were girlish even when he was growing up in the 1920s, was to become, thanks to E.H. Shepard's drawings in the books, instantly recognizable across the world.

Five years before his autobiography and after he had retired, Milne wrote another book, *The Enchanted Places*, about his childhood. It is about growing up with fame, and how one child came to terms with it. It is significant that *The Enchanted Places* was written before *The Path through the Trees*; Milne had to deal with this most difficult aspect of his childhood before he could talk about the rest of his life. He says he had spent years trying to escape being a literary celebrity. The epilogue to *The Enchanted Places* begins 'If the Pooh books had been like most other books – published one year, forgotten the next – there would have been no problem. If I had been a different sort of person there might well have been no problem. Unfortunately the fictional Christopher Robin refused to die...For the first misfortune (as it sometimes seemed) my father was to blame. The second was my fault.'[24]

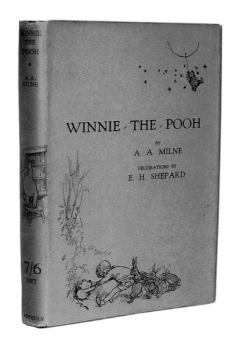

A first edition of *Winnie-The-Pooh* showing 'Christopher Robin', from whom Milne spent his adult years trying to escape...

E.H. Shepard

Christopher Milne, c.1974. In his book *The Enchanted Places*, Milne describes himself as 'shy, solitary, awkward...becoming worse as I grew older...'

Andrew Holmes/Dartmouth & Kingswear Society

Dartmouth became Milne's safe haven, where he was 'free, my own master'.[25] Here, he established his own identity as a bookseller and protagonist for the town. Although people did come looking for Christopher Robin, they were often disappointed. He lived as anonymously as he could. The 'Robin' in his name had been dropped by the time he went to the army. Although as a bookseller he could have profited from his connection with the Pooh books, he stocked but never displayed or publicised them. People remember a quiet, unassuming man, who built up a good bookshop and became a focal point for preserving the uniqueness of the town.

Harbour Bookshop, Tim Wood. It closed in 2012.

Courtesy Tim Wood

C A R N

I V A L

14/250

THE DARTMOUTH FIVE

Twenty-five odd years after the Dartmouth Five came here, Dartmouth has many artists. But in the early 1980s, when John Gillo, then Andras Kaldor, Simon Drew, John Donaldson and Paul Riley first arrived, there were very few.

Dartmouth was different then – very quiet, they say. Kaldor remembers Foss Street, where Drew found a place to live and work, as a back alley. On the South Embankment there was a coal merchant and a petrol station with a great crane supporting the fuel pipe. But it always had a solid group of people involved with sailing and/or the navy, and had supported a good bookshop for some thirty years. Bruce and Nicolette Coward, who owned the Harbour Bookshop from 1981, remember hosting the first Gillo-Kaldor exhibition after Andras had come in to chat carrying a big pot of paint. When he dropped it, the lid came off, and the floor was covered in paint. He was so mortified that he returned with a bottle of wine, and the friendship began. This exhibition, says Gillo, sowed the seeds for the group.

The Dartmouth Five, c.1985. Clockwise, from top right: John Donaldson, Andras Kaldor, John Gillo, Simon Drew and Paul Riley.

Jeff Waddington

They promoted their art through joint publicity and exhibitions. Stunts were never far behind. During an exhibition at the Lymington Gallery in Hampshire, celebrated in a restaurant afterwards, Donaldson played a piano suspended from the ceiling – hoisted up on the chair. They painted a mural at Café Alf Resco's on Lower Street. It's partially hidden by an extension, but you can still see it from the other side of the street. They exhibited jointly in Henley, Newmarket, Cowes, and the Country Living Fair in Islington. They did Christmas shows for their children – synchronised swimming behind a blue cloth, wearing bathing hats, trunks and clothes pegs on their noses, and a nativity in which Kaldor, the Virgin Mary, had to carry Riley (the smallest) as Jesus to a manger under the supervision of Drew as the Archangel – but Riley was still dropped into it. At the dress rehearsal for the swimming, Donaldson

Dartmouth Happy Families, organised by Elizabeth Cooper for the Dartmouth swimming pool fund. Dartmouth has an extraordinary number of families with names that describe their occupations – Cutmore the butcher, Swindell the banker and Pillar the builder, plus these. Simon Drew painted the Nashes, John Gillo the Legges, Andras Kaldor the Carrs, and John Donaldson the Sleeps.[1]

Two Ferries, acrylic on board, by John Gillo, 2012.

remembers that they were standing on a dais in the exhibition room, mostly in underpants with noseclips, practising receiving their gold medals, when in walked a family to look at the paintings. They froze. Very slowly, the family went from painting to painting, until they came to the unmoving tableau, considered it, and moved on. They had created their first piece of installation art, a true Gilbert and George.

Wives were always an integral part of it, critics of the art, managers of the business, organisers and morale boosters. They remember lots of dinners, particularly at Sally's Bistro at the Kaldors' place and regular eating at the Gillos', Drews' and Rileys'. They went on holidays together, to the vineyards of Bordeaux (this spawned an art exhibition in the restaurants of Dartmouth with a food-and-wine theme), and elsewhere in the south of France.

What held them together? They all say Dartmouth, they all say friendship and they all say food. Was it the art? Gillo says 'the group meant a huge amount to me for both inspiration and support. They have all been true friends over the last thirty years or so. It has been great to watch our work develop with shared inspiration and ideas. We all work in our own way, but we all pursue visual goals that are ultimately philosophical.' Drew points out that because art is fairly solitary, being with like-minded artists was tremendously encouraging, and that combined exhibitions attracted attention and helped sales. But for him and the others, the company and having a good time were equally important. As Riley says 'There was great camaraderie and mutual respect. We had a good time and we supported each other'.

John Gillo

The first to arrive of the five, John Gillo set up a gallery in Dartmouth in 1976. He had studied at Brighton School of Art, and in the early days taught art, first in Falmouth School of Art and then Churston Grammar School. 'During the winter of 1976', he says, 'I realised that the idea of teaching art for the next thirty-plus years was totally abhorrent and one particularly boozy evening with a friend...we decided to go out and set up a gallery.'

At first, Gillo's work was about abstract ideas to do with colour interaction, often on a large scale. Since this did not work commercially, he turned to traditional watercolours, mostly of Dartmouth and the surrounding villages. Within that discipline he found himself still trying to develop complex patterns and structures. 'Some of the work I now shudder to think of' he says. But some he still likes. Now, he has gone back to acrylic and more abstraction. Still within what he calls a 'landscape format', it is an exploration of distortion.

River Mouth (on the cover of this book) nudges the architectural chaos perched on Dartmouth's hills to make a subtle vortex of houses tipping off their foundations with the same shifting landscape appearing through the colours of the water while the clouds above scud off to the far right. The buildings, water and clouds become a maelstrom, with the painter and viewer inside; his painting *Two Ferries* moves with the same dynamic.

Mackerel uses complementary colours to create a sense of constant movement caught by shifting light from above and below. He says 'Fish lend themselves to this composition, highly directional, they flash through the water reflecting light and colour.'

Mackerel, acrylic by John Gillo, 2010.
Courtesy John Gillo

Horne Hill Steps, Dartmouth, acrylic by John Gillo, 2007. 'I like the idea of steps being a way to somewhere' he says. 'Horne Hill' is a traditional town view but it's been sucked upwards, the elongations and modest contrasts of planes of light saying something about the way the town is chaotically put together.   *Courtesy John Gillo*

Andras Kaldor

Andras Kaldor is a man of contradictions. He is an architect who is a painter. His passion is the *belle époque* of European baroque, or, failing that, of grand historic city houses and terraces, and he lives in a small town that has only one – the Naval College.[2] He paints buildings but never uses a ruler. He is Hungarian and has exhibited and worked in, among other places, New York, Washington, Berlin, Budapest and Paris, but always comes back to Dartmouth.

Kaldor thinks of terraces like musical scores, moving through repeated but not identical architectural motifs, harmony but punctuated with contrasts to give it a dynamic. But then he thinks one can get too esoteric about art and should just enjoy it.

The Opera House, Budapest, ink and gouache, by Andras Kaldor, 1988. A neo-Renaissance building, this leading European opera house was designed by Miklos Ybl. Gustav Mahler was musical director for years, and Kaldor's grandfather sang in the back of the choir.   *Courtesy Andras Kaldor*

Opposite: Saint Saviour's Church from the back, watercolour, by Andras Kaldor, 1986. The lines are supple, shadows more important than edges and repeated shapes of differing widths give rhythm. St Saviour has a blunt presence, filling the space, cut off two-thirds of the way down by a gable, a mass of medieval masonry with deep protrusions and a range of flat surfaces catching the soft light at slightly different angles. The watercolour was done very wet and fast, on a slope, then flat, then sloped again, over the ink work. 'Please notice', says Kaldor, 'the optimistic upward angles of the hands on the clock.'
Courtesy Andras Kaldor

261

The South Embankment, Dartmouth, print of ink and gouache original, by Andras Kaldor, 1998. The work was done for Joyce Molyneux, celebrated chef of the Carved Angel restaurant (with the blue awnings), in memory of many happy dinners.
Courtesy Andras Kaldor

Compare *The Budapest Opera House* with what he calls 'the stark concrete years of the sixties and seventies' and you can see why Kaldor gave up architecture – although he stuck at it for twenty years. The tough early times of full-time painting ended when Prince Charles called the proposed extension to the National Gallery 'a carbuncle', and Kaldor mounted 'Carbuncles or Masterpieces?' in a London gallery on historic London buildings and terraces. (He denies England has much proper baroque, but he found a bit.) Commissions followed for more paintings of buildings in London and Washington, and then came European railways and opera houses, combining his love of the music of the grand opera and the architecture of opera houses.

Turning to art was one of the dodgy times in Kaldor's life. But the dodgiest, he says, was when he left Hungary at seventeen as Russian tanks were rolling in on the revolution of 1956. Once safely in Vienna he organised travel to England, and found a place at Edinburgh University to study architecture. His architectural career in London and Yorkshire brought him to Plymouth and sailing the coast to Dartmouth.

Paul Riley

Paul Riley has always been a painter. Both his parents were artists and he studied at the Kingston School of Art, first exhibiting at the Royal Academy in 1960 aged fifteen. He came to Dittisham by chance twenty years later while working as an architect. His studio and art school at Coombe Farm outside Dittisham have been his centre of operations ever since. Many exhibitions and one-man shows followed in England, Scandinavia, continental Europe, the US and Australia.[3]

After art school Riley's palette was dark, and his inspiration, influenced by the early painting of van Gogh, was drawn from working communities, particularly mining villages in south Wales. Palette, medium and focus changed with travels to the Mediterranean. Once in Devon, Riley returned to watercolours, using a free-style brushwork as far removed from architectural drawing as possible. He met Kaldor, Drew and Gillo when he was keen to get to full-time painting again.

Riley's dictum now is restraint, the painting of suggestion. With watercolour it requires above all looking, then patience, skill and a deep knowledge of tools and techniques, and how they interact. The changing waters of the Dart around Dittisham retain a fascination for Riley, who was brought up on the Thames. The following four paintings he plays with different ways of capturing its moods.

Misty River, Dart, watercolour, by Paul Riley, 2009.   *Courtesy Paul Riley*

Frosty Autumn Morning, Sharpham, watercolour, by Paul Riley, 2011.   *Courtesy Paul Riley*

Top right: River Dart, Autumn, watercolour, by Paul Riley, 2011.   *Courtesy Paul Riley*

Bottom right: Early Morning, Dittisham, watercolour, by Paul Riley, 2009.   *Courtesy Paul Riley*

When the mists come, they can wriggle up the river, leaving patches of landscape clear, blurring others, hiding joints between water and tree, tree and its reflection. In the first painting, which is quite small, he uses an oriental-style brush with goat and wolf hair, and plays with wetting the paper, patch by patch, to capture the moving air, reflection and depth.

During the snow of 2011 he went out to find the frost had sharpened the light, clarifying the colours, so that every slope, tree and curve of the river was outlined. Riley uses different brushes here, and a range of masking techniques to get the precision and clarity he wants.

In *Early Morning* the light is bouncing off the water around the jetty, hardly penetrating enough to create reflections. Shapes are sharp and black or shrouded, tones are hinted at. The structure is minimal, but the place could be nowhere else.

Snow, South Hams, oil, by John Donaldson, 2011. Place and mood are Donaldson's focus. *Courtesy John Donaldson*

The Beekeeper's Staircase, oil, by John Donaldson, 2007. *Courtesy John Donaldson*

John Donaldson

John Donaldson can't recall a time when he didn't paint; one of his earliest memories is watching his grandfather paint watercolours. By thirteen, he had discovered oil; he liked its tangibility, the way he could push it around. Now, he does watercolours too. He grew up with music in the same way. In his late teens, he studied composition and classical organ before switching to modern jazz and electronic music. Donaldson came to Dartmouth in 1975 and met the other four of the Dartmouth Five some ten years later. Here, he paints, plays the organ in local churches and does local gigs. He still composes and records music. In painting he tries to catch 'a place where something has just happened, some shadow has passed, a moving cloud has changed a look.' He wants to be honest about the unusual and beautiful and the effects of light. He thinks 'impressionist' describes his work best, in that it has no hidden narrative, but attempts to interpret a visual moment.

Donaldson is inspired by the Dartmouth area, the south of France and Italy, as much by the countryside as by intimate scenes of historic houses on the river or cobblestone embankments in the sun, by the energy of bars and cafés, or the peace of sunlit steps rising against the corner of a vine-clad house. He can spend days searching for everyday views that crystallise a transitory but modest moment.

Paint and music are synergistic in his work, although he finds the connections between colour, texture and sound less conscious with time. 'In the simplest terms', he says, 'I hear sounds when I paint and see colour when I make music'. In the early 1970s, he painted mostly large abstracts as he listened to music – he remembers Bartok, the

266

Bayard's Cove, Dartmouth,
oil, by John Donaldson, 2004.
Courtesy John Donaldson

Modern Jazz Quartet, Jimi Hendrix and Olivier Messiaen – and actively interpreted what he heard and felt in colour and form. Trying to paint watery pictures more recently to Chopin's *Études* and *Barcarolles* really failed; the process was too literal. Mood is paramount for John in music and he may listen to the more frenetic passages of Verdi's *Requiem* or The Prodigy to help reach the 'speed' he needs to start painting, but then paints in silence, hearing the music in his head.

Painting is more of a physical challenge than music. He has to be really fit to paint; why, he's not sure. But he can compose, record or 'construct' music in almost any state, despite even hangovers or head colds. Perhaps, he thinks, it's because he's not a greatly gifted musician technically, so the need to concentrate can dispel aches and pains and negative feelings. Painting draws more on a subconscious that can't be forced. The subject has to be allowed to fill and occupy the mind.

the animals came in four-by-four

Simon Drew

Simon Drew, half wit and half artist as he describes himself, came to Dartmouth in 1981. He studied zoology (his drawings of animals and birds are basically accurate), and after six years training as and being a teacher, he retired, supported by his wife Caroline, to make something of himself.

dali havidson

Once here, he galloped off in all directions. He writes prose and poetry and draws to go with it.[4] His work is exhibited in art galleries in Britain, the US and Australia. It appears in books, and on mugs, tee-shirts and postcards. He has designed for Friends of the Earth, the Millennium Dome and the eternally running BBC programme *The Archers*. He has far-flung admirers. Alberto Grimaldi, producer of the iconic Marlon Brando film *Last Tango in Paris* bought the original of his drawing *Last Mango*. Couturier Jean-Paul Gaultier bought 100 of his cards showing a goat with E and A on its side. Günter Grass called to order some books – was it the author of *The Tin Drum*? Local postmen know him; a letter from Hong Kong to 'Simon Drew, Y-front, Dartmouth', arrived.

Verbal and visual puns get Drew going. But they have to work together. With *Dali Havidson* the caption doesn't do it, the image of the motor bike with the melting wheels doesn't do it, but the combination does. A very visual pun is *Camp David*, Michelangelo's *David* holding a handbag – the head of security at Camp David apparently has it hanging in his office.

Ideas can come spontaneously. For *Dali Havidson* he was sitting under a palm tree in Mauritius thinking about a book on art. They can arise from mishearing, mole for *moules*, or from misspeaking, like the old lady who said her grandson was a drum maisonette. Wherever he is, Drew is always listening, scribbling ideas in his little book.

But puns aside, Drew's work above all displays his pure enjoyment in doing the art. *Carnival* has no other point. *Dali Havidson*, *The Animals Came in Four-by-Four* and *Mole Marinière* do have another point, but the drawings could stand alone.

Some enjoy Drew's wit, some his imagination, some his art, and some just like him. His appeal is broad enough to have made him a celebrity.

All images on this spread and pp. 254-5 courtesy Simon Drew

prawn to be wild

mole marinière

269

A Conversation with the Past

This book has been about the people who have made Dartmouth. Inevitably, most are well known. But walk down the high street or read the local papers and many names crop up that, though not famous, connect with names here hundreds of years ago. Like their medieval houses hidden beneath later façades, the people of Dartmouth carry a living history.

What we know depends on the written records, and those we have, from manor and borough, ecclesiastical, naval and commercial documents, record generally unexciting things like land transactions, property ownership and minor offences. But just some can suddenly illuminate a glimpse of a lost way of life.

Lloyd **Attree** has a jeweller's shop on Duke Street. In June 1318, a John de Attry was mandated to take to Ireland a force from 'Dertemuthe, Tengmuthe and city of Exeter' to repel the invasion of Ireland by the Scots, under 'Rober de Brus and Edward his brother'.[1] This was four years after Edward II had been defeated by Bruce at Bannockburn and was fighting to keep Ireland. In 1327 he was to be deposed and the losses of Scotland and Ireland were among the reasons given by Parliament for declaring his son Edward III as king. John de Attry's ships – with those from Dartmouth listed ahead of Teignmouth and Exeter – were deployed in a futile effort and must have cost this port at the far reaches of the kingdom dear.

Fulfords is a property company with an office on the South Embankment. Fulfords still live in the area, although the company carries the name of the Exeter Fulfords that began it. Of the many Fulfords in the medieval records, the most prominent was Baldwin, 'escheator' of Devon, who came to Dartmouth in 1433, probably to enquire into the town's persistent piracy. The famous John Hawley was by then dead, but John, his son, was not. Baldwin was set upon by 'forty persons armed and arrayed as if for war and insurrection [who] so struck wounded and ill treated Baldwin, his clerks and servants so they could hardly get away alive...'. We know of the attack because in July that year Henry VI established a commission of enquiry and in December Baldwin, in an extraordinary apology, 'remits all personal actions against the following 73 persons'. The list begins with the mayor and is thought to include the town freemen. The story demonstrates once again the town's muscular independence. But John Hawley is not on Baldwin's list; he stops being MP in 1432 and disappears from the records in 1435.[2] Perhaps the burgesses had to deal with Hawley before Baldwin Fulford would forgive them.

LAST WORD

The Dartmouth area is one of uncommon natural beauty. It has been celebrated in film and on television, with local extras getting close to Kris Kristoffersson, Meryl Streep, Donald Sutherland and Faye Dunaway.[1]

It is unusual not only because of its green rolling countryside wandering or tumbling suddenly to river and sea, but also because of its villages and towns. Christopher Milne, who ran a bookshop here, talks about Dartmouth's townscape, pressed into the river by its hills, and the 'charm of small-scale, compactness, giving the pedestrian a very strong sense of being in the town. To the left and right he can almost touch it. In front and behind he can throw a stone and hit it.'[2]

Small and remote as it is, the area has a remarkable history. Explorers and pioneers have sailed and still sail from here. Merchants made fortunes from cod and wine. Royalty came to engage Dartmouth in its wars and arrived later for the naval college. Its strategic location involved it in national wars, from the crusades to the Second World War. The reputation of the town attracted extraordinary people – entrepreneurs and inventors, writers and artists, some, like George Bidder, John Masefield and J.M.W. Turner, with national standing, many, like Thomas Newcomen, locally produced. The footprint of the past falls everywhere, still visible because generations of people have valued and kept what was there before.

Dartmouth is crowded again with people attracted by the harbour, the mild climate and the invitation of the sea. Most come back year after year, many to live. Dartmouth does not let go.

Endnotes

Chapter 1: BURGESSES AND KINGS

1. *Dartmouth: Pre-Reformation*, by Hugh Watkin, The Devonshire Association, 1935, pp. 4, 280, 354.
2. Watkin, op.cit, pp. vi, 280.
3. *The Black Death*, by John Hatcher, Weidenfeld & Nicholson, 2008, p. 176.
4. Watkin, op.cit, Plate IX, facing p. 141.
5. Estimates from Maryanne Kowaleski, 'The 1377 Dartmouth Poll Tax' in *Devon & Cornwall Notes & Queries*, pp. 286-95. The estimates exclude the clergy (who paid taxes to the church) and those too poor to pay.
6. Watkin, op.cit, p. 59.
7. *Chaucer's Canterbury Tales, an Interlinear Translation*, Barrons' Educational Series, 1970, by Vincent F. Hopper, pp. 25-7.
8. Watkin, op.cit, p. 297.
9. *Dartmouth and its Neighbours*, by Ray Freeman, quoting E.H. Back, Richard Webb, 2007, p. 144.
10. Watkin, op.cit., churchwardens' accounts, p. 294.

Chapter 2: MEDIEVAL TURBULENCE

1. *Dartmouth, Pre-Reformation*, by Hugh R. Watkin, The Devonshire Association, 1935, p. 365.
2. Watkin, op. cit., pp. 368-7.
3. Watkin, op. cit., p. 82.
4. Maryanne Kowaleski, 'The 1377 Dartmouth Poll Tax' in *Devon & Cornwall Notes & Queries*, pp. 286-95. The tax excluded the clergy (who paid taxes to the church) and the very poor.
5. Watkin, op. cit., p. 72.
6. Originally drawn for 'Hawley's Fortalice' by Terry Edwards, Dartmouth History Research Group.
7. Watkin, op. cit., p. 60.
8. Watkin, op. cit., p. 66.
9. Watkin, op. cit., p. 370.
10. Watkin, op. cit., pp. 375-6; and *Dartmouth: a History of the Port and Town*, by Percy Russell, B.T. Batsford, 1950, p. 43.
11. In the original, '*Tout fut perdu par une imprudence qui tient de la folie.*' The *Chronique* was a history of France written for the king by the monks of Saint-Denis.
12. *Dartmouth and its Neighbours*, by Ray Freeman, Richard Webb, 2007, p. 38.
13. Russell, op.cit., p. 46-7.
14. Watkin, op. cit., pp. 378-9; Freeman, op. cit., p. 39, records the king claiming 50 percent of the ransom of two knights.
15. Watkin, op. cit., p xii.
16. 'Concerning Mr Huncks' by Larry Gragg, *Journal of the Barbados Museum and Historical Society*, 1996/7, Vol. XLIII, pp. 1-3.

Chapter 3: THE DART EXPLORERS

1. References from *The Second Voyage attempted by M. John Davis...for the Discoverie of the Northwest Passage*, reproduced in *R. Hakluyt, Voyages and Documents*, OUP, 1958, pp. 307-08.
2. List quoted in 'The Champernowne Family' unpublished manuscript by C.E. Champernowne, Dartington Hall Trust Archive, 1954. p. 86. Cited with kind permission of the Dartington Trust.
3. Champernowne, op.cit., p. 85.
4. Champernowne, op.cit., p. 101.
5. Quotation from Hooker in Champernowne, op.cit., p. 101.
6. *Life of Sir Walter Raleigh*, by James Augustus St John, 1868, Vol 1, Chapter XIII.
7. St John, op.cit., Chapter XIII.

8. St John, op.cit., Chapter XIII.
9. St John, op.cit., Chapter XIII.

Chapter 4: THE SEAS THAT BIND

1. *Compton Castle*, National Trust brochure, p. 18.
2. *True Relation of the Voyage of George Waymouth*, by James Rosier, 1905.
3. *Kingswear and Neighbourhood*, by Percy Russell and Gladys Yorke, Kingswear Historians, 2008, pp. 16-18, quoting Exeter City Library DD 12071, 12005/6 and 12021.
4. 'The Champernowne Family,' unpublished manuscript by C.E. Champernowne, Dartington Hall Trust Archive, 1954, p. 246. Cited with kind permission of the Dartington Trust.
5. *Torre Abbey*, by Deryck Seymour, James Townsend & Sons, 1977.
6. Champernowne, op. cit., p. 258.
7. Champernowne, op. cit., p. 256.
8. John Prince, author of the *Worthies of Devon*, was lecturer of St Mary's Church, Totnes and then vicar of Berry Pomeroy, so his description is from experience. Quoted in Edward Windeatt, *The Borough of Clifton-Dartmouth-Hardness and its Mayors and Mayoralties*, p. 6.
9. *A Briefe and True Relation of the Discovery of the North Part of Virginia*, by John Brereton, London, Bishop, 1602.
10. Log books of the *Mayflower* and the *Speedwell*.

Chapter 5: SLAVERY AND SIEGE

1. See *Dartmouth: a History of the Port and Town*, by Percy Russell, B.T. Batsford, 1950, pp. 71-2; *Dartmouth and its Neighbours*, by Ray Freeman, Richard Webb, 2007, pp. 65-6.
2. William Holborow, 'Building Development in Dartmouth, 1580-1660', in *Dartmouth Papers IV*, 1980, p. 20.
3. Freeman, op.cit., p. 78.
4. Holborow, op.cit., p. 4.
5. Russell, op.cit., p. 108.
6. *A Faithful Account of the Religion and Manners of the Mahometans*, by Joseph Pitts of Exon., 1738, ed., republ. by Gregg International Publishers, 1971, p. 3.
7. *Devon and The Slave Trade* by Todd Gray, The Mint Press, 2007, pp. 31-9.
8. Freeman, op.cit., p. 89 quoting DRO DD 61981, 61978 and 62067.
9. Russell, op.cit., p. 90.
10. *Histoire de la Barbarie*, by Father Pierre Dan, quoted in *White Gold: the Extraordinary Story of Thomas Pellow and North Africa's One Million European Slaves*, by Giles Milton, Hodder and Stoughton, p. 288.
11. Abraham Browne, quoted in Milton, op.cit., pp. 68-9.
12. Okeley wrote a memoir called *Ebenezer: or, A Monument of Great Mercy, Appearing in the Miraculous Deliverance of William Okeley*, 1675. Reprinted in Daniel Vitkus ed. Piracy, Slavery and Redemption, New York, 2001, and quoted in Milton, op.cit., p. 69.
13. Robert Adams, quoted in Milton, op.cit., pp. 16, 20.
14. *The Diary of Samuel Pepys*, Vol. II, 1661, The Chaucer Press, 1970, pp. 33-34.
15. *The Barbary Corsairs*, by Stanley Lane-Poole, 1890, p. 229, quoted in Milton, op.cit., p. 13.
16. 'The Famous Sea-Fight Between Captain Ward and the Rainbow', a ballad in *Naval Songs and Ballads*, Naval Record Society, C.H. Firth ed., 1908, quoted in Milton, op.cit., p. 285.
17. Russell, op.cit., p. 90.
18. *Barbary Pirates off the Devon Coast*, by Sadru Bhanji, Orchard Publications, 1996, p. 23; and Freeman, op.cit., p. 89.

19. Russell, op.cit., p. 113.
20. Freeman, op.cit., p. 112.
21. Freeman, op.cit., pp. 112-3; Wheeler accounts quoted in Russell, op.cit., p. 121.
22. *Dartmouth, Pre-Reformation*, by Hugh R. Watkin, Devonshire Association, 1935, p. 354.
23. *The Borough of Clifton-Dartmouth-Hardness and its Mayors and Mayoralties*, by Edward Windeatt, p. 53.
24. Freeman, op.cit., p. 117.
25. *Hostage: A Year at Gunpoint with Somali Gangsters*, by Paul and Rachel Chandler with Sarah Edworthy, Mainstream Publishing, 2011, p. 61.

Chapter 6: THEIR DAY IN THE SUN
1. *Dartmouth and its Neighbours*, by Ray Freeman, Richard Webb, 2007, p. 135.
2. *England in the Eighteenth Century*, by Roy Porter, The Folio Society, 1988, p. 177.
3. *A Tour Through Great Britain*, by A Gentleman (Daniel Defoe), 1724.
4. *A Living from the Sea*, compiled and edited by M.G. Dickinson, Devon Books, 1987, p. 71.
5. 'Discourse and Discovery of Newfoundland', by Captian Richard Whitbourne, 1621, quoted in *Dartmouth: a History of the Port and Town*, by Percy Russell, B.T. Batsford, 1950, p. 83-4.
6. *Oporto Old and New*, by Charles Sellars, 1899, p. 122.
7. 'The Story of Hunt, Roope & Co., Oporto', a company document, pp. 4-5.
8. Russell, op.cit., p. 124.
9. See *The Portugal Trade*, by H.E.S. Fisher, Methuen & Co. Ltd., 1971, for a comprehensive account of English-Portuguese trade in the 18th century.
10. Fisher, op.cit., p. 27.
11. *The Englishman's Wine*, Sarah Bradford, Macmillan & Co. Ltd., 1969, p. 55.
12. Bradford, op.cit., p. 15.
13. Sellars, op.cit., p. 21.
14. Quotations from *Sketches of Society and Manners in Portugal*, by Arthur William Costigan, London, 1788, quoted in Bradford, op.cit., p. 58.
15. John Teage letterbook, by kind permission.

Chapter 7: MY ONLY SECRET IS DAMNED HARD WORK
1. *Past Celebrities Whom I Have Known*, by Cyrus Redding, 1866, p. 47.
2. The sketchbooks are with the Tate Gallery.
3. Redding, op.cit., p. 47.
4. *Standing in the Sun: a Life of J.M.W. Turner*, by Anthony Bailey, Sinclair-Stevenson, 1997, p. 326.
5. Bailey, op.cit., p. 326.
6. Description by Turner's colleague C. R. Leslie in Bailey, op.cit., p xv.
7. Letter from Samuel Rogers to John Ruskin, quoted in Bailey, op.cit., p. 174.
8. Redding, op.cit., p. 53.
9. *Colour in Turner: Poetry and Truth*, 1969, by John Gage, p. 32, quoted in Bailey, op.cit. pp. 171-2.
10. Bailey, op.cit., p. 379.
11. Comment made by Jane Fawkes and quoted in Gage, op.cit., p. 225.

Chapter 8: THE WILD FREE LIFE
1. *Dartmouth and its Neighbours*, by Ray Freeman, Richard Webb, 2007, p. 143.
2. PRO, Exeter Letterbooks CUST 64/4, quoted in *Smuggler: John Rattenbury and his Adventures in Devon, Dorset and Cornwall 1778-1844*, by Eileen Hathaway, Shinglepecker Publications, Swanage, 1994, p. 11.
3. *Parish of Stoke Fleming, Devon, Elizabeth I (and before) to Elizabeth II Coronation, 2nd June 1953*, edited by Major J.H. Scott-Tucker, p. 75.
4. *Parson Peter, a Tale of the Dart*, by Arthur Norway, John Murray, 1900, p. 13.
5. Norway, op.cit., p. 68.

6. 'A Smuggler's Song' in *Puck of Pook's Hill* by Rudyard Kipling, Macmillan & Co. 1906.
7. Hathaway, op.cit.
8. Hathaway, op.cit., pp. 60-63.
9. Norway, op.cit., p. 4.
10. Norway, op.cit., p. 391.
11. Hathaway, op.cit., p. 169.
12. Hathaway, op.cit., p. 159.
13. *Jim Davis*, by John Masefield, Wells Gardner, Darton & Co., London, 1911; or *The Captive of the Smugglers*, Page Company, Boston, 1918, p. 163.
14. Janet Ashbee's journal, quoted in *John Masefield: a Life*, by Constance Babington Smith, OUP, 1978, p. 87.
15. Masefield, op.cit., pp. 80-81.
16. 'Christmas, 1903', *Ballads and Poems*, by John Masefield, London: Elkin Mathews, 1916.
17. Scott-Tucker, op.cit., p. 59.
18. Note from Nicholas Teague, 2004.
19. Leaflet of St Peter's Church, Stoke Fleming.

Chapter 9: THE LONG FUSE
1. L.T.C. Rolt and J.S. Allen, *The Steam Engines of Thomas Newcomen*, Landmark Publishing, 1977; and Eric Preston, *Thomas Newcomen of Dartmouth*, Dartmouth History Research Group and Dartmouth and Kingswear Society, 2012, p. 29.
2. *The Wealth and Poverty of Nations*, by David Landes, Little Brown and Company, 1998, p. 187.
3. *Dartmouth: a History of the Port and Town*, by Percy Russell, B.T. Batsford, 1950, p. 136.
4. Teage Letterbook, by kind permission.
5. *Standing in the Sun: a Life of J.M.W. Turner*, by Anthony Bailey, Sinclair Stevenson, 1997, pp. 364-5.
6. *Torquay Directory, and South Devon Journal*, Wednesday, August 17, 1864. The Dartmouth & Torbay Railway was leased to the South Devon Railway Company in 1866.
7. *The Newton Abbot to Kingswear Railway (1844-1988)*, by C.R. Potts, Oakwood Press, 1988, pp. 25-6.
8. *Torquay Directory*, 1864, op.cit.
9. Figures for Torquay from *A Regional History of the Railways of Great Britain: the West Country*, by David St. John Thomas, David Charles, 1960, p. 86; those for Dartmouth from Potts, op.cit., p. 62.

Chapter 10: THE 'JUST-DO-IT' VICTORIANS
1. *Torquay Directory, and South Devon Journal*, Wednesday, August 17, 1864.
2. Appendix to the pamphlet *Holdsworth's Water-Bulkheads*, London, J.D. Potter, 1852, p. 13.
3. *George Parker Bidder: the Calculating Boy*, E.F. Clark, KSL Publications, 1983, p. 197.
4. Clark, op.cit., p. 202.
5. Information from R.S. Hamlett and his papers in the Brixham Heritage Museum & History Society.
6. *The Liwentaal Enigma; the Story of a Local Aviator*, by Bob Marsh, pamphlet, c.1967, pp. 2-3, and *A History of the Dartmouth Cottage Hospital*, by W.G. Keane, Dartmouth History Research Group, Paper No. 2.
7. Letter to the editor, *Dartmouth and South Hams Chronicle*, 8 December 1894.
8. Lecture to the Camera Club, 1897, reported in *Autocar* and quoted in *Victorian England*, G.M. Young, The Folio Society, 1999, p. 525.
9. Inder family papers.
10. The Kingsbridge Branch, Ken Williams and Dermot Reynolds, Oxford Publishing Company. 1977, pp. 117-8.
11. *Dartmouth and South Hams Chronicle*, 23 June, 1939. Inder was especially pleased because Philip had been vehemently opposed to petrol-driven cars.

Chapter 11: THE VILLAGE AND THE SEA
1. *Hallsands: a Village Betrayed*, by Steve Melia, Forest Publishing, 2004, pp. 52-53.
2. *Sisters against the Sea*, Ruth and Frank Milton, Halsgrove, 2005, p. 42. Frank Milton is descended from the Trouts of Hallsands who were driven out in 1917, and the book draws from first-hand accounts of events then and later.
3. Melia, op.cit., p. 34.
4. Milton, op.cit., p. 17.
5. 'Hallsands and Start Bay', paper given by Richard Hansford Worth to the Devonshire Association in 1904, p. 329.
6. There has been a great deal of analysis of how the dredging affected the village. This synopsis is taken mainly from Hansford Worth's papers published in *Transactions of the Devonshire Association* of 1904, 1909 and 1923, and Melia, op.cit.
7. Milton, op.cit., p. 55, source for much of the other information on Elizabeth Anne.
8. *Hallsands, a Pictorial History*, by Kathy Tanner and Peter Walsh, p. 17.
9. Milton, op.cit., p. 54.
10. Milton, op.cit., p. 62.

Chapter 12: THE FRIGATE ON THE HILL
1. See *The Buildings of England: Devon*, Bridget Cherry and Nikolaus Pevsner, Penguin, repr. 1999, pp. 105 and 325.
2. Reminiscences of Captain Moore's niece quoted in *Britannia Royal Naval College*, by Dr Jane Harrold and Dr Richard Porter, Richard Webb, 2012 edn., p. 42. I am indebted to the authors for much of the material in this chapter.
3. 'John Ward of Hull (1798-1849)' by Arthur Credland, *Antique Collecting*, March 2012, p. 33.
4. Harrold and Porter, op.cit., p. 108.
5. Harrold and Porter, op.cit., pp. 80-1.
6. *The Newton Abbot to Kingswear Railway (1844-1988)*, by C.R. Potts, Oakwood Press, p. 92.
7. Harrold and Porter, op.cit., p. 99, from P. Ziegler, *Mountbatten*, Collins, 1985, p. 687.
8. Harrold and Porter, op.cit., p. 110.
9. Reported in *The Chronicles of Dartmouth*, 1854-1954, by Don Collinson, Richard Webb, 2000, p. 104.

Chapter 13: TOUCHING NATURE
1. *Lucien Pissarro*, by W.S Meadmore, Constable, 1962, p. 148.
2. Meadmore, op.cit., p. 132.
3. The Prints and Drawings Room at the Ashmolean Museum, Oxford kindly provided access to Pissarro's letters. The paintings shown appear in the *Catalogue of Oil Paintings by Lucien Pissarro*, by A. Thorold, 1983.
4. *Since I was Twenty-Five*, by Frank Rutter, Constable, 1927, quoted in Meadmore, op.cit., p. 107.
5. Meadmore op.cit., p. 108.
6. As well as: Walter Bayes, Henry Lamb, Wyndham Lewis, M.A. Lightfoot and Daman Turner.

Chapter 14: LOST WORLDS
1. *A Country Calendar and other Writings: Flora Thompson*, selected and edited by Margaret Lane, OUP, 1979, p. 28.
2. Lane, op.cit., p. 130.
3. Letter from Winifred Thompson to Mrs Tettmar, 8 June, 1951, Exeter University Library, Special Collections.
4. *Lark Rise*, by Flora Thompson, OUP, 1939, p. 1.
5. Letter in Lane, op.cit., p. 8.
6. Letter to Arthur Ball, 22 December 1931, Exeter University Library, Special Collections.
7. 'From a Devon hill-top' by F.T., *Peverel Monthly*, July 1930.
8. Thompson, op.cit., p. 272.
9. *Lucien Pissarro*, by W.S. Meadmore, Constable, 1962, p. 194.
10. 'From a Devon Hillside', by Flora Thompson, *Peverel Monthly*, Summer 1932.

11. Thompson, op.cit., p. 271.
12. *A Living from the Sea*, compiled and edited by M.G. Dickinson, Devon Books, 1987, pp. 32-3.
13. Letter to Arthur Ball, 16 August, 1942, Exeter University Library, Special Collections.

Chapter 15: AT WAR
1. *A Prophet at Home*, by Douglas Reed, Jonathon Cape, 1941, p. 252.
2. *Britannia Royal Naval College, 1905-2005*, by Jane Harrold and Richard Porter, Richard Webb, 2005, p. 118.
3. *Dartmouth & Kingswear during the Second World War, 1939-45*, by Arthur L. Clamp, 1994, p. 13.
4. *Parish of Stoke Fleming, Devon, Elizabeth I (and before) to Elizabeth II Coronation, 2nd June 1953*, edited by Major J.H. Scott-Tucker, p. 95.
5. *Most Secret*, by Nevil Shute, Heinemann, 1945, discussed in the chapter 'Pictures Writers Paint', is about clandestine naval operations out of Dartmouth. See also *Kingswear at War*, by David Williams, Kingswear Historians, 2011, p. 80 et seq.
6. Translation by Sheila Little of archives in the Naval War Records in Cherbourg.
7. *A Wren's-Eye View of Wartime Dartmouth*, compiled by Ray Freeman, DHRG, Paper 12, 1994, p. 18.
8. *The Land that Changed its Face*, by Grace Bradbeer, Devon Books, 1997, p. 88.
9. See the chapter 'Pictures Writers Paint' for a discussion of Leslie Thomas's *Magic Army*, on the American view of the occupation.
10. *We Remember D-Day*, compiled by Ray Freeman, DHRG, 1994, quoting *Once Around the Block*, by Bernhardt Krein, pp. 11-12.
11. Numbers from Arthur L. Clamp, *Preparing for D-Day*, Orchard Publications, p. 6.
12. *Dartmouth and its Neighbours*, by Ray Freeman, Richard Webb, 2007, p. 193. Leslie Thomas's *Magic Army*, discussed in the chapter 'Pictures Writers Paint', culminates in a description of Exercise Tiger.
13. Freeman, op.cit., 1994, p. 23.
14. *The Land we Left Behind*, by Robin Rose-Price and Jean Parnell, Orchard Publications, 2004, p. 79.
15. Rose-Price and Parnell, op.cit., p. 74.

Chapter 16: MYSTIC RIVER
1. This and the earlier quotation from *Goodbye to All That*, by Robert Graves, Penguin 2000, p. 11.
2. Graves op.cit., p 281.
3. Robert Graves, 'A Talk for the YMHA Centre, New York, February 9 1957, reprinted as Appendix B in *The White Goddess*, Faber & Faber, 1997.
4. 'The Nature of the Goddess: Ted Hughes and Robert Graves', by Nick Gammage, p. 151 in *New Perspectives on Robert Graves*, edited by Patrick Quinn, Associated University Presses, 1999.
5. Graves op.cit., 1997, p. 224.
6. Gammage in Quinn, op.cit.
7. Graves op.cit., 1997, p. 231.
8. Graves op.cit. 1997, p. 238.
9. *The Complete Poems*, by Robert Graves, edited by Beryl Graves and Dunstan Ward, Penguin Classics, 2003, p. 427.
10. Exeter City Library document DD 12002, quoted in *Kingswear and Neighbourhood*, by Percy Russell and Gladys Yorke, Kingswear Historians, pp. 8-9.

Chapter 17: CAPTAIN'S GOLD
1. *3 Great Houses, 54 Families, 800 Years*, by Elizabeth Jarrold, 2010, p. 49 – numerals have replaced words in this quotation. I am indebted to Jarrold for much of the information on Sharpham.
2. *Art in Devonshire*, by George Pycroft, Hamilton, Admans & Co, London, 1883, p. 125.
3. Advertisement in *Woolmer's Exeter and Plymouth Gazetteer*, August 1841, quoted in Jarrold, op.cit., pp. 68-71.
4. *The Buildings of England: Devon*, by Bridget Cherry and Nikolaus Pevsner, Penguin, 1999, pp. 722-3.

5. Jarrold, op.cit., pp. 64-6.
6. See the chapter 'The Wild, Free Life', on smuggling and customs in the area in Napoleonic times.
7. West Country Studies Library index cards. Peter Carey begins his *Parrot and Olivier in America* (Faber and Faber, 2010) with a printer in Dittisham forging bank notes at the end of the century.
8. Cherry and Pevsner, op.cit., p. 328.

Chapter 18: MANSIONS OF THE ENTERTAINERS
1. I am indebted to Nicholas Dimbleby for this story.
2. *Agatha Christie, an Autobiography*, Harpercollins, 1993, p. 497. See the chapter 'The Pictures Writers Paint' for a discussion of Christie's books based on the Dart.
3. Christie, op.cit., p. 527.
4. Christie, op.cit., p.60.
5. Christie, op.cit., pp. 416-7.
6. Christie, op.cit., p. 69.
7. See the chapter 'The Dart Explorers'
8. *Dartmouth: a History of the Port and Town*, by Percy Russell, Batsford 1950, p. 106.
9. Russell, op.cit., pp. 122-23.
10. As Osbert Lancaster said of art when talking about the Russian ballet in *Homes, Sweet Homes*, John Murray, 1939.
11. Reviews in *The Paignton and Newton Directory*, *Paignton Gazette* and *Daily Telegraph*.
12. Lancaster, op.cit., pp. 68, 72.
13. 'A Modern Country House, Coleton Fishacre, Devonshire', by Christopher Hussey, *Country Life*, 31 May 1930.
14. Lancaster, op.cit, p. 54.
15. *On the Margin*, by Aldous Huxley, Chatto and Windus, 1923, p. 117.
16. *Kingswear at War*, by David Williams, Kingswear Historians, 2011, p. 63.

Chapter 19: RIVERSONG
1. *Dart*, by Alice Oswald, Faber and Faber, 2002.
2. 'Paul Goddard' in Pyne, op.cit., 2005, pp. 28-9.
3. 'Ode to Joyce Gundry's fruit cake' in *Further up the River and Fifty Other Poems*, by Kevin Pyne, Richard Webb, 2004, pp. 80-81.
4. 'Freewheeling down to the harbour' in *First Across the Line and Fifty Other Poems*, by Kevin Pyne, Richard Webb, 2005, p. 33.
5. 'Elizabeth Mary' in Pyne, op.cit., 2004, pp. 44-5.
6. 'Light Airs' in Pyne, op.cit., 2004, p. 52.
7. 'Near Death' in Pyne, op.cit., 2004, p. 16.
8. 'Joe Mugford' in Pyne, op.cit., 2005, pp. 60-1.
9. 'A Round Turn and Two Half Hitches' in Pyne, op.cit., 2004, p. 28.
10. 'Schooldays' in Pyne, op.cit., 2005, p. 56.
11. 'River Dogs' in Pyne, op.cit., 2004, p. 39.
12. 'Bright Water Light Mark' in Pyne, op.cit., 2005, p. 15.
13. 'There is a Boat down on the Quay' Brian Patten, *Selected Poems*, Penguin Books, 2007, p. 163.
14. 'Travelling between Places' in Patten, op.cit., p. 30.
15. 'The Cynic's Only Love Poem' in Patten, op.cit., p. 105.
16. 'A Blade of Grass' in Patten, op.cit., p. 111.
17. 'Drunk' in Patten, op.cit., pp. 71-3.
18. 'For Harry Fainlight', Brian Patten, unpublished.

Chapter 20: THE PICTURES THAT WRITERS PAINT
1. *The Magic Army*, by Leslie Thomas, Arrow Books, 2004, first published 1981.
2. *Most Secret*, by Nevil Shute, Heinemann, 1945, and House of Stratus, 2000. Shute also wrote *Lonely Road*, Cassell, 1932, about this area.
3. *The Path through the Trees*, by Christopher Milne, Eyre Methuen, 1979.
4. A useful compendium is *The World of Pooh*, by A.A. Milne, Methuen & Co. Ltd., 1971.
5. Shute, op.cit., 2000, p. 109.
6. Shute, op.cit., 2000, p. 109.
7. See the chapter 'At War'.

8. *Nevil Shute: a Biography*, by Julian Smith, The Paper Tiger, 2002, p. 143.
9. Smith, op.cit., p. 53, letter to David Martin, Australia, novelist and critic, 11/1/1960.
10. Published in *The Regatta Mystery and Other Stories*, Bantam Books, 1939.
11. 'Queen of Crime' by Joan Acocella, *New Yorker*, August 16 & 23, 2010, pp. 86-7.
12. *Agatha Christie, an Autobiography*, Harpercollins, 1993, p. 262.
13. Christie, op.cit., 1993, pp. 260-1.
14. *Bodyguard of Lives*, by Anthony Cave, W.H. Allen, 1976.
15. Michael Morpurgo wrote *The Amazing Story of Adolphus Tips*, Harpercollins, 2005, about a child caught up in the evacuation.
16. *In My Wildest Dreams*, by Leslie Thomas, Arrow Books, 2006, p.xii.
17. Thomas, 2004, op.cit., p. 164.
18. Thomas, 2004, op.cit., pp. 297-8.
19. Thomas, 2004, op.cit., pp. 176-82.
20. Thomas, 2004, op.cit., pp. 260-70.
21. Thomas, 2004, op.cit., p. 616.
22. *The Path Through the Trees*, by Christopher Milne, Eyre Methuen, 1979, p. 143.
23. Milne, op.cit., 1979, pp. 227, 247.
24. *The Enchanted Places*, by Christopher Milne, Eyre Methuen, 1974, p. 163.
25. C. Milne, op.cit., 1979, p. 122.

Chapter 21: THE DARTMOUTH FIVE
1. A set of these cards, printed by Tozer & Co., Dartmouth, is reproduced in the end-papers of *The Chronicles of Dartmouth, 1955-2010*, by Phil Scoble, Richard Webb, 2012.
2. See Kaldor's *The Opera Houses of Europe* (1996), *Great Opera Houses* (2002), *New York, Masterpieces of Architecture* (1999), and *Berlin, Masterpieces of Architecture* (2002), all Antique Collector's Club.
3. Riley's publications include *Flower Painting*, Broadcast Books, UK, Northlight Publications USA, 1990; *Intimate Landscapes*, David Porteous Publications, 1991; *Watercolours: Paul Riley's Watercolour Workshop*, David Porteous, 2001; *Mastering the Medium*, Galerie Diamant, 2011.
4. Drew has published thirty nonsense books, too many to list he says, all published by ACC.

A CONVERSATION WITH THE PAST
1. *Dartmouth, Pre-Reformation*, by Hugh R. Watkin, The Devonshire Association, 1935, p. 354.
2. Watkin, op.cit., pp. xi-xii, 112-3.
3. Tucking is a west-country word; elsewhere the process was called fulling or walking and gave us Fullers and Walkers.
4. *Sports People of Dartmouth*, by Alan Coles, Dartmouth History Research Group, 1999.
5. Recorded by Todd Gray in *Devon and the Slave Trade*, The Mint Press, 2007, pp. 35-9.
6. Watkin, op.cit., p. 242.
7. Watkin, op.cit., pp. 11, 371-2.
8. See 'The Seas that Bind.'
9. *William Veale, Master Mariner, 1791-1867*, by Linda King, Dartmouth History Research Group, 1999.
10. Watkin, op.cit., p. 300.
11. See 'The Mansions of the Entertainers'.
12. Coles, op. cit., pp. 1-3.

LAST WORD
1. *The Chronicles of Dartmouth, 1955-2010*, Richard Webb, 2012, lists these on pp. 65-66. Highlights include *The Sailor who fell from Grace with the Sea*, 1976; *The French Lieutenant's Woman*, 1981, and the nine-year BBC television series *The Onedin Line*.
2. *The Path Through the Trees*, by Christopher Milne, Eyre Methuen, 1979, p. 232.

Acknowledgements

Pierre Landell-Mills has been an untiring source of support and ideas throughout this project; any recognition of his contribution would be inadequate.

The modern art scene in the Dartmouth area is vibrant and growing. I am grateful to many artists for discussions and ideas, but particularly to Bridget McCrum and to The Dartmouth Five.

Three families have been particularly generous with their time and enthusiasm – Sue and Nick Holdsworth; Gwen and Nick Teage; and Teresa and Brian Head – and I am especially grateful to them. The National Trust English Riviera is doing sterling and imaginative work to identify, save and make accessible the local heritage and Robyn Brown and her team – notably Heather Ball, Lucinda Heron and Katherine Ward – have given valuable time and support and I am deeply in their debt. Richard Porter has been a continuous source of help, advice and information, and this and his valuable work with Jane Harrold on the Britannia Royal Naval College have greatly improved this book.

History is the sum of its records. The book owes a great deal to modern historians Ray Freeman and Percy Russell; also to Stuart A. Moore who saved fine medieval documents in 1879, and to Hugh R. Watkin who rediscovered them in the old gaol and transcribed them half a century later.

I should particularly like to acknowledge the people who brought a spark to the endeavour. R.S. Hamlett found a Kingdon engine in Canada, transported it to New Zealand and built around it a replica of the original vessel, so now, after well over a century, the *Flirt* from Dartmouth plies Lake Roitoti. The Inder family shared their wealth of records about their ancestor Harry Inder, who built the engine of Dartmouth's first petrol car in a bedroom. The Chandlers suffered the same ordeal from pirates that seamen from Dartmouth faced in the 17th century – then repaired their yacht and set off again. In the Barbados Museum, a receptionist pointed out the *Journal of the Barbados Museum and Historical Society*, in which I found the reference to Henry Hauley, tying a knot with medieval Dartmouth. These and many others have made writing this book surprising and rewarding.

But thanks are due to all the artists, collectors, dealers, friends, historians, librarians and archivists who helped to move this project along: Nicky Alford, Savills; Philip Armitage, Britannia Museum & Archive; Brixham Heritage Museum and History Society; Richard Alexander; Jenny Bailey; Margaret Barlow; Jane Blair; Britannia Museum and Archive; John Bowden; Sophia Brothers, Science & Society Picture Library; Christina and Andrew Brownsword; Bob Cann; Dave Carter, Hayle Gallery; Rachel and Paul Chandler; Marion Clements; David Cobb; Don Collinson; Melanie Correia, New Bedford Whaling Museum; Nicolette and Bruce Coward; Laurence Daeche; Emma Darbyshire, Fitzwilliam Museum, Cambridge; Dartmouth Library, who supplied endless reading matter with cheerful grace; Nicholas Dimbleby; John Donaldson; Diana and Jock Douglas; Simon Drew; Helen Drury, Oxfordshire History Centre, Oxfordshire County Council; Nigel Evans; Rosemary Elford, of Elford Fine Art, Tavistock; Jenny and Paul Folca; Nicola Fox and Tim Burr, Kingsbridge Cookworthy Museum; Andre Gailani, Punch Ltd; Francis and Geoffrey Gilbert; Sarah Gillespie; John Gillo; Christabel Grimmer; Fran Gynn;

Carolyn Hayward; Father Will Hazlewood and Wendy Rendle, St Saviour's Church, Dartmouth; Daphne Hine-Haycock; Alice Hogg, DACS; Nikita Hooper, for sterling help at National Trust Images; Chris Horan, Dartmouth Town Clerk; Professor Ken Howard OBE, RA; Elaine and Lea Humphreys; Matthew Imms and Amelia Morgan, Tate Gallery; Sally and Tom Jaine; Elizabeth Jarrold; Andras Kaldor; Daragh Kenny, National Gallery, London; Susan Keracher, Dundee Art Galleries & Museums; Nicole Kluk and Megan Young, Art Gallery of New South Wales; Emma Lefley, Royal Museums Greenwich; Ann Lincoln; David Lingard and Brian Langworthy, Dartmouth Museum; Reg and Sheila Little; Patricia Llopis, M. Moleiro; John Madin, Victoria and Albert Museum, Exeter; Harry Major; Louisa Mann, Plymouth & West Devon Record Office; Don Manning, Cambridge University Library; John McWilliams; Messum's; Jane Mitchell; Patrick Morley (Glasshouse Art); Susan Morris, of Richard Green, who was most helpful; Imogen and Paul Moynagh; Mark Myers; Ruth Neave, Leisure and Culture Dundee; Milly Newman and Tony Pawlyn, National Maritime Museum Cornwall; Chris Nicholls, Sharpham Trust; Rita O'Donoghue Imperial War Museum; Stephen C. O'Neill, Pilgrim Hall Museum, Plymouth, Massachusetts; Alice Oswald; Peter Parker; Brian Patten; Nathan Pendlebury and Laura MacCulloch at National Museums, Liverpool; Richard Perera, Perera Fine Art; Luke Piper; Brian Pollard; Mark Pool and Leslie Byers, Torquay Library; Richard Porter and Jane Harrold, Britannia Royal Naval College; Gemma Poulton, Special Collections, University of Exeter; Noelle Pourret, Musée de Cluny, Paris; Eric Preston and Wally Fleet, Dartmouth History Research Group; Jane Price, Mayne Gallery, Kingsbridge; Kevin Pyne; Marlies Rahm, Osterriechisches Nationalbibliothek, Vienna; Caroline Rhodes, Hull City Council; Robin Rose-Price; Paul Riley; Tony Rouse, West Country Studies Library; Mandy Shepherd; Jacqueline Sherriff; Rokie and Robin Shiffner; Simon Shorvon for permission to use Pissarro paintings and to quote his letters; Peyton Skipwith; Melinda Smallwoood, Tony Swainston and Chris Cooper of the Royal Dart Yacht Club; Michael Stevens; James Stewart; Melvyn Stone; Laura Summerton, Bridgeman Art; Jilly Sutton; Michael Sutton-Scott-Tucker; Elizabeth Ann Swaffield, for permission to publish material by Flora Thompson; Michael Swain; Elizabeth Taylor, National Portrait Gallery; Robert Upstone, Fine Art Society; Rowena Weatherly; Barry Weeks, Totnes Image Bank; John Whiteley and Hannah Kendall, Ashmolean Museum, Oxford; Yvonne Widger, Dartington Trust Archive; David Williams; Rose and Steve Williams; Valerie Wills; Barbara C.G. Wood, National Gallery of Art Washington D.C.; Jan Wood, Devon Record Office; Violet Woodgate; and David Wright.

The idea for this book came from Richard Webb, long-time local publisher and supporter of Dartmouth, whose work stands as a valuable record of the town and its people; it would not have been possible without him.

And finally, my thanks to Diana Steel, herself a lover of Dartmouth, and the staff at The Antique Collectors' Club, particularly Pam Henderson, Catherine Britton, Susannah Hecht and Craig Holden, who have been professional, helpful and with whom it has been a pleasure to work.

Index

Page numbers in **bold** refer to illustrations and/or captions

Aboukir, HMS 155
Aceh, Sultan of 40
Acts of Uniformity 65
Adams, Robert 62
'Aerostat' glider **128**; 127
Alabaster, Cdre Martin **155**
Albert Victor, Prince **156**
Albert, Prince **120/1**
Aldewyche, Nicholas 31
Aldridge, John Arthur Malcolm **201**
Alexander, David **99, 243/4**; 10
Algiers **63**; 60-64
Allington 102
Altenberg an der Lahn Abbey **15**
Alyn, Thomas 273
American War of Independence 72, 97
Anchor Stone 245
Andrew, Prince 153
Anglican Whigs 65
Archangel 49
Armada 8, 44
Ash Ruth 215, 238
Ash, Maurice 215, 238
Ashburton 44
Ashe, Captain Edward **98**; 215-6
Ashprington 212
Asshenden, Thomas 27
Astley, John 41
Astley/Ashley (*née* Chambernowne), Kat **41**; 41
Attree, Lloyd 272
Aube 187
Autori **227**
Avelle, Oliver 32

Baird, Nathaniel Hughes John **247**
Baker, John the 16
Balfour Steam Navigation Company 127
Balkham, William **195**
Ball, Arthur **182**; 171, 182
Bankart, Edward 147
Barbary Coast (*see also*: pirates) p63
Barney, Thomas **111**
Bastard, Edmund 214
Bastard, John 212
Bawden, Edward **229**; 229
Bayard's Cove (Bearscove) **89, 91, 98, 99, 267, 270/1**; 87, 88, 91, 96, 216
Beacon, The **116/7**
Beavis, H.E. **189**
Beesands 135, 138
Belfort, HMS 190
Bellerophon Medal **9**
Benz, Karl 129-130
Bertha 124
Bevan, Robert 166
Bidder, George Parker **125**; 86, 118, 122-5
Black Death, The *see*: plagues
Blackalre, John 274
Blackawton

Blackler, P. 274
Blackpool beach **248**
Blackpool Sands **24/5, 31, 32, 129, 160**; 9, 30-1, 96, 102-5, 161, 193
Blackpool Sands battle 30-1
Blackpool Vale **160, 162**; 161, 162, 164
Boatfloat **6/7**
Boleyn, Anne 22
Bone, Henry **44**
Boone, Thomas **64**
Boulton, Midshipman 155
Bowden, John 273
Bozomzeal Hill **128**; 127
Brantyngham, Thomas de (Bishop of Exeter) 21
Brereton, R.R. **114**; 113, 118
Brereton, Rev. **52/3**
Brighton Art School 258
Britannia (train) 152
Britannia Royal Naval College (BRNC) **115, 144/5, 146, 147, 153, 157, 171, 193**; 144-57, 170, 186, 190, 245, 260
Britannia, HMS **148, 149, 156**; 118, 128, 148, 154
British Rail 112
Brixham Road 113
Brocklesby, HMS 188
Bromsgrove Guild 147, 154
Brookhill **110, 190, 191**; 119, 190
Brown, Anthony Cave 250
Brown, Mr 166
Brown's Hill 16
Browne, Abraham 62
Brunel, Isambard Kingdom 112-3, 115, 118, 123
Bufferis, P. **288**
Burghley, Lord 44
Burgin, Margaret 64
Burroughes, Sir John 44
Busk, Charles 126
Butler, Gustav **128**
Butterwalk, The **59, 224**; 60, 66, 108, 217, 224

Café Alf Resco mural 256
Calley, John 108
Camden Town Group 166
Campbell family 164
Campeador V **190**
Campo Pequeño **80**
Carey family **104**
Carlisle, Earl of 33
Carr family 256
Carter, J.H. 112
Carter's of Poole **229**; 229
Carved Angel (restaurant) **262**
Cashlauna Shelmiddy 102
Castelle, Lord of 32
Castle (Dartmouth) **12/13, 34-5, 68/9, 71, 77, 82/3, 87, 88, 92, 178, 198/9, 275**; 10, 28, 70, 87, 90, 119, 155, 189
Castle Drogo 228
Castle Road 86

Catesby, Mark **38**
Catholic School 178
Cayley, Sir George 129
Cecil, Sir Robert 44, 45, 49
Chambernoun, Otto 273
Chambers, George **63**
Champernowne, Arthur 50
Champernowne, Francis **51**; 50, 274
Champernowne, Katheryne *see*: Ashley, Kat
Champernowne, Richard 45
Champernowne Family 49, 50, 273, 275
Chandler, Rachel and Paul 67
Charite, la 274
Charles, Prince 153
Charles I, King 16, 63
Charles II, King **22, 56/7, 59, 66**; 21, 22, 65, 66, 108
Charming Molly **75**; 74-5
Châtel, Guillaume du 30
Châtel, Tangui du 30-31
Chaucer, Geoffrey **19**; 14, 18-9
Chaunpernum, Nicholas 273
Cherub, The **29**
Chomeley, Sir Roger 41
Christie, Agatha **192, 221, 222, 223, 247, 248**; 9, 201, 221-5, 245, 247-249
Christopher Robin *see*: Milne Christopher
Chronique de Saint-Denis 30-1
Churchill, Winston **188, 192**
Churston Grammar School 258
Cicala, HMS 189
Cinedrome 176
Civil Service Rifle Volunteers 150
Civil War (1642-51) 64-5, 72, 274
Clarence Hill 130
Clarence Street **39**; 78
Cleveland **66**; 66
Clifton **39, 59**
Cluny museum embroidery 15
Coat of Arms, Dartmouth **122**
Cobb, David **41**
Coffin, Sir Isaac 101
cog Johan, la 26
cogs **17**; 16
Cole, Mrs 162
Coleton Fishacre **218/9, 226, 228, 229**; 157, 225-9
Collins, G. **48**
Combecote 125
Compass Cove **183**; 178
Comper, Sir Ninian **157**; 148
Compton Castle **42**; 49, 222, 223
Concord **52/3**; 49
Conspicuous Gallantry Medal 155
Conygree Coal Works 108
Cooke, W.B. 84, 85
Coombe 126
Coombe Cottages 124
Coombe Farm 263
Coombe Mud 70, 125, 178, 183
Cooper, Elizabeth
Coquerel, Captain Léon 190
Cormorant 122
Cornwall, Duke of 16

Coronation Park **186**; 124, 178
Coronel, Battle of 155
Corporation of Bramble Tor 217
Costigan, Captain 81
Cottage Hospital, Dartmouth 128
Cottingham, Sir Francis 62
Coventry Canal Co. 112
Coward, Bruce 256
Coward, Nicolette 256
Cromwell, Oliver 65
crusades 14
Cundall, Charles Ernest **187, 188**
Cushman, Robert 51, 55
Customs House, Dartmouth **97, 98, 99, 101**; 96
Customs House, Exeter 96

D-Day **184/5**; 193, 196, 201, 249
D'Oyly Carte, Bridget 229
D'Oyly Carte, Dorothy, Lady **227**; 225-7, 229
D'Oyly Carte, Michael 229
D'Oyly Carte, Richard 226
D'Oyly Carte, Rupert **218/9, 227**; 225-7, 229
D'Oyly Carte opera company **228**; 226-7, 229
Damascus, 'Bishop' of 21
Dan, Pierre **62**
Darby, Abraham 108
Darke, Captain **126**
Dart (Alice Oswald) **232**
Dart River and Estuary **54, 67/8, 71, 72, 85, 88, 92, 97, 121/2, 152, 167, 173, 175, 180/1, 210/1, 215, 230/1, 232/3, 238, 239, 243/4, 263, 265, 273, 275, 276**; *and throughout text*
Dart Yacht Club *see*: yacht club
Dartington 50
Dartington Hall **51**; 45, 49, 228
Dartmeet 233
Dartmouth & Kingswear Society 252
Dartmouth & Torbay Railway 114
Dartmouth Bank 120
Dartmouth Five, The **256**; 254-69
Dartmouth Market Act 119
Dartmouth Pottery **195**
Dartmouth Steamer **120/1**
Dartmouth, Earl of *see*: Fitzcharles, Charles
Dartmouth, Lord George **48**
Dartmouth, Massachusetts 49
Davis Quadrant **37**
Davis, Sir John 9, 37-40, 44, 58, 222
de Attry, John 272
de Gaulle, Charles 190
de Gaulle, Philippe 190
de Grineau, Bryan **147**
de Lamérie, Paul **217**
de Ruyter, Admiral 76
de wint, Peter **233**
Dead Man's Folly (Agatha Christie) 247-8

Defoe, Daniel **73**; 73
Delfshaven 51
Deller, S. **130**
Devis, Arthur **70**; 75
Devon, Earl of 29
Devonport 138
Dimbleby, Nicholas **221**
Dirty New Ground 176
Discovery **156**
Disraeli, Benjamin 227-8
Dittisham **97, 246, 248, 265**; 113, 202, 221, 234, 245, 263
Dixon, Robert 16
Dolphin 153, 156
Donaldson, John **157, 256, 266, 267**; 10, 256-258, 263, 266-7, 268-9
Douglass, Sir James 123
Drake, Sir Francis 41
Drew, Caroline 268
Drew, Simon **254/5, 256, 268, 269**; 256-8
Drewe, Julius 228
Driftwood Quay 86
Drummond, Malcolm 166
Dudley Castle, Staffordshire **111**; 108
Duke Street **59**; 272
Dunkirk **188**; 187, 189
Durant, Elizabeth Jane 214
Durant, Richard 214
Durant family 214-5
Dutch Wars 76
Dyer's Hill 172

East India Company **41**; 40, 58, 222
École des Arts et Métiers, Paris 129
Edinburgh, Duke of *see*: Philip, Prince
Edmunds, John 232
Edward I, King **14**; 14, 16, 66
Edward III, King **15**; 14, 15, 18, 21, 26, 27
Edward VII, King 156-7
Edward, Prince (later King Edward VIII) **152, 156**; 152, 156
Edward, Prince (Prince Albert Victor) **156**; 153, 156
Edward, Prince of Wales (later Edward VII) **122, 123, 156**; 118-9, 122, 153, 156
Edyth 124
Eisenhower, General 196
Eleanor, Queen 14
Electric Telegraph Company 123
Elizabeth I, Queen **41, 43**; 22, 40, 44, 45, 49
Elizabeth II, Queen **154, 155, 191**; 154
Elizabeth, Princess *see*: Elizabeth II, Queen
Elmhirst, Dorothy **51**; 215
Elmhirst, Leonard **51**; 215
Elton family 2245
Embridge 161
Emett **193**
Enchanted Places, The (Christopher Milne) 252
Enock, Arthur Henry **118/9**
evacuation, WWII **192**; 193
Evans, Nigel **6/7, 12/3**
Exercise Tiger **196**; 249-51
Exeter 14, 17, 45, 63, 66, 96, 112, 115, 186
Exeter, Bishop of 20-21
Exeter gaol 97, 101

Exeter Inn, Ashburton 44
Exmouth, Lord *see*: Pellew, Sir Edward

Fairfax, General 64
Fairfax Place **172**; 178
Falkland Islands 38
Falmouth 80
Falmouth Art School 258
Fegen, Captain 154
First Across the Line (Kevin Pyne) 236-7
Fisher, Admiral Sr John 152
Fitzcharles, Charles (Earl of Dartmouth) 66
Five Little Pigs (Agatha Christie) 247
Flavel, John 65
Flirt **127**; 126-7
Floating Bridge 157
Florence 124
Flying Dutchman 114
Forrest, Captain Henry **116/7**
Forrest, George 225
Fort St George, Maine, USA 49
Fortalice (Hawley's) **28**; 28
Fosse Street **39, 59**; 29, 256, 274
Freake, Lady 157
Freake, Sir Charles **123**; 119
Freake, Thomas **123**; 119
Freake family **123**
Frederick, Captain G.C. 134, 139
Free French Flotilla (*Force Navales Françaises Libres*) **190, 191**; 8, 186, 189, 190
Froude, Robert Hurrell **125, 152**; 125
Froude, William 123
Fulford, Baldwin 272
Futter, James 33

Gallant's Bower **54**
Galleas **62**
Galmpton 200-201, 238
Gay, Karl **202**
George, Prince (later George VI) **152, 156**; 156
George I, King **217**
George III, King 63, 96, 212
George IV, King 96
George V, King 152, 153
George V statue **194**; 192
Gerston Hotel, Paignton 227
Gifferdandgorge 49
Gilbert, Adrian **41**; 40
Gilbert, Bartholomew 49
Gilbert, Humphrey 234
Gilbert, John **41**; 40, 44
Gilbert, Raleigh 49
Gilbert, Sir Humphrey **41, 42**; 9, 37, 44, 49, 222, 223
Gilbert, Sir John 223
Gilbert, W.S. 150
Gilbert & Sullivan **218/9, 227, 228**; 150, 226-7
Gilbert family 222-3
Gillespie, Sarah **11, 196, 200, 239**; 10
Gillo, John **97, 256, 257, 258, 259**; 11, 256-8, 263
Gilman, Harold 166
Ginner, Charles 166
Giverny 166
'Gold' beach 193
Gommerack 50
Gordon, G.T. 122
Gore, Spencer 166
Gorges, Sir Ferdinando 49, 50, 62

Gosnold, Captain Bartholomew **52/3**; 49
Grandisson, Bishop (Bishop of Exeter) 21
Graves, Robert **201, 202, 207**; 200-203, 238
Great Western Railway **113, 179**; 112, 114, 131, 141
Greenland 50
Greenway Court 223
Greenway ferry **246, 248**
Greenway House **114, 192, 220, 223, 224, 247**; 37, 49, 81, 113, 118, 200, 201, 221-3, 225, 247, 274
Grundy, Joseph 141
Guide, The 141
Guildhall 29, 65
Gundry, Joyce 236
Gurrow Point 127
Gynn, Frances **11, 139, 202, 234**; 10

Hallsands **132/3, 135, 136, 137, 138, 139, 142/3**; 132-143
Hanover Street (now Anzac Street) 176
Harbour Bookshop **253**; 252, 256
Harbour Breton, Newfoundland **74**
Hardnesse **39, 59**; 70, 273
Hardwick Hall **43**
Harris, Roope 274
Harvey, Harold **244**
Hauley ferry 26
Hauley Road 178
Hawkins, Sir John 41
Hawley, Henry (d.1573) 33
Hawley, Henry (Governor of Barbados) 33
Hawley, John (1340-1408; *see also*: Fortalice) **27, 28, 32**; 22, 26-33
Hawley, John 272, 275
Hawley, John (son) 27, 272
Heath, Charles 85
Hemy, Charles **102/3**
Henley, William **110**
Henri, Adrian 238
Henry IV, King b; 27, 30, 32
Henry VI, King 272
Henry VIII, King **36**; 21, 22
Henry, Charles Napier **73**
Henry, Richard 274
Hermione **213**; 212
Hicks, Anthony **221**; 221
Hicks, Rosalind 221
High Cross House 228
High Street 273
Higher Street **29, 110, 252**; 112
Hilliard, Nicholas **43**
Hilloways field 105
Hindostan HMS **148, 156**; 118, 148
HMS Pinafore (Gilbert & Sullivan) 226-7
Hodge, Beryl 200, 201, 238
Hody family 66
Holand, John 50
Holdsworth, Arthur (1668-1726) **75, 78**; 75, 76-8
Holdsworth, Arthur Howe **62, 71, 110, 125, 126, 217**; 23, 70, 75, 118, 119-20, 217
Holdsworth, Henry 120
Holdsworth, Olive & Newman 79
Holdsworth Bowl (Paul de

Lamérie punch bowl) **217**
Holdsworth family 72, 118
Holy Trinity Church (see also St Saviour's) 16, 23
Home Guard **188**
Hook, James Clarke **143**
Hopewell 63
Horne Hill **259**
Houtman, Cornelius 39
Howard, Ken **146**
Huckham school 136
Hundred Years' War 26
Hunt, G. 118
Hunt, Helen **252**
Hunt, Newman & Roope 79
Hunt, Roope & Teage 76, 78, 79
Hunt & Newman 79
Hunt family 72
Huntingdon, Earl of 50

Illustrated London News **156**
Impressionists 166
Inder car **131**; 130-1
Inder, James Henry and family 130, **131**; 130-131
industrial revolution **109**, 108, 118
Innes, J.D. 166
Institute of Civil Engineers 118
Iolanthe (Gilbert & Sullivan) **228**
Isère 187

Jackson, Sir John 138, 139
Jaille, de la 30
James I, King 44, 62
James II, King 65
João IV, King of Portugal 80
John ('an Indian of the Fort') 49
John V, King of Portugal **217**
John, Anthony 32
John, King 14
Jouette, la 26
Jubilee Flotilla (2012) **191**
'Juno' beach 193

Kaldor, Andras **177, 236, 237, 256, 260, 261, 262**; 256-8, 260-262, 263
Ketch's Hole 105
Keyne, Richard 32
Khadiye, Dahir Abdullah 67
Kingdon, George 125, 126
Kingdon engine **126, 127**; 126, 127
Kingsbridge **114**; 119
Kingsley, Rev. William 93
Kingston School of Art 263
Kingswear **55, 82/3, 87, 88, 100, 101, 106/7, 110, 115, 164/5, 168/9, 182, 189, 190, 288**; 26, 49, 50, 66, 85, 87, 98, 99, 112, 113, 114, 118, 131, 155, 157, 190, 196, 224, 245
Kipling Rudyard 98
Kittery **55**; 49, 50, 208
Klinghoffer, Clara **161**
Knight, John Henry 130
Knox, Wilfred **175**
Kyng, William 273

Lake, Samuel 122, 124
Lancaster, John 40
Lancombe valley **192**
Land family 72
Langtry, Lily 119
Lark Rise to Candleford (Flora Thompson) 170-82
Lee, Lieutenant Marshal L. **192**; 222

Leitch, W.L. 91
Leland, John 10
Levant Company 58
Levett-Prinsep, Thomas **116/7**
Lewis, John **215**
Leyden Pilgrims 51
Lidstone, Reuben 23
Lidstone, Thomas **110**; 112
Lidstone, W. **135**; 137
Lighthouse Cove **182**
lighthouse, Start Bay/Point
139, 196; 135
lime kilns 86
Linnell, John **84**
Little Dartmouth **183**; 274
Little Ice Age **75**; 74-5
Liwentaal, Alexandre 'Levento'
128; 127-9
Lobb, George 134-5
Local Defence Volunteers (Home
Guard) 189
Lock, Christopher 66
Locke, Joseph 123
London Inn, The, Hallsands
134-5, 137
Longcross Cemetery **183**; 183
Longford 190
Lorraine, Cross of **190**
Lower Knowle (Dr Barnado's
Home), Kingsbridge 250
Lower Street **110**; 29, 112, 256
Luny, Thomas **76/7, 94/5**;
Lutyens, Edwin 228, 229
Lyme 63
Lysons, Daniel, **36**

Madre de Deus 38, 44-5
Magic Army, The (Leslie
Thomas) 249-51
Mahler, Gustav **260**
Major, Mrs 164
Mallowan, Agatha *see*: Christie,
Agatha
Mallowan, Max **248**; 201, 221-
2, 224, 247
Manby, Charles 118
Mann, Miss 178
Mansfield, Richard 150
Mansion House **98, 216, 217**;
215-217
Manson, James Bolivar **173**;
164, 166
Margaret, Princess 154
Market Square **175**
Martin, Christopher 51, 55
Mary I, Queen 22, 41
Masefield, John **10, 102**; 102-4
Masonic Meeting House 217
Maurice of the Palatinate, Prince
64
May Fly 123
Mayflower **46/7, 55**; 51, 55
McAndrew, Vernon **190**
McCrum, Bridget **203, 204,
205, 206, 207, 208, 209**; 10,
202-208
McGough, Roger 238
Médaille d'Argent **190**
merchants 8, 16, 26, 37, 38
Mersey Sound, The (Brian
Patten, Roger McGough, Adrian
Henri) 238
Methuen Treaty (1703) 78
Mew 187
Mewstone 232
Middleton's blacksmiths 16, 178
Mighel, la 26
Mildmay, Frank 138, 140
Mill Creek 245

Mill Pool 119
Mill Vale **160**; 163
Mill, The 162
Miller, Agatha *see*: Christie,
Agatha
Milne, A.A. 253
Milne, Christopher **252, 253**; 9,
252-3
Milne, Oswald **218/9**; 225,
228-9
Milner-White 229
Milner, Edward 229
Molyneux, Joyce **262**
Monet, Claude 166
Monmouth HMS 155
Montgomery, Field Marshal
195; 196
Morris, William **59**
Most Secret (Nevil Shute)
245-6
motor-cars **129, 130, 131**;
129-30
Mount Boone **54, 64, 167**; 10
Mount Boone House **288**
Mount Galpin 78
Mountbatten, Lord 154
MTB 777 **189**
Mudd, Ambrose 76, 79
Mugford, Joe 237
Municipal seal **16**; 16

Napoleonic Wars 72, 96, 97
Naseby 64
National (Board) School 178
Natural History of Carolina 38
Naval College *see*: Britannia
Royal Naval College
Nelson, Admiral Horatio 152
Nethway House 66
New Bedford, Mass. **52/3**
New England, USA 50
New Ground (now Royal Avenue
Gardens) 114
Newcomen, Elias 108
Newcomen, Thomas **106/7,
109, 110**; 65, 108-10, 112, 115
Newcomen Cottage **110**
Newcomen engine **109, 111**;
108-10, 115
Newcomen Society of London 112
Newcomin Street 112
Newfoundland **74, 75, 78**; 33,
58, 60, 70, 72, 75, 76, 78, 79,
97, 99, 222
Newham 141
Newman family **74**; 72
Newman, Land & Hunt 79
Newman, R.L. **130**; 118
Newman, Sir Lydston 273
Newman, Thomas 61-2, 67, 70,
76
Neyle, William 63
Nigris, Johan de 19
Normandy **196, 197**; 186
North Cape, Battle of 155
north-west passage **40**; 37
Norton, Thomas 17, 63
Norway, Arthur **10**; 98, 99,
101, 105
Noss Point 122, 125, 127, 186
Nuestra Señora del Rosario 223

Okeley, William 62
Old Mill Creek **88, 177**; 127
Oldreive Brothers **172**
Olive family 72
'Omaha' beach 193, 197
Opera House, Budapest **260**;
262

Operation Overlord **195**; 190
Oporto **79**; 72, 78
Ordeal by Innocence (Agatha
Christie) 247, 249
Orion 112
Orisina Silent Night Daimler
130
Oswald, Alice **234**; 232-235
Outlook, The **171**; 170

Paignton 112, 115, 123
Paignton Pudding 115
Palladium cinema 176
paper mill **125**
Papin, Dionysius 109
Paradise (Paradise Fort;
Paradise Point; *see also*:
Ravensbury) **125**; 64, 68, 123
Parfitt, George 130
Parnoll, Captain Philemon
210/1, 213, 215; 212-3, 215,
216
Patey, Edith 134
Path Through the Trees, The
(Christopher Milne) 252
Patience (Gilbert & Sullivan)
228
Patten, Brian **237**; 10, 237-41
Paxton, Joseph 229
Payne, William **105, 220**; 223,
224
Peasant's Revolt (1381) 17, 28
Pellew, Sir Edward (Lord
Exmouth) 64
Pellow, Thomas 64
Penfound, Ambroe 72
Pepys, Samuel 62
Peter the Great, Tsar of Russia
217
Petyfen, Emelina 22
Pevsner **214**; 146, 212, 213,
216
Philip, George **131**
Philip, Prince (Duke of
Edinburgh) **154, 190, 191**;
153, 154
Phillip II, King of Spain 60
Philip & Son 125, 127, 131
Piggott, Mary 81
Pilgrim of Dartmouth 76
Piper, John **51**
pirates and privateers **56/7,
61, 62, 63**; 37, 40, 41, 58-67,
70, 72, 97, 273
Pirates of Penzance (Gilbert &
Sullivan) **227**; 226-7
Pissarro, Camille 161, 166
Pissarro, Esther **173**; 162-66
Pissarro, Lucien **158/9, 160,
161, 163, 164/5, 167, 173**;
10, 158-67
Pitts, Joseph 60
Place, Lieutenant 154
Plague of Children (1361-64) 16
plagues 16, 17
Plymouth 17, 41, 55, 89, 93,
115, 186, 250
Plympton, prior of 29
Popham, Colonel 80
Popham, Sir George 49
Popham, Sir John 49
port wine 72, 78-79
Portland 101
Post-Impressionists 166
Prettyjohns, Elizabeth Anne
140; 134, 140
Prince, John **54**
Princess Royal 216
Prospect House 142

Prout, Miss 178
Prout, Samuel **92, 105**; 91
Punch **193**
Pyne, Kevin **236**; 236-7
Pyne, Lyzie 236

Quay House 86

Ragamuffin 188
railway station **164/5**
Raleigh, Sir Walter **41, 44,
220**; 37, 40, 43-44, 45, 49,
222
Ratcliffe, William 166
Rattenbury, John 97, 98, 99,
100, 101
Ravensbury (*see also*: Paradise)
125; 86, 123
Red Portugal (*see also*: port
wine) 78
Redding, Cyrus 84, 86, 90
Reed, Douglas **188**; 187
Regatta **116/7, 157,
158/159**; 118, 153, 157
Regatta Fair 176
Regatta Mystery (Agatha
Christie) **222**; 247
Regatta, The **158/9**
Regency, The 96
Retriever **74**
Reynolds, Joshua **213**; 212
Richard I, King 14
Richard II, King 26, 27, 29, 50
Ricketts, Charles 229
Ridge Hill **110, 186, 288**; 125
Riley, Midshipman 154
Riley, Paul **237, 256, 263,
264, 265**; 256-8, 263-5
Ritchie, Leith 90
Riversbridge **160**; 162
Riversbridge Farm **163**
Riversbridge, 161
Rock & Co. **20**
Rogers, Samuel 90
Rolle, Lord 97
Rolls Royce 208
Rooke, Matthew **59**
Roope family **220**; 72, 81, 222,
223, 224
Roope, Harris Roope 223-4, 225
Roope, John **59**
Roope, Nicholas 86, 223
Roope, William 223
Roosevelt **192**
Rotoiti, Lake, New Zealand **127**
Rowe Bucke **44**
Rowlandson, Thomas **101**
Rowpe, Nicholas 274
Royal Academy 263
Royal Avenue Gardens 112,
114, 176, 274
Royal Barge **120/1**
Royal Bijou theatre, Paignton
150, 227
Royal Castle Hotel **222**
Royal Dart Hotel **164/5**; 189,
190
Royal Dart Yacht Club *see*:
yacht club
Royce, Frederick Henry 130
Ruskin, John **59**
Ruszkowski, Zdzisław **239**
Rutter, Frank 166

Salé pirates/Sallee Rovers 60,
273
Sanders **80**
Sandquay **131**; 122, 125, 126
Sandridge **120/1**; 37, 190

Sandy Cove **105**
Sargent, Malcolm 229
Savery, Thomas 109
Sawyer, Herbert 212
Schellinks, Willem **8, 54, 167**; 9, 164
Scott, Robert Falcon **156**
Seale, Sir Henry Paul **288**; 118
Seale-Hayne, Charles **288**; 112, 115, 118
Seaman's Secrets 38
seine boats and nets **143**; 136, 137
Seint John 30
Seint Nicholl 30
Shambles, The **252**
Shapleigh, Alexander 50
Shapleigh, Nicholas 50
Shapleigh family 49
Sharpham **239, 264**; 238
Sharpham House **210/1, 214, 215**; 212-5, 216
Shepard, E.H. 253
Shepler, Dwight C. **197**
Sheringham, Admiral 118
Sheringham, George **228**
Ship in Dock pub **186**
Shovell, Sir Cloudsley 80
Shute, Nevil **244, 246**; 9, 98, 245-6
Sickert, Walter 166
Simon, Lady **113**
Simpson family 118
Simpson, Francis Charles **126**; 122, 125, 126
Simpson, Strickland & Co. **127**; 125, 126, 127, 130, 131
Slapton **239**; 193, 194, 273
Slapton Ley **196**; 194, 273
Slapton Sands **105, 184/5**; 30, 99, 103, 134, 250
slavery **62, 63**; 60-66
Smith, John 252
Smith Street **39**
smugglers **10, 94/5, 97, 99, 100, 101, 102/3, 104, 105**; 96-105
South Devon Railway 112, 118
South Embankment **262**; 256, 272
South Hams **266**; 202
South Pole **156**
Southampton 51
Southtown 17
Spanish Civil War 200
Spanish Succession, War of 70
Speedwell **46-47, 55**; 51, 55
Spicer, Nicholas 63
Spurway, Thomas 63
St Barnabas Church 183
St Clare's Terrace 130

St Clement's Church, Townstal **23, 88**; 10, 16, 64, 65, 223
St Columba **193**
St John's, Newfoundland **74, 78**; 75, 76
St Mary and St George 19
St Matthew **65**; 22
St Peter's Church, Stoke Fleming **104**; 105
St Petrox Church **88, 198/9**; 60, 155
St Saviour's Church **12/3, 15, 18, 20, 21, 27, 39, 58, 65, 88, 164/5, 261**; 9, 14-23, 30, 60, 64, 66
St Thomas, Kingswear **88**
stage coach **114, 129**
Stalin **192**
Stancombe, Captain **71**; 70
Stanley Steamer (car) **131**
Staplehill, Samuel 65
Start Bay 70, 105, 135
Start Point 101, 104, 139, 188
Staverton 232
Stephan, Fitz 16
Stephenson, George 108, 118, 123
Stephenson, Robert 118, 123
Stewart, James **28, 240**; 11
Stoke Fleming **80, 104, 105**; 96, 98, 102, 104, 161
Stoke Gabriel **152**; 63, 190
Stokenham 70
Stokenham Church 194
storms 134-137
Strang, William **102**
Strete **192**; 102-3, 135, 161, 189
Sullivan, Arthur 150
Sunday Times 166
Sutton, Jilly **235, 273**
Swete, Rev. John **100**
Sword beach 193

Tange Castelle 32
Taylor, Sir Robert 212
Taylor, Thomas **71**
Taylor & Newman 79
Teage, Dixon 81
Teage, John **81**; 112, 114
Teage, Nicholas Dixon Land **80**; 105
Teage family **81**; 72
Tewkesbury, Nicholas de 16
Thistle 124
Thomas, Leslie 9, 249-51
Thompson, Edwin 182
Thompson, Flora **10, 168/9, 170, 182, 183**; 168-83
Thompson, John 170, 182
Thompson, Peter **182, 183**; 182-3

Throckmorton, Elizabeth 44
Tirpitz 154
Tissandier, Gaston 129
Topsham 63
Torbay 186
Torcross **184/5**; 103, 134, 193
Torquay 113, 115
Torre 113, 115
Torre, Abbey of/Abbot of, Paignton 16, 20, 23, 29
Totnes **54, 233**; 14, 17, 45, 115
Totnes Castle 127
Townesend, Nicholas **21, 39**
Townstal, **88**; 16, 21
Townstal manor 16
Traverse Book 38
Treaty of Utrecht 70
Trenite, la 273
Tresilian, Robert (Chief Justice) 27
Triewald, Martin 108
Trout family 141
Trout, Ella **139, 141**; 141-3
Trout, Patience **141**; 141-3
Tucker, Frederick **10, 180/1**
Tucker, Jim 273
tucknetting 137
Tukker, John 273
Turner, J.M.W. **11, 82-9, 91-3, 113, 167**; 10, 84-93, 164
Turner, William, 84
Tygress 70, 71

U forces 190, 193
Underhill, William **55**
US Coastal Reserve **192**
US Naval Advanced Amphibious Base (USNAAB; *see also*: U forces) 190
'Utah' beach **196**; 190, 196-7

Vale House 200
van de Velde the Younger, Willem **56/7, 61, 66**
van Gogh, Vincent 166
Veale, Theodore 274
Veale, William 274
Veitch 225
viaduct **114**; 113
Victoria, Queen **120/1**; 96, 118, 153
Victoria Cross 154, 274
Victoria Road 119
Virginia, USA 44
Vosse, William atte 16

Waddeton 190
Walker, Dr Jane 166
Wall, William Allen, **52/3**
Walpole's Excise Bill (1733) 216

Walsingham, Thomas 14, 30
Walters, F. **171**
Ward, John **149**; 62
Warfleet **82/3, 87**; 64, 86, 90, 274
Warfleet Creek **54**
Warfleet House **123**; 119, 123, 157
Warfleet Lodge **122, 123**
Waterhead Creek **164/5**; 164
waterwheel **125**; 120
Watt, James 108
Waymouth, Captain George 49
Webb, Ashton 147
Webb, Lt Colonel Richard 252
Wellington Barracks 150
Wellman, Walter 129
Wells cathedral 33
Weymouth 63
Wheeler, Laurence **65**; 65
White Goddess (aka *The Roebuck in the Thorn*; Robert Graves) **202**; 201
Widdicombe 70, 78
Wilcox, Leslie **46/7**
Wilford, Willaim de 30
Wilkes, Petty Officer Fred 155
Willcocks, John **75**
William III, King **78**
William of Orange 274
William, Prince 153
Wimbush, John **241**
windmill **72**; 73
Wise, Enid **175**
Wolfe, George **120/1**
Wood, Frank **153**
Wood, Tim **253**
Woodmass, Thomas 80
Woolacombe, Thomas 118
Woolley, Emanuel 66
World's Hydrographical Description 38
Worth, Richard Hansforth 139, 140
Wright, Wilbur and Orville 129
WWII 8, 184-97
Wyllie, Willaim Lionel **148, 150/1**; 152

xebec **62**; 60, 61, 67

yacht club **116/7**; 118-9, 122, 125
Ybl, Miklos **260**
Yeats, Jack 102, 104
Yeats, W.B. 102

Zion Place 178
Zion Street 176

Conservative Festival given in Mount Boone Park, August 25th, 1852, by P. Bufferis. Set back from Mount Boone House at the top of Ridge Hill where there is now an orchard, this engraving gives a lively picture of Victorian Dartmouth, with its barouches and Indian shawls, its boisterous youth and its serried ranks of guests watching some entertainment. The conservative win, by 11 votes, was to be overturned for fraud, but they won again the following year. The battle between conservatives and liberals, which entertained and enriched much of Dartmouth in mid-century, was a family affair, fielding Sir Henry Paul Seale, giving this festival, supporting the conservatives, and his nephew, Charles Seale-Hayne of Kingswear, for the liberals.
Valerie Wills